THE BOOK OF
ENGLISH
PLACE NAMES

For Niki and Julia, without whose generous purchasing power my books wouldn't have been anything like as successful as they have been – and because it's Wednesday.

THE BOOK OF
ENGLISH
PLACE NAMES
HOW OUR TOWNS AND
VILLAGES GOT THEIR NAMES

CAROLINE TAGGART

EBURY
PRESS

1 3 5 7 9 10 8 6 4 2

Published in 2011 by Ebury Press, an imprint of Ebury Publishing
A Random House Group company

The Random House Group Limited Reg. No. 954009

Addresses for companies within the Random House Group can be found at
www.randomhouse.co.uk

A CIP catalogue record for this book is available from the British Library

The Random Hou... ...ardship Council
(FSC), the leading ...our titles
that are printed ...rtified paper carry the
FSC log...

Designed and set by seagulls.net

Printed and bound in Great Britain by CPI Mackays, Chatham, ME5 8TD

ISBN 9780091940430

To buy books by your favourite authors and register for offers visit
www.rbooks.co.uk

CONTENTS

ACKNOWLEDGEMENTS

I am, as always, most grateful to all the friends and relations who gave me encouragement and, this time, suggestions for places to include. Special thanks to Peter for lending me books and coming up with the story of Twenty and to Heff for wondering about Indian Queens. Thanks also to Rebecca for thinking this book was a good idea, to Andrew for taking it on and to Liz, Kasi and everyone else at Ebury for making it happen.

INTRODUCTION

It's a proud boast among us British that we haven't been successfully invaded since 1066. We fended off Napoleon, Hitler and goodness knows who else besides. What we tend to overlook, though, is how often we were invaded *before* 1066. Starting in AD 43, four waves of invaders settled in what the Romans called Britannia (that's four if you lump each group together; many, many more if you choose to separate the Angles from the Saxons from the Jutes and if you count the number of individual Viking incursions). Each brought its own culture, its own language and its own way of doing things. As the power of each waned, as armies withdrew, royal lineages died out and yesterday's conquerors became today's settlers, mingling and intermarrying with the people they had overthrown, they left behind one indelible marker: the names they had given to places.

   The name of a place gives us hints not only about who used to live there, but about how they made their living, who their leaders were, what gods they worshipped. It tells us why people chose to settle in a particular spot rather than in another just down the road – perhaps there was a ford at A; perhaps B was a farmable valley in a mountainous area and C a hilltop site that was easy to defend. In the most primitive cultures, place names are basic: if you never move far from home, it's enough to call your local river 'the river', because it is the only one – or the only one that matters. (The same attitude leads Londoners to routinely call the Thames 'the river' to this day.) As civilisation develops, however, place names need to be more sophisticated. Once you start trading with nearby villages, you need to be able to tell them apart, even if you do nothing more inventive than name them 'North Village', 'Middle Village' and 'South Village' (that's where all those Nortons, Middletons and Suttons come from). A village with one outlying farm can refer to 'the outlying farm'. Once there are two of them, you need to come up with names such as 'the outlying farm by the bridge' (Brigstock) and 'the outlying farm by the road' (Radstock). If there are two southerly villages, they might become 'the southern village by the bridge' (Sutton Bridge – it isn't always rocket science, this place-naming business) and 'the long southern village' (Long Sutton). A village large enough to have two churches might split in two and become, say, Chalfont St Peter and Chalfont St Giles. And so it goes on. Some English place names date back two thousand years, a few were created for 'new towns' in the nineteenth century, and there are many thousands in between – but all have a story to tell.

Before we get into those stories, though, let's have a quick look at the people who created them.

In the beginning, there were the Celts or Britons. (Actually, the Celts weren't the first inhabitants of Britain, which is why you'll occasionally see the word 'pre-Celtic' in the entries later on, but we know almost nothing about them and they were a long time ago, so…) It's an over-simplification to speak of the Celts as one people, because they were made up of a number of tribes who fought a great deal among themselves. For our purposes, though, they had one important thing in common: their language. It differed from place to place, as local dialects differ the world over, but it was fundamentally the same language. Its descendants are Welsh, Cornish, Gaelic and Irish and we'll call it Old Celtic.

To defend themselves, the Celts built hill forts; when they weren't fighting they farmed and lived in small communities headed by a chieftain. They were also skilled metal workers and had established trade routes with Europe, notably for the export of Cornish tin. Crucially, there weren't very many of them: the population of Britain in 750 BC was probably about 150,000, although it grew quite a bit over the next few centuries as certain tribes gained in importance and held sway over an area equivalent to several modern counties, reducing the need to skirmish. But settlements in the earliest times were few and far between and place names were workmanlike. To a large extent the names of the Celtic settlements themselves have been superseded and lost (LONDON is a notable and mysterious exception); most of the place names that have come down to us in Celtic form are those they gave to major rivers and hills. Avon comes from the Old Celtic for 'river'; the names of the THAMES, Severn, TRENT and many others also date back to these early days. *Penn*, meaning 'head' and thence 'hill', survives in names such as PENZANCE, PENRITH and the Pennines.

These, then, were the people who were in residence when the Romans arrived.

The first Roman invasion of Britain took place under Julius Caesar in 55 BC, but didn't last long. However, the link had been established: the following century saw an expansion of trade between Britain and the Roman Empire; some chieftains' sons were sent to Rome to be educated. So when a quarrel broke out over the succession to the leadership of a tribe, the offended party appealed to Rome for help – and Rome took the opportunity to annex Britain as part of the empire. In AD 43, during the reign of the

Emperor Claudius, Roman soldiers landed in what is now Kent and spread across the country.

Given the divided nature of Celtic society, it is not surprising that some tribes were friendly to Rome and others were hostile. The conquest of Sussex and Hampshire was easy, while Dorset, Wales and the northern part of the country occupied by the particularly belligerent Brigantes gave trouble and led to considerable blood-shed, and the far south-west established a reputation for impene-trability that would stand it in good stead for centuries to come.

But in the end the Romans prevailed and they remained in charge of most of England, except Cornwall, for almost four hundred years. They took over the sites of many of the Celtic hill forts – after all, a good defensive site is a good defensive site, whoever had the idea in the first place – and established military bases and supply depots; in times of peace, these became the build-ing blocks of towns. These weren't the only towns, though; the Romans soon set about building more. They loved towns. To them, towns were the centres not only of trade but of cultured life. The important buildings – baths, theatres, temples – were made of stone, which is why so many remnants survive to this day. And, of course, they were linked by the famous Roman roads, still notice-able on the map because they run so nearly straight. Under Roman rule the population of Britain grew to three to four million – a level it didn't hit again until at least the fourteenth and possibly the sixteenth century – and although most people continued to farm much as they had always done, towns flourished as they had never before.

The Romans were great expansionists, but one name stands out as the exception to that rule: Hadrian. Emperor from AD 117 to 138, Hadrian decided that the empire had expanded far enough and consolidation became the order of the day. He instigated the building of a wall to protect 'his' part of Britain from the depredations of the tribes to the north. Hadrian's Wall is important for our purposes simply because it gave the Romans another excuse to build camps – and to give them names.

Very few Latin names from the period of the Roman occupation are still in use (the Anglo-Saxons, about whom there will be more in a minute, translated and adapted them), but many towns and camps survived. The Latin word for a garrison or military camp was *castra* and it would have been familiar all over the Roman Empire. Certainly it was familiar to the Angles and Saxons before they came to Britain, because it is their version of the word, *ceaster*, that has found its way into many modern names. It wasn't the Romans who added these endings: they were great ones for adapting what was already there. So, for example, in COLCHESTER, they took over a place called Camulodunon, Latinised it to Camulodunum and left it at that. Similarly, in CHESTER, the Celtic Deoua became the Latin Deva. Names ending in *–ceaster* emerged during the Anglo-Saxon period. So they really mean not so much 'the Roman fortified town' as 'you remember, that place where the Romans used to be'.

It's a cliché that all good things must come to an end and by the time the Roman Empire came to an end it hadn't been a good thing for a long time. AD 410 is the date usually given for the 'fall' of Rome, but by then the empire had been in serious trouble for more than a century. Roman troops had been gradually withdrawn from Britain as they were needed to quell uprisings elsewhere. They were certainly all gone by the middle of the fifth century, creating, of course, a vacuum.

Enter the next wave of invaders.

Even in Roman times, Saxons from across the Channel had been conducting raids on the east coast of Britain, and now the time was ripe for a full-scale takeover bid. The Saxons were not alone in grasping this opportunity. Two other tribal groups from northern Europe, the Angles and the Jutes, took control of parts of Britain in the fifth and sixth centuries. Culturally and linguistically related, these three groups are usually referred to (inaccurately but conveniently) as the Anglo-Saxons and their language was what we now call Old English. Unlike the Romans, the Anglo-Saxons were largely illiterate, so local records from this period are – to put it mildly – scant. But we know that the Jutes settled in Kent, the Isle of Wight and the mainland opposite it, while the Saxons took over the south and west of the country and the Angles the east and north. From these beginnings there eventually emerged four power-ful kingdoms: Wessex, which extended south from the Thames and included the modern counties of Hampshire and Dorset; East Anglia, covering roughly the same area as it does now; Mercia, across the middle of England south of the Humber; and Northum-bria, much of England north of the Humber. Like the Romans, the Anglo-Saxons never quite got to grips with Devon and Corn-wall, which is why so many Celtic names remain there.

But they took over the rest of the country pretty thoroughly. After the departure of the Romans, Britain's population had declined drastically – and not just because of the absence of Romans. Society had fallen apart. Disease was probably rife, many Britons fled the country and many of those who remained became slaves or at best subservient to the invading tribes: they had been subservient to the Romans for years, so what difference did it make? The Anglo-Saxons didn't go in for towns in the way that the Romans did, but they established an enormous number of smaller settlements which survived and grew. Any place name ending in –*ham* or –*ton*, –*hampton* or –*hampstead* is likely to have started life as an Anglo-Saxon homestead or farm (see the box *Farming Country 1,* page 50), and they were responsible for most of the –*fields* and the –*leys*, the –*downs* and the –*eys*, too. In fact, the vast majority of modern English settlement names have their origins in Old English; most of the other contributions are either oddities or window dressing.

Before we come to the next invasion, we need to digress for a moment and look at another great influence on English place names: Christianity. Christians were persecuted throughout the Roman Empire until the Emperor Constantine converted to the religion in the fourth century and, with a few notable exceptions (see St Albans and St Helens in the box on *Saints*, page 33), the religion had little lasting impact on Britain in Roman times. Thereafter, it arrived in three principal phases. Missionaries, most now regarded as saints, travelled to Cornwall from Brittany, Wales and Ireland from about the fifth century and are commemorated in a number of place names (see, for example, the entries for PADSTOW and KEYNSHAM). In the following century, St Columba came from Ireland to Iona in Scotland. From there he sent out missionaries who founded the great monastery at LINDISFARNE and spread the faith across Northumbria. One of the most notable converts of this period was Oswald, whose story is told under OSWESTRY and who was responsible for the founding of two other great monasteries, those at WHITBY and JARROW.

Finally, in 597, Pope Gregory the Great sent a mission, headed by St Augustine, to see what he could do with the rest of the country. Some pagan kings among the Anglo-Saxons had already married Christian princesses from the Continent and converted, but nominal religious faith seems to have gone hand in hand with actual political advantage, so to what extent Christianity filtered down to the populace at large is open to debate. Be that as it may, Augustine founded a monastery at CANTERBURY and converted the East Saxons – the first St Paul's cathedral in LONDON dates back to this time. Thereafter, monasteries abounded: dominated by minster churches (the words 'monastery' and 'minster' derive from the same root), they were the homes of monks who generally lived apart from the rest of the world but who offered hospitality to travellers and 'ministered' to the sick. For almost a millennium, monasteries were the greatest centres of learning in the country. The monks compiled and illuminated manuscripts which were both objects of great beauty and works of phenomenal scholarship. The monasteries also became immensely rich – as we shall see in a moment. William the Conqueror endowed them with vast tracts of land, and it was common for kings and noblemen to make generous donations to the church in the hope of saving their souls in the long term and keeping the local abbot on side in the meantime. These are the establishments that were looted during the reign of Henry VIII in the act of institutionalised vandalism known as the Dissolution of the Monasteries. Before that, however, towns had grown up around them, just as they had grown up around fortresses in earlier times.

But we're getting ahead of ourselves. Let's go back to the Anglo-Saxon kingdoms, which struggled for supremacy among themselves for several hundred years. In theory, a king's son would inherit from his father; in practice, a kingdom went to the man who mustered the largest army and wielded the mightiest sword. King Offa of Mercia, who built the dyke that bears his name, remained in power for forty years during the eighth century, a remarkable achievement suggesting he was a very great warrior indeed. But soon after his death Mercia was playing second fiddle to Wessex. And by this time there was a new set of players on the scene: from Denmark and Norway came the Vikings.

The Vikings – also known as Norsemen – were great seafarers (some would say pirates). They were also pagans and their most serious initial attacks were on the monasteries at Jarrow, Lindisfarne and Iona in the closing years of the eighth century. A generation later they had built up to almost yearly raids and in 865 came a full-blown invasion. The Vikings landed in East Anglia and turned north, taking control of the kingdoms of East Anglia and Northumbria within three years. Wessex, however, put up more of a fight.

In 871 the man we now know as Alfred the Great became King of Wessex and in 878 he won a battle against the Danes that enabled him to negotiate a deal. The two powers drew an imaginary line across England roughly from LONDON to CHESTER. They acknowledged Danish control of everything to the north and east of it: an area that became known as the Danelaw. Danish influence – on life, the universe and place names – was profound in East Anglia, Lincolnshire and the north-east. The Old Scandinavian equivalent of the Old English *–ham*, meaning a homestead, is *–by*, and from WHITBY to DERBY to ASHBY DE LA ZOUCH that memento of Danish occupation remains.

A combination of diplomacy, prudent marriages and luck kept Alfred and his descendants in charge of the south and west; the kingdom of Mercia ceased to be a political giant. Alfred was, in fact, one of the first to use the name England, 'land of the Angles'. Inspired by the example of the Venerable Bede (see page 24), he was thinking about a united country. It was about this time that the Anglo-Saxons – who, for all their scrapping, were pretty hot on admin – invented the *shire* as a way of governing the country at a more grassroots level (see the box on *Shires and Counties* on page 62). Peace – of a sort – reigned.

It couldn't last, though, could it?

Skating quickly over Wessex's incursions into Danelaw, Norwegian raids on the north-west, and disputes with and among the

Welsh and the Scots, we come to the year 960. The Danes have been thrown out by a succession of powerful English kings. England is more or less united under Alfred's great-grandson Edgar. But by 1000, under Ethelred the Unready, it is in trouble again and in 1016 it accepts a Danish king, Cnut or Canute. Cnut, being also King of Denmark and Norway, is something of an absentee landlord as far as England is concerned. To aid administration, therefore, he divides the country into four earldoms, corresponding with the four great kingdoms of earlier times – Wessex, Mercia, East Anglia and Northumbria. Which, inevitably, creates four powerful earls…

Fast-forward another half-century and we find a mess. The Danish line has died out and England has been ruled for twenty-four years by the Saxon Edward the Confessor, son of Ethelred. When he dies at the beginning of 1066, the strongest of a number of men aspiring to the throne is Harold Godwinson, Earl of Wessex. Also in the race is a Norwegian called Harald Hardrada, whom Harold G defeats on 25 September at a place called Stamford Bridge, near YORK; Harald H is killed. So far so good, if you are on Harold G's side. But now the remaining contender moves to stake his claim. William, Duke of Normandy, lands at PEVENSEY on 28 September, a mere three days after the battle of Stamford Bridge. Pevensey, as you may know, is in Sussex. Some distance from York.

There had been a treaty between England and Normandy since Ethelred the Unready's time. Indeed, Ethelred had married the then Duke's daughter, so there were ties of kinship too. William was illegitimate, but had succeeded to the title because he was his father's only son; in terms of pure genealogy, he had the strongest claim to Edward the Confessor's throne. Some also say that Harold Godwinson, as Edward's ambassador to Normandy, had previously promised to support William's claim when the time came. Whether that is true or not, Harold raced south to confront William, who, almost inevitably, defeated the exhausted Saxon army at Hastings on 14 October. Harold was killed (arrow in the eye? Maybe, maybe not) and William, who had started the autumn as William the Bastard, was on Christmas Day crowned William, first Norman king of England – 'William the Conqueror'. Not a bad three months' work.

Three things happened in Norman times that were relevant to William's ability to rule his kingdom and remain relevant to place names today. The first was that, having confiscated the land held by Saxon nobles, he proceeded to give lots of it away – to his own nobles and to the church. These nobles – whom we describe colloquially as 'lords of the manor' – didn't generally change the names of the estates they acquired; they simply added to them. SHEPTON MALLETT, LEIGHTON BUZZARD and MILTON KEYNES are all places whose original name (Shepton, Leighton, Milton) was Old English but whose Norman landlords satisfied their egos by tacking on their own name. The church did the same, often using its official language – Latin – to give us roll-it-round-the-tongue-and-savour-it names such as Kingsbury Episcopi, 'the king's manor that now belongs to the bishop'. Dorset boasts a village called Toller Fratrum: Toller (Old Celtic for 'hollow stream') from the name of the river, Fratrum from the Latin for 'of the brothers' – that is, the monks or priests. With just a hint of bathos, there is a village on the same river called Toller Porcorum, 'of the pigs'. Well, the brothers had to eat.

The second thing that happened was that William and his successors built castles: about five hundred of them within a generation of the Conquest. Primarily designed for defence, many became residences with support staff and service industries – cue the development of more towns.

The distribution of both Norman names and Norman castles across the country is interesting. Winterborne Clenston, Askham Bryan, Acton Pigott and their ilk are found as far south-west as

Somerset and Dorset, as far west as Shropshire and as far north as Yorkshire. They are less common in the far south-west and the far north. We have already reflected on the impenetrability of Cornwall; William the Conqueror also had trouble persuading the people in the north of England to accept his rule. What with that, and the ongoing conflict with the Welsh that is the theme of the chapter on Western England (page 203), it should be no surprise to note that these are the areas where most castles were built and where names suggesting that the Normans had just settled down and got on with their lives are comparatively rare.

Finally on that list of three things, William commissioned the most remarkable document that any student of place names anywhere in the world could ask for: the Domesday Book. This was a survey, carried out in a matter of months in 1086, of all the lands that made up England; everything that the king, the church or the nobility owned; who had owned it in Edward the Confessor's time and how much it had been worth then; who owned it now and how much it was worth; who sublet which parts of it and how many ploughs, horses and other animals they possessed; what sort of state the land was in; and – most importantly – how much tax was paid on each holding. It was invaluable to William and his successors for the purposes of raking in money; it is equally invaluable in the examination of place names because it records more than 13,000 of them and tells us how they were spelt (or how the Normans decided they were spelt) at that one precise moment: 1086. Although the Domesday Book is written in Latin, the names are not Latinised: what is written down is exactly what places were called in the vernacular. For many names, Domesday is the first record we have; for many others it is an indispensable halfway house between the Old English found in earlier documents and the modern form.

Although names continued to evolve for several centuries before modern usage and spelling were settled upon, the Norman Conquest is the final of the five great contributions to English place-name development. The earlier ones, as we have seen, were the Celts, the Romans, the Anglo-Saxons and the Danes. But that does not mean that every name is either Celtic or Latin or Old English or...

It's worth noting at this point that none of these conquerors attempted to exterminate the people they conquered. Subjugate, yes, but after they had established their supremacy they settled down, intermarried and had children. It's one of the reasons the Danes were able to take control so easily under Cnut: half of England thought of itself as more Danish than English anyway.

This practice of intermingling rather than suppressing is reflected in place names, which are often as hybrid as the people who produced them. As we shall see in the individual entries, names were added to, translated, changed, misheard, misunderstood, mispronounced or any random combination of the above. Many clearly went through a stage in which the person writing it down thought, 'That can't be right', even though it was, or 'It looks a bit like so-and-so, so I guess that's what it must be', when it was nothing of the sort. Before the age of mass communication, a scribe in the north (with his ear attuned to a Scandinavian tongue) might write a name one way, while his counterpart in the south (used to Old English) understood something if not completely different, at least different enough to cause confusion to posterity. And in a time when few people travelled and no one watched Australian soaps on television, regional variations – a bit more Danish here, a little less Norman French there – would have taken a much firmer hold than they do today.

I said a moment ago that the Domesday Book was often an invaluable halfway house between the oldest recorded form and the modern one. But where no earlier record exists, sometimes we have to fall back on educated guesswork to establish a place's meaning. For example, in addition to the *hām* that meant a homestead, Old English had a word *ham(m)* or *hom(m)* meaning 'a flat piece of land in the bend of a river' or some other partially enclosed piece of land. Early spellings of Twickenham, not to mention its position on a kink in the THAMES, tell us that this was definitely a *hamm*. With Beckenham in Kent, however, there is no clear evidence – the earliest record is ambiguous and we have to admit that we can't be sure. Going back to Twickenham, although we are confident of the *–hamm*, we don't know whether the piece of land belonged to a man named Twicca, or was in a fork in the river. That's why words such as 'probably' and 'maybe' occur so often in the entries of this book.

Although the Normans didn't generally change place names beyond the 'lord of the manor' additions mentioned above, they had a huge influence on spelling and pronunciation, because of differences between their own language and Old English. In the latter, a *g* at the end of a word was a guttural sound which didn't exist in Norman French. Thus the word *burh* and more particularly its dative form *byrig*, meaning '(at) a fortified place', caused them problems. And remember, they were the bosses: no one was going to tell them they were getting it wrong. Eventually, therefore, Norman pronunciation became standard and the written language evolved to mimic it, producing the *–bury*, *–burgh* or *–brough* of many names. Similarly, the Old English *c* was hard – either *k* or *ch* – and words beginning with *sc* (pronounced *sk*) were common. No problem to the Danes and Norwegians, whose languages contained similar sounds. In Wessex, however, even before the Conquest, they were often softened to *s* and *sh* – a tendency that would have been reinforced when the Normans started to struggle with them. This goes a long way towards explaining why *kirk* and *church* are fundamentally the same word, and why a place whose first syllable refers to sheep (*scēap* in Old English, with the *c* originally pronounced *k*) is now Skipton in Yorkshire but Shipton in various towns further south.

Mention of the dative case introduces another point that is worth expanding: Old English nouns were inflected in a way that Modern English nouns are not. This means that they changed endings to indicate details that we show with prepositions: the basic (nominative) form of the word for king was *cyning*, but if you wanted to say 'of the king' (genitive) it was *cyninges*, 'to or at the king' (dative) *cyninge*, 'of the kings' (genitive plural) *cyninga* and 'to or at the kings' (dative plural) *cyningum*. All these variations turned up in early records and could lead to names with similar meanings evolving in different ways. The genitive *s* ending survives in Modern English as the *'s* that shows possession and is to be seen in many place names along the lines of KINGSTON and SHREWSBURY.

Some of the evolutions from Old to Modern English seem inexplicable at first glance. For example, a ninth-century document records the name of Sodbury (now Chipping Sodbury, see the box on *Market Towns*, page 102) as Soppanbyrig. In fact, this transition gives four useful examples of the many ways in which changes occur. First, when two consonants that the lips and tongue produce in similar ways (in this case the *p* and *b*) occur in close proximity, one tends to be changed over time to give something easier to pronounce. Second, an unstressed middle syllable may simply be swallowed. Third, the final *g* was the tricky sound mentioned above. And fourth, if a name can be made shorter, it will, even if it means losing any clue as to the meaning. These changes were well under way by the time of the Domesday Book, a mere twenty years after the Norman Conquest. It records Soppanbyrig as Sopeberie (that pesky ending has been disposed of). Sobbyri is found in 1269 (middle syllable has gone, name is getting shorter) and Sodbury in 1316 (tongue-twisting consonants sorted out). These changes did not happen overnight or systematically, but they all made some sort of sense.

Before moving on, it would be wrong to give the impression that every place name in England dates back to the Middle Ages and beyond. The Industrial Revolution in general, and the arrival of railways in particular, led to the creation of a number of new towns in the eighteenth and nineteenth centuries, so that we find places such as FLEETWOOD, founded by and named after a local MP who thought it would serve as an entrepôt for goods being transported from London to Scotland. The names of MORECAMBE and BLACK-POOL are ancient, but the towns themselves barely existed before the arrival of that other eighteenth-century invention, tourism. And early twentieth-century philanthropy came up with the concept of the 'garden city', giving new life to places such as LETCHWORTH and WELWYN. Of course, the fortunes of settlements also wax and wane: some prosperous medieval wool towns now barely make it on to the map; some towns that grew up to service mines, mills, factories and railways fell into near oblivion when their 'core industries' declined. See BELPER, NEEDHAM MARKET and TWENTY for three examples of places whose glory days have passed by.

This book is not intended to be comprehensive. Names whose origins are neither certain nor particularly interesting have been shamelessly omitted – although space has been found for some, such as HOUGHTON CONQUEST, that sound as if they should be more interesting than they are. These mild disappointments are more than counterbalanced by the serendipitous discovery of innocent-sounding places such as PURBROOK and BALDOCK, and by the wild speculation attached to peculiar names such as INDIAN QUEENS. Much repetition has been avoided by the use of boxes covering recurring themes. Many names ending in *–ford* or *–bridge*, which started life as 'the place where you can get across the river', are listed in the boxes on *Crossing Places* (pages 117 and 242) and those named after a long-forgotten chieftain appear in *Whose Place Is It Anyway?* (page 189). In addition, a list of the most common place-name elements is given on page 291. If a name that interests you is not included, this information should set you off on the road to working out its meaning for yourself. If not, the more encyclopaedic works that I have consulted are listed in the Bibliography on page 296. From the many thousands of possibilities for inclusion, I have chosen to concentrate on those whose stories interested me the most and to illuminate the intriguing, the amusing and the downright bizarre. I hope you'll agree that there is no shortage of those.

SOURCES REFERRED TO IN THE TEXT

In addition to the Domesday Book (see above), the following sources and authors crop up repeatedly in the course of the book.

Ptolemy – Claudius Ptolemaeus – was a second-century Greek astronomer and geographer who worked in the great library of Alexandria. His studies of astronomy formed the basis for that science until Copernicus came along in the sixteenth century, but it is his *Geographia* that concerns us here. It was a treatise on the art of cartography, followed by four books of detailed maps of the Roman Empire – including Britain – of the time. Ptolemy used a very precise grid system with measurements of latitude and longitude, which has enabled subsequent historians to make a fair guess at the location of Roman settlements which have since been lost, and to reconstruct their relative importance.

Tacitus (c. AD 55–117) was a Roman historian whose *Annals* are one of our most important sources on early Roman Britain.

Bede (c. AD 673–735), known as the Venerable Bede, was a monk living at the monastery of JARROW in Northumbria. His great work was an *Ecclesiastical History of the English People*, written in Latin and translated 150 years later under the auspices of Alfred the Great. The book begins with Caesar's invasion in 55 BC and continues up to Bede's own time. The Latin title was *Historia ecclesiastica gentis Anglorum*, the last part meaning 'the people of the Angles': Bede was preaching a unified church, and with it a unified England, long before Alfred adopted both the term and the concept. Bede's history is our great source of information on the seventh and early eighth centuries and, thanks to the magnificent library on which he drew, one of the best for the earlier period. Bede is regarded as the father of English history, the most learned man in Europe at the time.

The Anglo-Saxon Chronicle, begun in Wessex in the ninth century, again probably under the auspices of Alfred the Great, gives a year-by-year summary of events from the fifth to the eleventh centuries, drawing on earlier sources and bringing them together for the first time. Not entirely unbiased – it is pretty hot on Alfred's own achievements, for example – it is nevertheless of at least equal importance to Bede for the Anglo-Saxon period.

Geoffrey of Monmouth (died 1155) wrote a *History of the Kings of Britain* and is the principal source for some of the stories about Arthur and Merlin (though not the Round Table), as well as 'Old

King Cole' and Shakespeare's Lear. He is also responsible for the
legend that Britain was founded by Brutus, a descendant of Aeneas,
Prince of Troy. Geoffrey claimed to base his history on 'a very
ancient book in the British tongue', but most scholars now agree
that he made most of it up.

William Camden (1551–1623) was an English antiquarian and
historian who compiled the first topographical survey of the British
Isles, *Britannia*, published in 1586. A county-by-county account of
his own travels and of the geography, history and legends surrounding each place he visited, it includes personal opinions of the landscape and local peculiarities and, crucially, many observations on
the origins of place names. If earlier documents and modern
research don't help us to winkle out the meaning of a name, we
can usually rely on Camden to have a good story to tell, often with
eyebrows unmistakably raised at the rubbish his informants chose
to believe.

1

❧

SOUTH-WEST ENGLAND

Although it is geographically convenient to lump Cornwall, Devon and Somerset together, Cornwall stands apart in terms of place names. It largely withstood the Romans, who had an important fort at EXETER but little impact further west; and it remained an independent kingdom, resisting the Saxons, until the eleventh century. It's difficult to be sure why the Cornish were so successful in fending off invaders: certainly the Tamar would have been a formidable barrier in the south, but a determined army could have marched north of Dartmoor and into north Cornwall without getting too bogged down. Yes, a lot of the land was barren and inhospitable, but this isn't the only part of the country of which that could be said. Perhaps the locals were just particularly belligerent; perhaps the fact that they were skilled metalworkers meant they had a better class of weapon. Perhaps the fact that the Cornish peninsula was so far from any invader's base camp meant that the Romans and the Saxons had rather run out of steam by the time they got here. Most likely the explanation is a combination of all these factors.

Anyway, this fierce independence accounts for Cornwall's large number of unusual (= Celtic) place names – the commonplace –hams and –tons of the Anglo-Saxon world cut little mustard here. On the other hand, Cornwall succumbed (if that is the word I want) to Christianity at an early stage and produced a plethora of saints barely known elsewhere. By comparison, Devon and Somerset are much more in tune with the rest of the country and, considering

....
26

that they gave us names such as Newton Poppleford and Beer Crocombe, we should all be grateful for that.

CORNWALL

The name of the county means 'the territory of the Cornovja tribe'; the Cornovja were a Celtic people whose name probably derives from **cornu**, *'horn', because of the horn-like shape of the Cornish peninsula. That's one version, anyway: see the box on page 29 for another, less prosaic account.*

Bodmin

A name of Cornish origin, this means something like 'house of monks' or 'dwelling by the monastery'. The monastery was founded in PADSTOW in the sixth century by St Petroc, one of the patron saints of Cornwall. It moved to Bodmin – already an important trading post – in the tenth century and dominated the town until Henry VIII had it closed in 1538.

Bude

'Muddy or turbulent river', though this is an unkind description of the river Neet today.

Camborne

Unrelated to other *–bornes* and *–bournes* 'up country' (see, for example, BOURNEMOUTH), the first part of this name comes from a Cornish word probably meaning 'crooked' (see next entry) and the second from a Cornish word meaning 'hill'.

Camelford

Not as exciting as it sounds. The *camel* bit is an Old Cornish name for a river, possibly meaning 'crooked' but certainly not 'hump-backed and useful in the desert'. The suffix *–ford*, as in other names with this ending, means that it was a place where you could cross the river. Camerton in Somerset and Cambridge in Gloucestershire were similarly built on crooked rivers; the more famous CAMBRIDGE has a different derivation.

Fowey

The town is named after the river, whose name means 'river where beech trees grow'. The ending *–y* or *–ey* in a West Country name often indicates a river that was named by the Celts: *Bovey* and *Cary* – see BOVEY TRACEY and CASTLE CARY – are two other examples in this chapter.

Indian Queens

Surely a contender for the oddest name in the book, and one that can't be explained satisfactorily. We know that the village was named after a pub, which was originally, and uncontroversially, called the Queen's Head; some time in the 1780s it became the Indian Queen (singular). There is no evidence to support a connection with the Native American princess and Disney heroine Pocohontas – and in any case she died in 1617, so why bother to change the name of the pub over 160 years later? The legend persists, however, as good legends tend to do. A slightly more probable story suggests that a Portuguese princess once spent a night here on her way from Falmouth to London and her dark complexion led people to assume she was Indian. Either way, there is still only one queen, Indian or otherwise. The plural came about towards the end of the eighteenth century, almost a century before Queen Victoria was proclaimed Empress (never Queen) of India. So although at one time the pub sign depicted Victoria on one side and a Native American on the other, that can't be the original reason for the change. It remains a mystery that has beguiled

The twelfth-century chronicler Geoffrey of Monmouth was not one to dismiss a good story, however improbable. He would have us believe that a Trojan hero called Corineus was given the territory we now know as Cornwall as a reward for conquering the giant Gogmagog, and that he named it after himself. Apparently, Corineus could have had his pick of the provinces, but chose Cornwall because 'it was a diversion to him to encounter these giants, which were in greater numbers there than in all the other provinces that fell to the share of his companions'. Gogmagog was 12 cubits tall – that's about 2.75 metres – and Corineus threw his victim over the nearby cliff that is still called Giant's Leap. Yes, right, thank you, Geoffrey.

Tradition has it, by the way, that the name of the Gogmagog hills in Cambridgeshire is a satirical one bestowed by Cambridge University students in the sixteenth century, because these gentle hummocks are the nearest thing to giants you are likely to find in that low-lying part of the world.

many a tedious drive along that winding bit of road between Newquay and St Austell.

Launceston

Nothing to do with a man called Launce, this town's name at the time of the Domesday Book, Lanscavetone, gives more of a clue. The Cornish prefix *lan–* means 'church site' (it's related to the modern Welsh *llan–*) and the middle part is a corruption of Stefan, the Cornish for Stephen. The *–ton* ending indicates a Saxon farmstead or village, so Launceston was 'farmstead near the site of St Stephen's church'. In the thirteenth century the wealthy priory dedicated to Stephen, the first Christian martyr, moved from its original site (north-west of the existing town) to the centre of town, near the castle; like so many it was destroyed during Henry VIII's Dissolution of the Monasteries, but the parish church of St Stephen-by-Launceston, built to replace it on the original site, still exists.

Liskeard

An old Cornish name meaning 'Kerwyd's court', but sadly no one seems to remember who Kerwyd was. By the time of the Domesday Book Liskeard was a small farming village, so all that can be said for sure is that the grandeur that was Kerwyd's had been and gone by then.

Lizard

Nothing to do with the animal, this means 'court on a height', the *Liz–* part having the same derivation as in LISKEARD.

Looe

The word means 'pool' or 'inlet', and the town derives its name from the river on which it stands, which in turn is probably named after the inlet at its mouth.

Lostwithiel

The *lost* element here means 'tail' and the whole name translates as 'place at the tail-end of the woodland', which is a sensible enough site for a settlement. That was certainly the Normans' opinion – they used it as a centre for the tin trade and made it the capital of Cornwall. A version of the name is first recorded in the twelfth century, but the fact that its origins are Cornish indicates that there were people living here before the French-speaking influence arrived.

Marazion

This exotic-sounding name is from Old Cornish – the local version of Old Celtic – which is why most of us wouldn't have a clue what it means. Sadly, it is nothing more exciting than 'little market'.

Mousehole

Believe it or not, this actually does mean 'mouse hole': it was the name given to a sea cave just to the south of the harbour. Of course, calling a place Mousehole after a cave that looked like a mouse hole would be too easy, so the locals pronounce it 'Mowzle' (rhyming the first syllable with 'cow'), just to keep the rest of us on our toes.

Newlyn

One of the few place names beginning with 'new' that aren't meant to convey newness. Newlyn was originally Lulyn, which was probably Cornish for 'a pool (*lynn*) for a fleet of boats (*lu*)'; by the fourteenth century it had become Newlyn, simply because enough people thought, 'No, that can't be right' for the change to occur. Confusingly, St Newlyn East is named after an otherwise forgotten saint called Niwelina. To make matters worse, St Newlyn East is nowhere near Newlyn but very near Newquay, whose name does indeed mean 'new quay' (see the box *Not Rocket Science*, page 286).

Padstow

Stow frequently means 'a holy place' and this one is associated with the sixth-century St Petroc, who – like many of his ilk – seems to have left his mark over much of the south-west. The parish church in BODMIN is dedicated to him, but there is also a St Petroc's in EXETER and an Our Lady of Lourdes and St Petroc in ASHBURTON. Two Devon villages, Petrockstowe and Newton St Petroc, bear his name. Petrockstowe is obviously pretty faithful to the original, whereas in Padstow the changing of *e* to *a* may have occurred through confusion with St Patrick, and Petroc has changed to 'Pad' through the same process that turns Patrick into Paddy.

Penryn

'Promontory', from the Celtic *penn* meaning 'head' and *rynn*, 'point of land'. The prefix *pen–*, which the Anglo-Saxons wrongly assumed meant 'hill', is found across the UK: it survives in Pen-y-Ghent in Yorkshire, Pen y fan and other Welsh peaks, PENZANCE, PENRITH and the tautological PENDLE.

Penzance

'Holy headland', the holiness being a reference to a chapel that once stood at the entrance to the harbour – for the meaning of *pen–*, see the previous entry. The town's symbol is the severed head of St John the Baptist, which is odd as the oldest church on record was and is dedicated to the Virgin Mary. It may be that John was chosen as a somewhat macabre pun on 'holy head'.

Redruth

The Cornish language is frequently a trap for the unwary, and Redruth is a prime example. It means 'red ford', but the *red* bit is the ford and *ruth* means 'red'. This was once important mining country, producing two-thirds of the world's copper and a substantial amount of tin, and the process of extracting the metals turned the water red. Retford in Nottinghamshire was also a red ford, in this case because of the red clay soil.

St Austell

Named after a sixth-century Cornish monk, who was normally spelt Austol. He was a follower of the Welsh saint Mewan, whose name lives on in a village just down the road, and helped him to found the abbey known as St-Méen in Brittany.

St Michael's Mount

So named after the Archangel Michael appeared to local fishermen in 495. History does not record why the archangel chose to do this, but there is an earlier Cornish legend that a giant named Cormoran once lived on the mount and used to wade ashore to prey on the local livestock. One night, a boy called Jack (associated by some sources with the fairytale Jack the Giant-Killer) rowed out to the island, dug a pit just below the place where the giant was sleeping and, as the sun was rising, blew a horn to wake him. The giant, not at his best at that hour of the morning, staggered out of bed, was blinded by the sunlight, fell into the pit and died. So it may be that St Michael had heard there was a vacancy. On the other hand, he popped up at Mont St-Michel in France, too, so perhaps he just had a thing about fishing villages with tiny mountains.

SAINTS

As I said in the introduction, Christianity came to various parts of Britain in various waves, but it was an important influence on society by the seventh century AD. Thereafter, place names containing Christian elements became common. ECCLES derives from a Celtic word for *church*, which had itself come from Latin. The Christian references in CHRISTCHURCH and CHURCH STRETTON are obvious. But many places simply dedicated their church to a local saint and took their name directly from that; or they added a saint's name to the existing one. Some of the saints – Peter, Michael, Mary – are still very familiar to Christians; others might have been forgotten if their names hadn't been immortalised in these towns.

St Alban was the first Christian martyr in England, his story recorded for posterity by the Venerable Bede. St Albans, now in Hertfordshire, was in those days (the third century AD) a Roman town called Verulamium and the ancient Roman religion still prevailed. Alban started life as a pagan, but gave shelter to a persecuted Christian priest and was so moved by the man's faith that he converted. He changed clothes with the priest, enabling the latter to escape, but was himself arrested and condemned to death. He was beheaded at the top of a hill just outside the town, where legend has it a spring appeared miraculously to enable him to drink; legend also maintains that the executioner's eyes fell out after he had done the deed. In due course a church was built to honour Alban's memory and it became a place of pilgrimage with a reputation for healing the sick.

St Helen or **Helena** was the mother of the Roman Emperor Constantine, who converted the empire to Christianity. Geoffrey of Monmouth popularised the idea that she was the daughter of King Cole of Camulodonum (Old King Cole), but Geoffrey of Monmouth always needs to be taken with a pinch of salt. Camulodonum is now COLCHESTER, but Helena's most enduring legacy is rather further north. St Helens in Merseyside didn't exist as a town until the nineteenth century, but the local church (originally dedicated to St Elyn, but they hadn't invented spelling back then) is recorded in 1552. After major rebuilding in 1816 it was rededicated and its name changed to St Mary's, a mere thirty-four years before four local villages were joined to create the parish of – St Helens. Precisely a hundred years after the rededication of St Mary's the church was burned to the ground; by the time the replacement was opened in 1926 the good people of St Helens had learned their lesson and went back to the original name. The new church is still going strong. Don't mess with the mothers of Roman emperors, that's what I say.

St Ives in Cambridgeshire was originally called Slepe, 'slippery, muddy place' (it is on the banks of the river Ouse). From AD 986 much of the land in the area belonged to RAMSEY Abbey, and one day a local ploughman accidentally ploughed up a stone coffin, clearly Roman in origin. The local abbot – or perhaps his marketing team – promptly decided that the body was that of a Persian bishop called Ivo and had him reburied in the abbey itself. People flocked to it from miles around, with the result that within a hundred years St Ives was a thriving market town.

St Ives in Cornwall is named after an Irish saint, St Ya, who is said to have floated across to Cornwall on an ivy leaf.

St Ives in Dorset was originally just 'Ives', meaning a place that was overgrown with ivy, but somewhere along the way someone decided that if Cambridgeshire and Cornwall could have a St Ives, Dorset could too.

St Neot was a Saxon monk who divided his time between Glastonbury, Cornwall and the town in Cambridgeshire that now bears his name – which makes him the Dark Ages' equivalent of David Attenborough in globetrotting terms. His relics ended up in the medieval priory of St Neots (Cambridgeshire), which may well be why that town is more substantial than the Cornish village of St Neot, though the absence of a railway from the latter may also have something to do with it.

Tintagel

This may be a spine-tingling setting for Arthurian legend, but it has a somewhat prosaic name: 'fort by the neck of land'. The Celtic *din* meaning 'fort' is found again in the name of another romantic ruin, Tintern Abbey in Monmouthshire.

Truro

Like LOSTWITHIEL and MARAZION, this is a name that is impossible to analyse, even if you have memorised all the common place-name elements listed in the Glossary. It is probably Cornish for 'place of great water turbulence'. The facts that the rivers Kenwyn and Allen meet here and form the river Truro and that the city was prone to flooding until defences were built in the 1980s help to justify this view. But they could equally well support the alternative opinion that the name means 'three rivers'. It has also been suggested that it means 'three ways', as three roads once met here. So, sadly, even if you learned Cornish you probably wouldn't be any the wiser.

DEVON

This area was once the home of a Celtic tribe called the Devonians or Dumnonii. In post-Roman, pre-Saxon times their territory included Cornwall and parts of Somerset as well as the modern county of Devon; their capital was Isca (now EXETER).

Ashburton

One of many names whose whole is more approachable than the sum of its parts: 'the farmstead (*tūn*) on the river (*burna*, as in BOURNEMOUTH and many others) where the ash trees grow'. Informative, yes; catchy – perhaps less so.

Barnstaple

This name is more exciting than it might at first appear: it means 'post of the battleaxe'. The 'post' element signifies a meeting place; the 'battleaxe' would have been a symbol distinguishing it from other such posts. All this reflects the fact that in Saxon times the town was both a stronghold built to withstand Danish invaders and the principal centre of commerce in North Devon, where people came to meet and to trade. The name of Dunstable in Bedfordshire – 'post associated with a man named Dun' – comes from the same source.

Beer

An Old English name meaning 'place by the grove'. The village on the south-east Devon coast has been happy with this unpretentious description for a thousand years; Beer Crocombe in Somerset and Beer Hackett in Dorset both became more impressive-sounding after the Norman Conquest when the name of the local lord of the manor was added.

Bovey Tracey

Sadly, no one seems to know what Bovey means – it is the name of the local river, and a Saxon settlement called Boffa existed here by the sixth century, but where the name came from in the first place is a mystery. The Norman family of de Tracey moved in some time after 1066, in time for William de Tracey to become one of the knights who murdered Thomas Becket in 1170 (see CANTERBURY). William is said to have built the parish church of St Peter, Paul and Thomas of Canterbury as a penance.

Budleigh Salterton

Budleigh is Old English for 'glade belonging to a man named Budda'; Salterton comes from the fact that, in the days before refrigeration, local salt was a valuable commodity, used as a preservative and collected, stored and sold here. A few kilometres inland, the same activity is commemorated in the name of Woodbury Salterton – 'salt-workers' farmstead near the fortified town by the wood'. Indeed, salt is a feature of a number of names in the south-west

– Salcombe in Devon means 'salt valley' and Saltash in Cornwall, once called simply Ash, 'place of the ash tree', had 'salt' added to the front of its name around 1300, when salt production was an important local industry.

Dartmoor

Dart is 'river where oak trees grow', and two branches of it rise on the moor which has taken its name. They meet – reasonably enough – at Dartmeet and flow down to the estuary on which Dartmouth sits. Dartington, where the glass of that name used to be made, was once 'farmstead on the river Dart'. Surprisingly, there isn't a Dartford in Devon, though the one in Kent was originally a place where you could cross the river where the oak trees grew.

Drewsteignton

This village might have been considered too insignificant to be included here if it weren't for the irresistible fact that Drewsteignton is an anagram of Downing Street. That is presumably not the reason for the name, which means 'Drew's farm by the Teign', the Teign being the local river (see the box *The Place by the River*, page 210) and Drew the name of the medieval gentleman who lived there. A couple of kilometres from the village, Castle Drogo picks up the theme: Drogo is the Latinised form of Drew or Drewe, which was the name of the early twentieth-century tea magnate who persuaded Sir Edwin Lutyens to design a castle for him.

Exeter

Exe comes from a Celtic word for water (see the box *The Place by the River*, page 210). The Latin *castra* meant a fort and it was adopted into Old English as *ceaster* or *caster*, lingering on in the names of many places that were originally fortified: CAISTER, CHESTER, LEICESTER, MANCHESTER and so on (see the Introduction, page

11). The ending *-ter* is a corruption of this, making Exeter, which was once the more explicit and more complicated Exanceaster, 'fortified town on the Exe'.

George Nympton

You'd expect this to be a pub named in honour of a local hero, but it is more complicated than that. Nympton means 'farmstead by the Nimet', which is probably an Old Celtic name for the river Mole and suggests a holy place. The local church is dedicated to St George, and if it seems perverse that they didn't call the place Nympton St George so that we could guess what the name meant – well, they did in the thirteenth century and then some bright spark changed it. This might have been out of a desire for symmetry: there is also a Bishop's Nympton (once in the possession of the bishops of EXETER) and a King's Nympton (owned by William I himself).

Germansweek

The *week* here is actually a *wīc* or dairy farm (see the box *Farming Country 2*, page 139) and the local church is dedicated to St Germanus, one of those lesser-known saints of whom the south-west is so fond (see PADSTOW and the box on *Saints*, page 33).

Honiton

Originally Honetune, 'farmstead belonging to a man named Huna'. So what? you might ask. Well, this becomes more interesting when you consider that the rather smaller Clyst Honiton was originally Hinatune, which meant 'farmstead belonging to a religious community' (it came under the jurisdiction of EXETER Cathedral). Presumably the distinction between the two names, which were similar enough to be confused by the uninitiated, was simply blurred into oblivion as time went by. Clyst, a tributary of the Exe, probably means 'sea inlet' (though both 'hallowed place' and 'clean stream' have been suggested). It has been added to a number of village names, of which the most intriguing is Clyst William. While Clyst St Lawrence, Clyst St George and Clyst St Mary are distinguished by the names of their parish churches, William isn't a saint or even a person: he comes from the Old English *aewelm*, 'river source' and sits at the source of the river Clyst.

Ilfracombe

'Alfred's valley', or possibly 'the valley belonging to Alfred's sons', is all we know. Tradition rather than history makes a link with Alfred the Great; it is more likely to be the name of a local lord in Anglo-Saxon times.

Lynmouth

This and nearby Lynton, situated by the river Lyn, might have gone under the heading 'not rocket science' were it not that *lyn–* means 'torrent', a fact which became tragically significant on the night of 15 August 1952. Some 23 cm of rain had fallen on Exmoor in the previous twenty-four hours, with the result that the two branches of the river came together and roared down the steep-sided valley to the seaside town. Gathering boulders as they went, they caused cottages to 'fold up like a pack of cards', as one onlooker described it, and drowned thirty-four people. Records tell of comparable devastations in 1607 and 1770, suggesting that the Anglo-Saxons who named the river knew what they were talking about.

Moretonhampstead

However you spell it and wherever it is in the country (there are Moretons and Mortons all over the place), the first part of this name means 'farmstead on a moor or marshy ground'. This particular Moreton is one of about a dozen that appear in the Domesday

Book. 'Hampstead' is a combination of two Old English elements
–ham, 'homestead', and *–sted*, 'site of a building', with the *p* inserted
to make it easier to pronounce. Like *–ton*, therefore, the compound
–hampstead ends up meaning little more than 'village'. It was added
to this name in the fifteenth century, by which time people had
forgotten where Moreton came from in the first place. See the box
Farming Country 1, page 50.

Newton Abbot

Newton, as you might expect, means 'new farmstead, estate or
village'; Abbot indicates that it was once under the jurisdiction of
an abbey, in this case Torre Abbey. Many Newtons – and there are
plenty of them across England – have a second part to their name
derived from their Norman overlords: Newton Burgoland in Leicestershire, Newton Ferrers in Devon and Newton Purcell in Oxfordshire are examples. Even the wonderfully named Newton Blossom-
ville in Buckinghamshire can be explained in this way: it was once
owned by the de Bloseville family, with no suggestion that they were
keen gardeners. Other Newtons are augmented by a description of
the terrain: Newton Aycliffe in Durham stood in a clearing among
oaks and Newton Poppleford in Devon grew up by a pebbly ford.
Finally, Newton Flotman in Norfolk reflects that age-old suspicion
of outsiders. Its name tells us that it was once owned by a sailor or
Viking – from the Old English for 'floating man', 'a man who came
from across the sea'.

Noss Mayo

This off-the-wall name is said to have arisen in the thirteenth
century, when Edward I gave the manor of Stoke to one Mathew
Fitzjohn. This, added to the shape of the peninsula on which it
sits, may explain why it came to be known as 'Mathew's nose' or
'Mathew's promontory' – rendered in Old English as Noss Mayo.

Okehampton

Okement is a Celtic river name meaning 'fast flowing' and Okehampton is the homestead on it. There is no connection with oaks. Similarly, the granite outcrop called Yes Tor, which overlooks the town, has nothing to do with anyone agreeing to anything: it's from the Old English for 'eagles' hill'. There are no eagles either, though if you are lucky you might see the odd harrier or buzzard.

Ottery St Mary

The town sits on the river Otter, so called because – yes, really – it was frequented by otters, and has a church dedicated to the Virgin Mary. Otterburn in Northumberland similarly means 'otter stream'.

Paignton

Nobody is certain about the origins of this name, but it was probably 'estate associated with a man named Paega'. Thus it might originally have been 'Paegington', the *–ing–* signifying 'associated with' or 'the family or descendants of' (see the box *Whose Place Is It Anyway?*, page 189). By the time of the Domesday Book this had been simplified – or corrupted, call it what you will – to Peintone. Over the ensuing centuries it was variously written Paington and Peynton until, in the nineteenth century, a railway company moved the *g* to create the current spelling, which neatly parallels that of Teignmouth (see the box on *The Place by the River*, page 210), just up the coast. Nobody is sure whether this was a marketing wheeze or a spelling mistake, but either way it hasn't been changed back.

Plympton/Plymouth

Plympton is somewhat unusual in that the name of the settlement pre-dates the name of the river. Plympton means not, as you might expect, 'farmstead on the Plym' but 'farmstead with plum trees'. The river Plym therefore got its name via a process called back-formation

– which means that, in this instance, people assumed Plympton meant 'farmstead on the Plym' and named the river accordingly. Plympton is first recorded early in the tenth century, Plymouth – 'place at the mouth of the Plym' – not until 1230. Oddly, given these dates, the name of the river does not appear until 1238, though it must have been well established in local usage by then.

Tiverton

The ninth-century spelling Twyfyrde is the clue here: it means 'two fords'. The river Loman flows into the Exe here, and the town developed because it was a point at which both rivers could be crossed. The *–ton* ending had been added by the eleventh century: the Domesday Book records it as Tovretone. If you pronounce Twyfyrde with a silent *w* (as in the modern word *two*), the change of spelling over the years becomes less of a stretch.

Torbay/Torquay

All the *Tor–* names in this part of Devon stem from Torre, originally a small Saxon settlement that grew more important after the founding of an abbey in the twelfth century (see NEWTON ABBOT). The name means 'rocky hill' and the later developments of Torquay and Torbay are simply the quay and the bay nearby.

Westward Ho!

The only place name in Britain that ends with an exclamation mark, this was originally the title of a romantic adventure novel by Charles Kingsley, published in 1855 and set largely in nearby Bideford ('ford across the river Byd). Kingsley had meant the title to mean something along the lines of 'Go west, young man' but when the popularity of the novel attracted people to holiday in that part of the world, it was annexed by a couple of entrepreneurs who were building a hotel to cash in on the new demand. From being the name of a hotel, Kingsley's title – and exclamation mark – extended to the surrounding area.

SOMERSET

Somerset is named after neither a Celtic tribe nor a giant-killer; like most other counties it takes its name from its principal town. The –set ending refers to the people who lived near and were dependent on a place. Somerset originally meant 'the people who live around SOMERTON', which was once an important trading centre.

Bath

People have been drawn to the healing waters around which Bath is built for 10,000 years, although the city was not founded until 863 BC, after the ancient British king Bladud had been cured of leprosy here. Or so the story goes. The Romans called the city Aquae Sulis, 'the waters of Sulis', Sulis being the local goddess of water and healing. It was they who built a reservoir round the spring and constructed the first bath-houses: earlier visitors bathed or drank in the open air. By the tenth century the Latin name had been ditched in favour of Bathan ('baths') and the modern form was established by the seventeenth.

Bristol

The governance of Bristol is such that you could argue for it to be included in Gloucestershire or to have a separate county listing to itself, but please keep these arguments to yourself – it has to go somewhere, so here it is. The name means 'assembly place by the bridge' and indicates Bristol's importance in commerce from the earliest times. In Anglo-Saxon/Viking days it was a centre for the slave trade and later thrived on exporting cloth and minerals and importing wine, grain and other necessities (before taking up the slave trade again, when its victims became Africans rather than

Britons). There has been a harbour here since the thirteenth century, created by modifying and diverting the rivers Avon and Frome; the first stone bridge was also built in the thirteenth century, but the name Bristol existed by the time of the Domesday Book, suggesting that there were earlier, wooden bridges. The latter part of the name comes from the Old English *stōw*. This often meant a place where people met for religious purposes (see, for example, PADSTOW and FELIXSTOWE), but that was clearly not the case here: people came to Bristol on business. So how did *–stow* turn into *–stol*, when it remains as *–stow* or *–stowe* in so many places? Well, if you are sitting comfortably, the local accent includes a phenomenon called l-vocalisation, which is a tendency to turn the consonant *l* into a vowel: think of the way some people pronounce 'middle' as something like 'middow'. As early as the twelfth century Bristolians were doing this to some words and then indulging in another phenomenon called hypercorrection – putting something right when it wasn't wrong in the first place. To get your head round this, think of people who habitually drop their h's but then say things like 'happle' or 'hanswer'. In other words, hearing the pronunciation 'Bristow', the posher locals assumed – wrongly – that this was a case of l-vocalisation and hypercorrected it to the modern form.

Castle Cary

The name of the river Cary dates from Celtic or even pre-Celtic times and may mean 'stony'. The castle didn't last long, by castle standards: it was built some time between 1066 and 1138, and before the end of the twelfth century the new dynasty of Plantagenet kings had allowed it to fall into ruin for 'political reasons'.

Chard

This is thought to mean 'building on rough ground'. Modern-day Chard is the highest town in Somerset; the slopes around it are steep and the soils notoriously poor, so it would certainly have been tough – and probably rough – ground for Saxon farmers to work.

Crewkerne

'Building by the hill'. The Celtic prefix *cruc*–, meaning tumulus or hill, also forms part of the endearingly named villages of Cricket St Thomas and Cricket Malherbie, just down the road. The –*et* part of 'Cricket' means 'little'; St Thomas was the murdered Archbishop of CANTERBURY, Thomas Becket, who was canonised in 1173 and subsequently had a lot of churches named after him; and Malherbie was the name of a local manorial family (whose name suggests an ancestor who came from a place overgrown with weeds).

Frome

Another Celtic river name, this one meaning 'brisk'. Frome in Somerset is simply named after the river on which it sits. The name of Frome St Quintin in Dorset derives from a different river and from a late medieval lord of the manor; 10 km downriver is Frampton, 'a farmstead on the Frome'. Yet another river Frome, this time in Herefordshire, boasts Bishops Frome, Canon Frome and Castle Frome, whose names all refer to the spheres of influence – religious or political – into which the settlements once fell.

Glastonbury

'The stronghold of the people living at the woad place' would never have caught on, would it?

Keynsham

This –*ham* was originally a *hamm*, 'enclosure in a bend in a river' (see the Introduction, page 20). This particular bend – in the river Avon – may have been named after a man called Caegin or possibly a saint called Keyne, who also gave her name to the village of St

Keyne in Cornwall. It seems unlikely that a pious virgin of the sixth century should have divided her time between these two places – they're about 250 km apart – but these Cornish saints do seem to have got around.

Langport

You may wonder what a place whose name sounds as if it means 'long port' is doing 25 km from the nearest sea. Well, two thousand years ago it occupied a strategic position on the river Parrett; the Romans built a causeway here and used barges to transport goods to and from the Bristol Channel. The river later developed a tendency to silt up and the town's importance as a trading post declined. However, in addition to the modern meaning of 'harbour' (which comes from the Latin *portus*) and the unconnected meaning of 'door or gate' (Latin *porta*), in Old English a 'port' might also be a market town, so the name may have come from this. Either way, it was once very prosperous and must also have been long.

Midsomer Norton

As with SOMERTON and Somerset, the pronunciation 'summer' is the clue; indeed, *somer* is an old spelling of the modern word. In medieval times the feast of St John, which falls on 24 June, was marked by a huge midsummer fair here. Norton, which occurs in many other place names all over the country, means 'farmstead or village to the north' – that is, to the north of wherever the person doing the measuring is standing.

Minehead

Nothing to do with mining, this is a combination of a Celtic word meaning 'hill' (it is related to the Welsh *mynydd*, as in the Long Mynd in Shropshire) and a later Old English addition which gives us the further information that the hill is on a promontory jutting out into the sea.

Nempnett Thrubwell

This ought to be a firm of solicitors in a Dickens novel, or possibly the name of a minor public school, but in fact is an amalgam of two earlier villages. Nempnett means 'place at the level ground' – fair enough, as it is just on the edge of the Mendip Hills. Thrubwell is a place at a well or spring (see WELLS, below), possibly a gushing one (if *thrub* is related to the modern *throb*, as one authority suggests). As is often the case with ancient wells and springs, there is a possibility that it was at one time sacred to the Celts. Whether or not there are Celtic gods hanging about, the village is home to the remains of an ancient burial mound or barrow which rejoices in the name of the Fairy Toot. According to an eighteenth-century source, 'the field in which this barrow stands has from time immemorial been called the Fairy Field and the common people say that strange noises have been heard underneath the hill'. The fairies playing their recorders, perhaps?

Norton St Philip

Another 'farmstead or village to the north' (see MIDSOMER NORTON), this tourist-luring village boasts a church dedicated to both St Philip and St James, but most people go there because of the pub dedicated to St George, one of the oldest hostelries in the country. Some say it dates back to 1223, which would make it older than the local priory, but then the people who built the priory had to sleep – and drink – somewhere. Although the name of the village is recorded, in its Latin version, as Norton Sancti Phillipi in 1316, the variations Philips Norton and Philip's Norton occur as late as the nineteenth century.

Peasedown St John

This is one of those quietly pleasing names that means what you would hope it might mean: 'hill where peas are grown', with the later addition of the name of the parish church. Peas were also grown (by the pond) in Peasemore in Berkshire, which was originally Peasemere; (in a nook of land) in Peasenhall in Suffolk (see LUDGERSHALL for more about this sort of nook); and (in marshy ground) in Peasmarsh in Sussex. The name of Pease Pottage in Sussex is first recorded as Pease Pottage Gate on a map dated 1724, too late for this etymology to be likely: it is more probable that it was a jokey reference to the marshy ground hereabouts. The 'gate' may refer to the fact that there was a turnpike or tollgate on the busy road, or to the village's position at the entrance to a forest – either way, it later became obsolete and was dropped.

Porlock

Anyone who has studied the poet Coleridge knows that he was interrupted in the composition of *Kubla Khan* by 'a person from Porlock', and much ink has been exhausted in speculation on who, why and what his business was. The name is less controversial: it means 'enclosure by the harbour', the *por–* element being a corruption of 'port' and *–lock* being connected to the modern senses of locks that can be opened with keys or enclosed in canals.

Radstock

'Outlying farmstead by the road', the reference being to the Fosse Way, the Roman road that ran from EXETER to LINCOLN and marked the boundary of the first phase of the Roman conquest in the mid-first century AD. It got its name from the Latin for 'ditch', because it had a deep ditch on either side.

Shepton Mallet

This was simply Shepton, 'sheep farm', in Old English times; in the Norman period it became part of the manor of a family named Malet. The smaller villages of Shepton Montague and Shepton

Beauchamp had different owners but a similar connection with sheep. The Malet family also owned Curry Mallet, not a utensil for crushing spices but a village near the river Curry. The meaning of

FARMING COUNTRY 1

The two most common elements in English place names are *–ham* and *–ton*, from the Old English *hām* or *tūn* respectively. *Hām* – the ancestor of modern 'home' – occurs in the earliest Anglo-Saxon place names and is usually translated as 'homestead', but the meaning expanded as settlements themselves grew in sophistication, to cover a village, manor or estate. *Tūn* first appears a bit later and was originally an enclosure, but soon came to mean 'farmstead' and eventually 'town'. As early as the ninth century the two elements were combined to form the ancestor of the modern *Hampton*, which acquired the meaning of 'home farm, farmstead or village proper', as opposed to any outlying places. It is worth pointing out, though, that not all *–hamptons* come from this combining of two simple elements. Hampton can also mean 'high farmstead', as in MINCH-INHAMPTON, or it can come from *hamm* meaning a bend in the river (see the Introduction, page 20, and SOUTHAMPTON).

Hām and *tūn* would have been pronounced 'hahm' and 'toon' until about the sixteenth century, when a phenomenon known as the Great Vowel Shift introduced the modern 'home' and 'town'. But by that time the place names of which these words formed part were well established and their origins largely forgotten: certainly the current pronunciations of such names as BIRMING-HAM and NORTHAMPTON, with almost no final vowel sound at all, are miles away from either their Old English sources or their Modern English equivalents.

the river name is unknown, but that seems a small price to pay for having such an excellent name.

Somerton

'Farmstead or village used in summer', this former county town lies on the fringes of the Somerset Levels. To this day these are quite, um, level and were once marshland amid which people lived on man-made islands. The land was too wet to be grazed in winter, so cattle were brought down from the surrounding hills only when the low-lying country was at its driest.

Taunton

'Farmstead on the river Tone', the name of the river meaning that it was sparkling and fast-flowing. In the eighth century the settle-ment was called Tantun and by the time of the Domesday Book it was Tantone, suggesting confusion between the two similar-sounding elements that made up its name. At some point over the centuries the river was also called the Thon before both it and the town settled on their current spellings.

Watchet

It's difficult to guess that a place name means 'under the wood' when the woods aren't there any more, but that is the case here. Watchet sits at the foot of cliffs that were once heavily forested.

Wellington

'Estate associated with a man named Weola'. The two other Wellingtons in England – a town in Shropshire and a village in Herefordshire – have the same derivation, but it is the town in Somerset that claims a connection with the first Duke of Welling-ton. The story is that when he was offered a peerage, Arthur Welles-ley, as he then was, didn't know what title to choose. His brother discovered a family link with Wellington – their ancestors had owned property in the area in centuries gone by. This was good enough for Arthur, though he made no serious attempt to become intimate with the place, visiting it only once in his long lifetime.

Wells

There are lots of natural springs in this area and that is what the Old English word *wella* means. A document dated 766 mentions a 'large spring', which is probably St Andrew's Well, now in the garden of the Bishop's Palace. Other settlements based round springs had to give themselves longer, more explanatory titles (see, for example, TUNBRIDGE WELLS and WELLS-NEXT-THE-SEA) because this one had bagged the name first.

Weston-super-Mare

If you know any Latin, this goes into the 'not rocket science' section, but in case you don't: *super mare* is Latin for 'on sea' and, as any glance at a map will tell you, this is a settlement on the west coast. It was given the 'on sea' tag in the fourteenth century to distinguish it from the wonderfully named Westonzoyland, and nobody has ever felt strongly enough to abandon the Latin. Zoyland simply means 'in the manor of [an old district called] Sowi' and Westonzoyland is to the west of Middlezoy. Why, in the nineteenth century, someone decided to add *–land* (meaning 'estate') on to Westonzoy but not Middlezoy is a matter for conjecture: best guess is that by this time they were owned by different people and the owner of Westonzoy had delusions of grandeur.

Wiveliscombe

It is most likely that this means 'valley associated with a man named Wifel', but it is more fun to go with the alternative suggestion that it was a beetle-infested valley, its name connected with the modern word *weevil*.

Yeovil

Once upon a time, Yeovil and the river Yeo had the same name, variously Gifl, Ivel or Gifle, which is Old Celtic for 'forked river'. The river flows through not only Yeovil and Yeovilton but also Ilchester ('Roman town on the Yle', which was the spelling in vogue at the time this town was named). There are a number of other rivers called Yeo in the West Country, but most of their names are of Old English origin: they derive from the word *ea*, which means a river or stream. A second Somerset Yeo is different again and may mean 'stream where yews grow'. Over the centuries the names of all these rivers have influenced each other, so that they end up taking the line of least resistance and coming out the same.

2

SOUTH-CENTRAL ENGLAND

Although the Jutes are known to have settled in Hampshire and the Isle of Wight in the fifth century, by the seventh they had given way to the West Saxons, who gave their name to the kingdom of Wessex. The most famous King of Wessex was Alfred the Great (871–99), whose achievements include preventing the Danes from overrunning southern England, building a number of fortifications which grew into thriving towns, and reviving literacy and learning in the wake of the Danish raids on the northern monasteries. He also managed to remain on good terms with his neighbours: no mean achievement given the history of this period. If there is one man who can take the credit for England becoming a united country, it is Alfred the Great. His capital was WINCHESTER, a city that was still strategically important at the time of the Norman Conquest: after his victory at Hastings, William the Conqueror marched a long way out of his way in order to subdue Winchester before heading for LONDON.

DORSET

Like Somerset, Dorset takes its name from the people who settled round a place – in this case DORCHESTER, which, then as now, was the most important town in the area.

Affpuddle

One of the most endearing names in the book, this has a disappointingly banal meaning: it is 'estate on the river Piddle belonging to a man named Aeffa'. Even Piddle, which you'd think was a cute name for a river, means nothing more giggleworthy than 'marsh' or 'fen'. However, it redeems itself by inspiring two other wonderful names: Piddlehinton, 'estate on the Piddle belonging to a religious community', and Piddletrenthide, 'estate on the Piddle assessed at thirty hides'. A hide was a measure of land reckoned as 'enough to support a household'; it was used in the Domesday Book and elsewhere to assess how much tax a landowner or tenant should pay.

Blandford Forum

Bland– comes from a Saxon word meaning gudgeon – a small fish caught and eaten by the poor. So Blandford stood at a ford in a river that gudgeon came from. Conveniently situated, as the estate agents say, at the point where the roads from POOLE to SHAFTES-BURY and from SALISBURY to DORCHESTER met (and crossed the river), it was a market town by the thirteenth century. It then became first Chipping Blandford (see the box on *Market Towns* on page 102) and later Blandford Forum, using the Latin rather than the Old English word for a market. This also distinguished it from nearby Blandford St Mary, named, since at least the thirteenth century, after its church. Blandford Forum was badly damaged by fire in 1579 and totally destroyed in 1731, so a lot of its early records have been lost: we don't know how its original church compared with St Mary's down the road, but the 1732 replacement, dedicated to St Peter and St Paul, is regarded as the finest Georgian church outside LONDON. So that's an ill wind...

Chesil Beach

Chesil comes from the Old English for 'shingle'. Try walking along the beach in bare feet and you'll see why.

Christchurch

One of the more self-explanatory names in the book. The church in question is an eleventh-century priory with the distinction of being the longest parish church in Britain (around 90 m). Before the name Christchurch appeared, about 1125, the settlement was known as Twynham, 'place between the rivers', because it is situated between the Avon and the Stour (see the box *The Place by the River*, page 210).

Cranborne

'Stream where cranes or herons are seen'. There were obviously a lot of these birds about in Anglo-Saxon times, as their presence explains the names of Cranbrook in Kent, Cranfield in Bedfordshire, Cranford in Greater London, Cranham in Gloucestershire and many more. Don't go running away with the idea that you have spotted a pattern, though, because Cranham in Greater London is so called because it was frequented by crows.

Dorchester

The Celts lived in this area at least 4,500 years ago: Maumbury Rings, the circular 'henge' just to the south of the town, dates back to that time. It would have been an important meeting place, possibly a religious one, for two thousand years before the Romans decided it was a great site for an amphitheatre. In due course the Romans also built walls round the town, and the mosaics that survive in a Roman town house discovered in the 1930s show a comfortable standard of living in the fourth century AD. As for the name, the Saxons called the place Dornwaraceaster, having adding *ceaster*, 'Roman fortified town', to the Roman name, Durnovaria. This in turn was a Latinised version of the Old Celtic, which for a long time was thought to mean 'place of fist play', referring to the fighting that went on in the amphitheatre. But the Celtic name is much older than the amphitheatre, so that can't be right; modern wisdom is that it is more likely to have meant 'place with the fist-sized pebbles'. If the pebbles had come from CHESIL BEACH, this would certainly have the ring of truth about it.

Durdle Door

'Pierced or drilled opening' – an apt description for this natural rock arch, which was formed by the sea beating away at the softer rocks, leaving the tougher limestone behind.

Lyme Regis

Lim was an Old Celtic word for 'stream', which became the name first of a river and then of the settlement at its mouth. *Regis* is Latin for 'of the king' and the regal suffix appeared in 1284, when the town was granted a Royal Charter by Edward I. A Royal Charter gave towns certain legal rights – effectively it made them into towns with governing bodies, rather than a group of people who happened to live near each other. The Crown still hands them out, turning towns into cities and allowing organisations such as the Royal Mint, the Royal Opera House and the Royal Institute of British Architects to have 'royal' in their names.

Poole

This is an old form of 'pool', so the name means 'place at the pool' – in this instance, Poole Harbour. Most names ending in –*pool*, including BLACKPOOL and LIVERPOOL, have the same derivation.

Purbeck

The name originally referred to the Purbeck Hills – 'beak-shaped ridge frequented by bittern or snipe'. The Isle of Purbeck, on which the hills sit, takes its name from them, and Purbeck stone and Purbeck marble are quarried there.

Sherborne

Old English for 'bright, clear river'. The town in Dorset with a famous school is the best known example of this name, but there are a number of others with the same sparkly derivation: one in Gloucestershire with the same spelling, Sherbourne in Warwickshire, and three Sherburns, one in Durham and two in Yorkshire. As you might expect, Monk Sherborne in Hampshire used to have a priory, but if you travel a few kilometres down the road you may be surprised to learn that the parish church of Sherborne St John is dedicated to St Andrew, and has been since about 1150. Robert St John was a thirteenth-century lord of the manor who clearly wasn't going to let a mere saint stand between him and posterity.

Sixpenny Handley

Handley means 'high wood or clearing', but disappointingly the 'Sixpenny' bit has nothing to do with its perceived value. Instead it comes from the name of the hundred – ancient administrative district – in which it is found. Break 'Sixpenny' down into the Old English *six*– or *sex*– and the Celtic *pen*– (see PENRYN) and you'll find that it means 'Saxons' hill'. Perfectly sensible, but not as much fun as the modern version.

Swanage

The Old English word for 'swan' was *swan*, which would be helpful if they hadn't also had a word *swān*, pronounced more like 'swain' and meaning 'young man, servant or herdsman' – the modern words 'swain' and 'boatswain' derive from this. There is nothing to tell us whether Swanage meant a farm where swans were reared or a herdsman's farm. The suffix –*age* derives, oddly, from the Old English *wīc*, meaning a farm (see the box *Farming Country 2*, page 139): Swanage was called Swanawic in the late ninth century, Swanwic in the Domesday Book and Swanewiz in 1183, gradually drifting closer to the modern pronunciation. See also SWANLEY.

Verwood

Say 'Fairwood' in a Dorset accent and you won't be far wrong. In fact, you'll be spot on, as long as you mean 'fair' in the old-fashioned sense of 'handsome' or 'beautiful'. The first mention of the name (1288) gives it as the Norman French Beuboys ('fair wood'); then in 1377 Fairwoode is mentioned in a charter granted by a local landowner named William de Bello Bosco, whose name is a Latin form of – funnily enough – 'fair wood'. The spelling Fairwood persisted into the nineteenth century, when Verwood was removed from the vast parish of CRANBORNE and established as a village in its own right. The new parish of Verwood included the intriguingly named Three-legged Cross, but sadly this probably means nothing more than that it sat at a place where three roads met. An attempt to make it more exciting points out that there may have been a gallows (known as a 'three-legged mare') here, because there often was a gallows at a crossroads, but there is no hard evidence.

Wareham

'Homestead by the weir'. There was certainly a weir by the twelfth century and probably much earlier than that – the name is first recorded in the ninth century, and there is evidence that there was a settlement here way back in the Iron Age. Wareham's strategic position between the rivers Piddle and Frome would always have made this an attractive site. Weirs, like fords, were an important feature of the landscape in olden times: they are also the source of Ware in Hertfordshire, and of Edgware ('weir associated with a man called Ecgi') in Greater London.

Wimborne

The river on which Wimborne sits is now called the Allen, but it used to be the Wimborne, which means 'meadow stream'. The town is strictly speaking Wimborne Minster, referring to the eighth-century nunnery round which the settlement grew. (This was destroyed by the Danes and replaced in Norman times.) Further upriver are Wimborne St Giles – no prizes for guessing the name of its parish church – and Monkton Up Wimborne, where there was once a monastic chapel. Allen, by the way, is another of those ancient Celtic river names whose meaning no one knows.

Winterbourne Abbas

Literally 'winter stream', this means a stream that flows most strongly in the winter and may even be completely dry in summer. Perhaps the people who founded a settlement here moved to SOMERTON when the time seemed right. Abbas refers to the village's association with the Abbey of Cerne, and lots of other Winterbournes or Winterbornes have additional names showing their connection with the church (Winterborne Monkton in Wiltshire, associated with GLASTONBURY Abbey), the nobility (Winterbourne Earls, also in Wiltshire, owned by the Earls of SALISBURY) or a particular manorial family (Winterborne Clenston, Winterborne Stickland, Winterborne Zelston and Winterborne Herringston, all in Dorset. Sad that Winterborne Herringston wasn't a fish market, but you can't always have what you want). Winterbourne Gunner in Wiltshire was once the property of a lady called Gunnora, some six centuries before anyone in the village had any chance of being an Arsenal fan. Winterborne Whitechurch tells us that the church was made of stone – comparatively unusual still in the thirteenth century. Winterton in Lincolnshire is nothing to do with winter, but comes from a personal name.

Wool

This name has nothing to do with sheep; it is the same derivation as anywhere called WELLS and means 'place at the spring'.

HAMPSHIRE

This was originally Hamtun-shire, 'the shire of SOUTHAMPTON'.
'Shire' names came into being around the tenth century and that
of Hampshire was presumably established before Southampton
acquired its 'southern' prefix.

Aldershot

Alder– is a common opening for place names and, irritatingly, it
seems to be connected with alder trees almost exactly half the time.
This is one of those occasions: Aldershot means 'projecting piece
of land where alders grow'. Others include Alderford in Norfolk
('ford where alders grow'), Alderholt in Dorset ('farm where alders
grow') and Alderley in Gloucestershire ('woodland clearing where
alders grow'). For examples of other meanings for *alder*, see ALDER-
MASTON and ALDERLEY EDGE.

Alton

'Farmstead at the source of a river', in this case the river Wey (see
the box *The Place by the River*, page 210). Alton Pancras in Dorset
sits near the source of the Piddle (see AFFPUDDLE) and is a rare
appearance of the name of this child-saint other than as a London
railway station. Alton in Derbyshire, home of Alton Towers, has a
different derivation and means 'old farmstead'.

Andover

'Stream where ashes grow'. The *–dover* element recurs in DOVER
and in Wendover ('white waters').

Bournemouth

'Mouth of the stream', the *bourne* element being connected to the
Scottish word *burn* and to other similar place names. The stream
in question is called the Bourne, which makes up in simplicity what
it lacks in imagination.

SHIRES AND COUNTIES

The concept of a *shire* came into being under the Saxons in the tenth century, after England finally became a single country. A shire was an administrative district with its own court and a bailiff or reeve whose task it was to represent the king in his area. This official became known as the shire-reeve or *sheriff* and he was a powerful man, as any fan of Robin Hood will know. The Normans inherited this system but introduced their own word, *county*, creating what are known as the historic counties of England – names and areas which have survived in popular use despite the occasional burst of official boundary redrawing over the years.

For the most part, shires were named after their principal town and the counties retained these names – Hertfordshire, Warwickshire, Yorkshire, etc. Those that kept their older names included the ancient kingdoms of Kent and Cornwall; and the various subdivisions of Wessex, including Sussex, Surrey, Somerset, etc, whose names are explained under their individual county entries. Cumberland and Northumberland were too sparsely populated and too subject to conflict with the Scots to be included in the original system.

In modern parlance the *–shire* ending occurs almost exclusively in counties that are named after a town: the only real exception is Berkshire, although you might think that the town names in Shropshire, Wiltshire and Hampshire were cunningly disguised. Over the years, however, there have been anomalies. Suffolkshire, for example, is found in some late medieval records, but Camden in the sixteenth century and Daniel Defoe, travelling in the 1720s, both refer to Suffolk and Norfolk without remarking on the name (and Camden is a great one for giving variants and 'folk' usage – if Suffolkshire had been a local alternative in his day, he would have told us). Devonshire was once a common form (Defoe uses it, though Bartholomew's 1887 gazetteer has the shorter version) and is still occasionally found, mostly in references to cream teas and in the title of the Duke of Devonshire, whose seat, bizarrely, is in Derbyshire (see RICHMOND).

The boundaries of the historic counties remained much as they had always been until the nineteenth century, when major reforms to local government were introduced. Notable later changes came in 1974, with the introduction of metropolitan and non-metropolitan boroughs (some of them subsequently abolished). This created, for example, Merseyside from parts of Cheshire and Lancashire, and divided Sussex into East and West. There were some apparent oddities, too: Bedfordshire was unchanged, but Oxfordshire took over parts of Berkshire. The areas that emerged least scathed from this sort of operation were again the ancient kingdoms – Kent, Devon and (now here's a surprise) Cornwall.

As far as individual town names are concerned, however, this higher-level administrative reshuffling has had little effect – most were established long before they needed to worry about whether they were in Staffordshire or the West Midlands.

Enham Alamein

Enham is an old name for an old place: in the eleventh century it was either a homestead or an enclosure where lambs were reared (this is one of those instances where we don't know if it was a *hām* or a *-hamm* – see the Introduction, page 20). In the thirteenth century it became Knight's Enham, because it was held by a knight called

Matthew de Columbers. But the real interest here lies in Alamein, which was of course the site of a famous Allied victory in North Africa during the Second World War – the one which caused Winston Churchill to remark that it was, perhaps, the end of the beginning. Many of the injured soldiers from El Alamein were sent home to a recovery centre in Enham, which had been set up at the end of the First World War but had run short of funds in the 1920s and 1930s. When the Second World War was over, a public subscription in Egypt contributed a substantial sum to allow the centre at Enham to be extended, and the change in the village's name was a token of gratitude.

Farnborough

'Hill or mound where ferns grow' (as in MARLBOROUGH, the ending comes from the Old English *beorg*, 'hill or mound', rather than *burh*, 'fortified place'). Other ferny places include Fareham in Hampshire, Faringdon in Oxfordshire, Farnborough in Kent, Farnham in Surrey, Farnworth in Greater Manchester, Ferndown in Dorset and possibly the Farne Islands off the coast of Northumberland. But to relieve the monotony of such a long list, the town of Ferns in County Wexford, although outside the remit of this book, takes its name from an Irish word meaning 'elder trees'.

Fleet

Too far from the sea to have anything to do with the navy, this means 'place on a stream, pool or creek'. The now largely underground river Fleet in LONDON, which gave its name to Fleet Street, comes from the same source. So do the towns of Fleet in Lincolnshire and Northfleet and Southfleet in Kent, which had acquired their distinguishing prefixes by the time of the Domesday Book.

Gosport

Although Gosport is on the coast and started life as a fishing hamlet, the *port* element here (as in LANGPORT) signifies a market town rather than a harbour. The whole name means 'goose town', either because geese were sold in the market or because wild geese gathered in the area. An alternative explanation that either King Stephen or the Bishop of Winchester sheltered here after being saved from a storm and suggested that the town be called 'God's port' seems to have no basis in fact. Though this doesn't stop it persisting.

Havant

The Old English version of this name was Hamanfuntan, which makes the translation of 'spring belonging to a man named Hama' more explicable: *–funtan* derives ultimately from the same source as the modern *fountain*. By the time of the Domesday Book the name had been corrupted to Havehunte and, if you consider that the *h* is usually silent in French, this is getting fairly close to the current form.

New Alresford

Another name to keep you on your toes: ALDERLEY EDGE may have nothing to do with alders, but Alresford (pronounced 'Allsford') does. It is, simply, 'ford where the alders grow'. A settlement of this name – now known as Old Alresford – is recorded as early as 701 but even the 'new' version dates back to 1200, when a Great Weir was constructed across a reservoir to the south of the old town. There is also an Alresford in Essex, but, confusingly, its name derives either from a man's name or from 'eels' ford'.

New Forest

This one is not as obvious as it might seem, being neither new nor entirely a forest. It became William the Conqueror's new hunting ground in 1079, when it was brought under Forest Law. This means that it was thereafter a protected area in which deer and other huntable animals were nurtured and the rights of the local populace severely restricted. It doesn't necessarily mean that it was heavily wooded or that a programme of tree-planting was undertaken: much of the area, then as now, was open heathland. Trees were in fact planted en masse in the seventeenth and eighteenth centuries, but that was to supply timber for England's thriving shipbuilding trade.

Petersfield

The vast majority of place names beginning with Peter refer to a church dedicated to the apostle, and this is no exception. Around the year 1100 St Peter's was built in an open space ('field') near the manor, because the existing church was an inconvenient distance away across marshy ground.

Portsmouth

'Mouth of the harbour' – a glance at a map will provide all the explanation needed. The harbour has been an important one for well over a thousand years and many local place names, such as Portchester, Ports Down and Portsea, refer to it. Portsea is nothing to do with the sea but means 'the island by the port'. Read it as *Port's–ea* and it will make more sense: an –*ea* or –*ey* ending, especially when preceded by a possessive *'s*, often means 'island' (see CHERTSEY, RAMSEY and many others). There is scope for confusion, though, because some –*ea* and –*ey* endings come not from *ēg*, 'island', but *ēa*, 'stream' – ROMNEY is one example. As with the *hams* and *hamms* discussed in the Introduction, it is a matter of going back to early spellings for clues.

Purbrook

A little place with a great name – it means 'brook haunted by a goblin'. The fact that the A3 now runs through the middle probably accounts for the lack of recent sightings.

Ringwood

'Wood situated on a boundary', possibly because it sits on the edge of the NEW FOREST, which, as we have seen, wasn't really a forest at all.

Southampton

Although –*hampton* is frequently translated as 'homestead', this is an example of the Old English *hamm* mentioned in the Introduction and meaning 'partially enclosed land, land hemmed in by water'. Homtun, as it was called in the ninth century, fits this description perfectly, as it lies roughly between the rivers TEST and Itchen. The 'south' had appeared in its name by 962, to distinguish it from NORTHAMPTON.

Southsea

Here's a name that means what it says – 'place in the south by the sea'; the ending doesn't refer to an island, as it often does (see Portsea under PORTSMOUTH). Southsea came into being after Henry VIII built a castle here in the sixteenth century, just in time to see his flagship the *Mary Rose* sink in front of it. For other names that do exactly what they say on the tin, see the box *Not Rocket Science*, page 286.

Test

Nothing to do with exams or cricket, this comes from an Old Celtic word, probably meaning 'fast flowing'. Nearby Testwood was simply '[the place at] the wood on the Test'.

Waterlooville

Named not, as you might expect, after the battle, but after a pub that commemorated the battle: the Heroes of Waterloo. The story goes that soldiers returning from Belgium in 1815 landed at PORTSMOUTH and stopped for a pint (or whatever) at a pub that had opened that very day and was subsequently named in their honour. This may sound too convenient to be true, but in fact a large area of forested land along the main road from LONDON to Portsmouth was divided up and sold off for development in or just after 1810; in 1815 the village that is now Waterlooville had precisely five buildings – four cottages and a pub. So it is just about possible that the pub had hastily opened for business because word had gone around that the returning heroes would be passing. Good story, anyway. Waterloo railway station in London is named after the battle, with no intervening hostelry; but Waterloo just north of LIVERPOOL is named after the Royal Waterloo Hotel, which opened in June 1816, on the first anniversary of the battle.

Winchester

One of the Celtic tribes that inhabited Britain in pre-Roman times was the Belgae; they also lived in what in those days was called Gaul, and have given their name to Belgium. But in Britain their capital was the place that became Winchester. The Celtic word for 'capital' or 'favoured place' was *venta*, and the Romans originally called Winchester Venta Belgarum – 'the Belgae's capital'. They quickly both displaced the Belgae and dropped their name, producing Ouenta in the second century (Classical Latin pronounced *v* as *w*, so this is a small step). After the Romans left, the Anglo-Saxons added the ending that indicates a former Roman settlement (see the Introduction, page 11) and Winchester was born.

ISLE OF WIGHT

Wight *comes from an Old Celtic word meaning 'place of a division' and the island is probably so named because it sits between the two branches of the Solent. This means that the island's name is older than the names of any of the settlements, the earliest of which* *are Old English. But that is fair enough, as people on the mainland could have seen and named a substantial island without feeling the need to go and live there. The name Solent is also Old English, but its meaning is unknown.*

Cowes

The name does actually mean 'cow', but has no connection with dairy or beef farming. Instead, it is inspired by two sandbanks that used to lie in the mouth of the river Medina and apparently resembled cows. They aren't there any more, so we have to take history's word for it.

Ryde

This means 'small stream', and that is where the town sits: the stream itself now bears the more impressive name of Monkton-mead Brook, which means 'the brook running through the meadow by the farmstead belonging to the monks'. (And surely prompts the response, 'Oh, *that* Monktonmead Brook! Why didn't you say so?') Thirteenth-century references to La Ride reflect Norman influence, but the original name is older than that – it is a local variation on the Old English *r̄th*, 'stream'.

Sandown

'Sandy enclosure or river meadow'. In the thirteenth century the settlement was called Sandham (a *hamm* rather than a *hām*, see Introduction page 20), a name which persisted until at least the eighteenth century and is still found in some local businesses. Henry VIII built Sandham Castle in 1541 as an important part of the defence of the realm, though it survived for less than a century, thanks to the sea eroding the cliffs. When the radical MP John Wilkes acquired a holiday home here in 1788 he called it Sandham Cottage (he also referred to it as his 'villakin', which must surely have been appallingly

twee even in those days). Wilkes was largely responsible for bringing
the seaside resort into fashion and the masses soon thronged. By
the nineteenth century, the name Sandown was prevailing, perhaps
because those masses were familiar with Sandown Park in Surrey
(whose name means 'sandy hill') and assumed that the locals on the
Isle of Wight had simply got it wrong.

Shanklin

Every now and then a name to which we have never given much
thought turns out to be richly evocative, and this is one of them. It
translates as 'bank by the drinking cup'. The 'drinking cup' is the
waterfall at Shanklin Chine, a beauty spot whose early visitors
included John Keats and Jane Austen. *Chine* is a local word for a deep
fissure in the wall of a cliff, which describes the topography exactly.

Ventnor

Probably 'farm or estate of a family called Le Vyntener', who may
or may not have been vintners or winemakers. This name doesn't
appear until the seventeenth century; before that the settlement was
called Holloway, 'way in a hollow', because of a road that runs out
of low-lying Ventnor and up into the downs just beyond.

Yarmouth

'Gravelly or muddy estuary' – an unglamorous name, perhaps, but
Yarmouth was a port in the time of Ethelred the Unready (978–
1016) and pre-dates by about 900 years the Isle of Wight's heyday
as a tourist resort. The name of the river Yar is a back-formation
(that is, it was named after Yarmouth, rather than the other way
round) and the derivation of GREAT YARMOUTH in Norfolk is
completely different.

3

❦

SOUTH-EAST ENGLAND

The south-east was the chosen landing place of many of the country's early invaders: the Romans almost certainly landed on the east coast of Kent; archae-ological evidence places the Jutes in Kent too. St Augustine, arriving to convert southern England to Christianity in 597, landed on the Isle of THANET and made his headquarters at CANTERBURY. The Vikings raided the Isle of SHEP-PEY. In 1066 the Normans landed at PEVENSEY. There is nothing surprising about any of this – for the most part the travellers simply made landfall at the nearest convenient spot – but it does mean that the south-east is particularly 'full of history'. From the Roman remains at ROCHESTER to the site of the Battle of Hastings, it covers all the waves of invasion that created our place names.

SUSSEX

–sex at the end of a place name refers to the Saxons, and Sussex was the home of the South Saxons. They invaded Britain inde-pendently of those who conquered Essex ('East Saxons') and Wessex ('West Saxons'), establishing their kingdom in 477 and remaining sparate until they fell under the influence of Wessex in 825. The evidence of Sussex place names tells us that this was one of the earliest areas the Saxons conquered; that they were well

established by the sixth century; and that they had suppressed the native Celts pretty thoroughly.

Arundel

This name is, unusually, more evocative than it sounds: it means 'valley where the horehound grows'. The ending *–del* comes from the same root as the modern word 'dell'; horehound, a wild herb related to mint, was once a useful remedy for coughs and colds.

Battle

Site of the Battle of Hastings, 1066. Among (many) other things, this was significant in introducing the last radical change in English place names – the influence of Norman French (see the Introduction, page 19). The abbey here was built by William the Conqueror as a penance for the great loss of life in the battle; the altar is said to mark the spot where Harold, who had been King of England for all of nine months, fell. For more about Hastings, see the box *Whose Place Is It Anyway?*, page 189.

Beachy Head

There isn't actually much of a beach below Beachy Head – none at all at high tide – but then the name has nothing to do with beaches. The Domesday Book spelling is Beuchef, which gets nearer the mark: it was, according to the Normans, a 'beautiful headland' (the 'head' in the modern name was added – tautologically – much later). Surprisingly few English place names are totally French in origin and a surprising number of those that are begin with 'beau' or something like it: Beauchief in Sheffield means exactly the same as Beachy; then there are Beaulieu in Hampshire ('beautiful place'), various places called Beaumont ('beautiful hill'), Belper in Derbyshire ('beautiful retreat'), Belvoir in Leicestershire ('beautiful view') and BEWDLEY in Worcestershire. Perhaps the Normans, being the ruling and therefore the leisured classes, had more time to look about them, say, 'That's a beautiful place' and decide to build there.

Bexhill

This name is a prime example of how mistakes creep in and mis-understandings are perpetuated. The earliest spelling we have is the eighth-century Bixlea, followed by the Domesday Book's Bexelei, 'glade where box trees grow'. This should have produced a modern name of Bexley or Boxley (both of which occur in Kent and have similar derivations). But we have a number of records that show how Bexhill came about. Some time between 1190 and 1248 it is found as both Bexle and Byxle. Pronounce the former with little emphasis on the second syllable (as in the modern 'little') and it is easy to see how people might have imagined this was 'Bex 'ill'. Camden mentions Beckes-hill, which looks as if it should be a hill belonging to a man named Beck, or associated with a *beck* or stream, and presumably that is what people thought when they settled on the modern spelling. Unlike Bexhill, Box Hill in Surrey is actually a hill and it used to have an abundance of box trees growing on it, as did the Boxfords in Berkshire and Suffolk, and Boxgrove in Sussex. However, the Old English for 'beech' was very similar to the word for 'box', with the result that Boxted in Essex and Boxted in Suffolk are reminders that these places once boasted beech trees. Boxworth in Cambridgeshire was once called something like Bucksworth, so was either the home of a man called Bucc or a place where bucks were kept. Just learn them off by heart – it's the only way.

Bognor Regis

Bognor has been around since Saxon times and means 'shore asso-ciated with a woman called Bucge'. It became 'royal' (*regis* meaning 'of the king') only in the twentieth century, after George V had been there to convalesce after a serious illness. His Majesty is alleged to have said, 'Bugger Bognor' on his deathbed, when assured that he would soon be well enough to go there again, but the mark of his earlier approval lives on.

Brighton

'Farmstead belonging to a man named Beorhthelm'. Variations on this tongue-twister persisted for a surprising length of time: Brighthelmstone is found as late as 1823, although by then the town had been a fashionable resort for some years and the idle rich were presumably too full of port and brandy to bother with such a complicated name.

Crawley

'Wood or clearing frequented by crows': there are a number of Crawleys with the same derivation scattered across the country. Crawcrook on the Tyne is 'bend in the river frequented by crows'. Crawshaw Booth in Lancashire was plain Crawshaw ('copse frequented by crows') until at least the fourteenth century; the 'booth' is a later addition of Scandinavian origin, meaning a herdsman's hut. Cromer in Norfolk was 'lake frequented by crows' (think 'crow mere'). The same meaning with a modern spelling recurs in Crowborough and Crowhurst in Sussex, another Crowhurst in Surrey, Crowcombe in Somerset and Crowmarsh Gifford in Oxfordshire, the last of these having been the property of a man called Gifford at the time of the Domesday Book. It is a matter for conjecture whether he spent a lot of time draining his land or trying to scare the birds away, but either way it sounds as if nature was against him.

Eastbourne

Like many places built on a river, this was initially called Bourne (see BOURNEMOUTH) and the prefix was added when it became necessary to distinguish between two nearby places.

Gatwick

'Farm where goats are kept'. Not any more, it's not.

Hassocks

The name of the cushion that you kneel on in church if you are that way inclined derives from an Old English word for 'matted grass'. Apparently clumps of grass were once taken from bogs and trimmed into a cushiony shape to make kneeling on the hard floor of a church more comfortable; when people started making proper cushions for the same purpose they hung on to the name. So did the people who developed this town in the nineteenth century: it was the name of the local railway station (on the main London-to-Brighton line, so a good place to have a town), which was in turn named after a field called Hassocks, where clumps of coarse grass once grew.

Littlehampton

This was merely Hantone ('homestead') in the Domesday Book, as was SOUTHAMPTON, although the derivation of the latter was differ-ent. The 'little' – which had been added by 1482 – may have been intended to distinguish between the two.

Peacehaven

You might think this was a tautology, on a par with the modern cliché 'safe haven', but in fact it was a deliberate choice for a new town. The resort was developed during the First World War and the name was chosen in 1917 not only to indicate that the town would be a peaceful place for people to live but also in recognition of the general desire that the war would soon come to an end.

Pevensey

With its links to Julius Caesar's landing in Britain and later to the beginnings of the Norman Conquest, this should mean something more exciting than 'island belonging to a man named Pefen' – it's the same *-ey* ending as the one mentioned under PORTSMOUTH. What excitement we can muster lies in the fact that, as the bay has silted up over the centuries, this former island, the landing place for both Caesar and William the Conqueror, now lies 2 km inland.

Polegate

This is a comparatively late coinage for this part of the world, first appearing in the records in 1563. Polegate is close to PEVENSEY (see previous entry) and may take its name from the fact that it lies on land reclaimed from the sea; the old word for this was *polder*, used today in the same context in the Netherlands.

Rye

Along large stretches of the coast of East Sussex and Kent there are towns that were ports in the Middle Ages and now lie a couple of kilometres inland. Rye, whose name means 'island or dry ground in the marsh', is one of them (see PEVENSEY for another). Over the centuries, construction of sea walls to protect the low-lying marshy areas from flooding, the resulting silting up of rivers and harbours and the changes of direction taken by the rivers have all contributed to these changes in topography.

Selsey

'Island of the seal', meaning the marine mammal. The peninsula on which Selsey sits was once genuinely on an island in the Channel, but by the nineteenth century it had become attached to the mainland.

Winchelsea

Unlike Chelsea (see under ROTHERHITHE), this is not a landing place. Instead the word should be broken up as *Winchels–ea* to produce 'island by a bend in the river'. In medieval times the town was on a sandbank protecting the estuaries of the Rother, the Brede and the Tillingham and was an important trading post and naval base. But after being encroached upon by the sea for several decades, it was finally washed away in a massive flood in 1287. By this time, Edward I had seen the writing on the wall and ordered a replacement to be built; the population moved a few kilometres inland to what we now know as Winchelsea, one of the oldest 'new towns' in the country.

Worthing

Probably 'settlement of the family or descendants of a man named Weorth', though Worthing in Norfolk means 'enclosure'. Various places called Worth, Wortham in Suffolk and Worthen in Shropshire are all also to do with enclosures (see the box *Farming Country 2*, page 139).

SURREY

This is an oddity among county names, the only one to derive from the Old English gē, meaning 'district'; Surrey is therefore 'the southern district'. The most likely explanation is that it was regarded as the southern part of Middlesex, the bit south of the Thames. The now-defunct county of Middlesex was the domain of the Middle Saxons (those who lived somewhere between the East, South and West Saxons of Essex, Sussex and Wessex).

Abinger Hammer

Abinger means 'enclosure at Abba's place' or 'enclosure associated with Abba's people', though sadly Abba does not refer to the Swedish pop group – it was simply an Old English personal name. The 'Hammer' part comes from a former iron foundry known as Hammer Mill and distinguishes this village from Abinger Common

ANIMAL PLACE NAMES

Animals have been hunted in the wild, or domesticated and farmed, from the earliest times and 'the place/ford/river associated with such-and-such an animal' is a feature of names throughout the country. Judging by the frequency with which they occur in place names, sheep were the most common domesticated animal: they are commemorated in **Shiptons** ('sheep farm') and **Shipleys** ('clearing where sheep are kept') throughout the country, as well as in **Shipbourne** in Kent ('stream where sheep are kept'), **Shipmeadow** in Suffolk and others. Confusingly, however, **Shippon** in Oxfordshire, comes from a different source and means 'cattle shed'.

Horses are not often mentioned in place names, but **Stodmarsh** in Kent and various places beginning with *Stud–* acknowledge the fact that horses were kept there. They were not stud farms as we would understand the term, but the Old English *stōd* is the source of both the place names and the modern word.

The Anglo-Saxons kept cattle, too, and pigs: OXFORD, **Oxenholme** in Cumbria and **Great Oxendon** in Northamptonshire were respectively the ford where oxen could cross, the river meadow where they grazed and the valley where they were kept. **Kilburn** in LONDON may once have been a stream associated with kine or cows. Pigs, known by their earlier name of swine, were kept on a hill at **Swindon** in Wiltshire, by a river in **Swinefleet** in Yorkshire and by the ford at **Swinford** in Leicestershire and Oxfordshire.

Pigs were not only domestic animals, though: wild boar were a favourite with hunters. The Old English word was *eofor*, so the various **Evertons, Evershot** in Dorset, **Eversley** in Hampshire and **Eversholt** in Berkshire were all associated with boar.

The other popular quarry was deer in their various ages and sexes. They were seen at **Hartland** in Devon, **Hindhead** in Surrey, **Buckden** in Yorkshire, **East** and **West Dereham** in Norfolk and **Darley Dale** in Derbyshire. **Buckfast** in Devon comes from the Old English for 'shelter for bucks'; the Benedictine abbey for which the village is famous (destroyed by Henry VIII and rebuilt in the nineteenth century) was founded in the eleventh century on the banks of the river Dart, at a sheltered spot where deer came down to drink. They also grazed in the woods at nearby **Buckfastleigh**, *–leigh* meaning 'glade' or 'clearing'.

Other wild animals are immortalised too, though some of them have not been seen in England for a long time. There were beavers at BEVERLEY in Yorkshire and **Bevercotes** ('place where beavers built their nests') in Nottinghamshire; wolves at **Wolford** and **Wolvey**, both in Warwickshire and both suggesting places that were protected against wolves. Wolford was not originally a ford but a *weard*, meaning 'protector' and connected with the modern sense of 'warding something off'; the ending of Wolvey comes from a word for 'hedge'. Badgers were to be seen at BAGSHOT in Surrey, **Brockhall** in Northamptonshire and **Brox-ted** in Essex. The Celtic *brocc* gives us Brock, still used as a nickname for a badger, though most places beginning with *Brock–* are associated with brooks. One place with no connection with badgers is, funnily enough, **Badger** in Shropshire, which comes from a personal name.

Bee-keeping was an early Anglo-Saxon occupation, reflected in **Beeby** in Leicestershire and **Beoley** in Worcestershire.

And finally, yes, there were dogs on the **Isle of Dogs** in LONDON. Almost certainly strays – contrary to a persistent rumour, there is no evidence of royal hunting dogs being kennelled here.

('by the open ground') and Sutton Abinger ('southern village') just a few kilometres away. Abington Piggotts in Cambridgeshire is similarly associated with a man named Abba, who was supplanted by a family named Pykot.

Bagshot

There has been much debate over the meaning of this name, but experts now seem to agree that the first part refers to badgers. The Old English *scēat* meant a projecting piece of land or, more probably in this case, the end of a wood, so this was a wood where badgers were seen. Oxshott ('belonging to a man named Ocga'), also in Surrey, and Heyshott ('where heather grows') in Sussex come from the same word. The twelfth-century spelling Bagsheta means that we can be certain at least of the second part of the name. Bagshot in Wiltshire, on the other hand, appears in the Domesday Book as Bechesgete, telling us that it was originally 'gap or gate belonging to a man named something like Beocc'.

Chertsey

This means 'island belonging to a man named Cerot', which is intriguing, because although Chertsey is close to the THAMES it is certainly not on an island. Camden records the fact that '[the Thames] after leaving Berks washes Chertsey, which Bede calls "Cerotus' Isle", now scarce a peninsula except in winter floods'. Bede lived eight hundred years before Camden, so the latter account reflects how the course or level of the river had changed since the writing of the former.

Haslemere

'Pool where hazels grow'. Hazlemere in Buckinghamshire means the same thing; the ending of Haslingden in Lancashire comes from the Old English for 'valley', so that name means 'valley where hazels grow'. Hazelhurst in Greater Manchester is 'wooded hill where hazels grow', Hazelrigg in Tyne and Wear is 'ridge…' and the various Hazelwoods mean what you would think they meant.

Horley

This town and the one in Oxfordshire with the same name probably both mean 'clearing in a horn-shaped piece of land'. This part of Surrey was once both marshy and densely forested, so perhaps the settlement was built on the only suitable piece of land, which happened to be horn-shaped.

Leatherhead

Nothing to do with leather, this comes from Old Celtic and means 'grey ford', a not very flattering description of the river Mole at the point where it cuts through the North Downs. The Mole, disappointingly, takes its name from the settlement of Molesey (now East and West Molesey), rather than from any burrowing animal. Molesey was once 'dry ground in a marsh belonging to a man named Mull'. Like CHERTSEY, it must have been a wetter place in Anglo-Saxon times than it is now.

Reigate

Rei– probably comes for the Old English for a female roe deer, which would make Reigate mean the entrance to a deer park, established in Norman times. It has, however, been suggested that it may refer to the course of a river, or to the town's position on a road that passes over the North Downs. Whatever the origin, a local history website proudly boasts that there are no other Reigates anywhere in the world – and the maps of North America, Australia and New Zealand show that this is a claim that cannot be made for many of the entries in this book.

Staines

Another place where people foregathered (see BARNSTAPLE and MAIDSTONE), presumably for trading purposes. The name comes from the stone that would have marked the meeting place.

Thorpe

–*thorpe*, meaning 'an outlying farmstead or secondary settlement' is a common element of place names in the north and east, because it comes specifically from Old Danish and so it is not found in the Norwegian-influenced north-west: Scunthorpe, once the property of a man named Skuma, is perhaps the best-known example. The Old English word *throp* has the same meaning but is very rare – see ADLESTROP. Outlying settlements in places where the Anglo-Saxons held sway tend to have names ending in –*stock* or –*stoke* (see, for example, RADSTOCK and the box *Farming Country 2*, page 139). Thorpe in Surrey is interesting, therefore, because it is found in a predominantly 'English'-speaking part of the country. It is spelt Thorp in the seventh century (too early for the Scandinavians), so the reason for it remains a mystery.

Walton-on-Thames

Many names beginning with *wal*– stem from the Old English for 'foreigner' or 'serf', a term which encompassed the Celts or Britons who were in the country when the Anglo-Saxons arrived. So Walton was 'village of the Britons', and this applies not only to Walton-on-Thames but to Walton-le-Dale (in the valley) in Lancashire and Walton-on-the-Naze (on the promontory) in Essex as well. Walbrook and Walworth in LONDON also have this root – as do WALLASEY and the principality of Wales. Full of foreigners, all of 'em, as far as the Anglo-Saxons were concerned.

KENT

This is one of the oldest county names in England. Julius Caesar mentions Cantium, Ptolemy Kantión ákron ('the promontory of Kent') and the Anglo-Saxon Chronicle Cent. Camden suggests that Kent comes from an old word canton, meaning corner, because 'here England shoots out in a corner eastwards'. This may sound reasonable, but most scholars now believe that it comes from an Old Celtic name meaning 'coastal district'.

Ashford

The Ashford in Kent has the derivation you might expect – 'ford where ash trees grow' – whereas an early spelling of Ashford in Surrey, Ecelesford, shows that it was 'ford of a man named Eccel'; it developed into 'Ashford' by analogy with other settlements beginning with *ash–*. In Shropshire, the two Ashfords are distinguished by the names of their late-medieval lords of the manor, giving rise to the delightful Ashford Bowdler and Ashford Carbonell.

Broadstairs

Well, yes, it does mean 'broad stairs', but why, you may well ask? Its earlier name of Bradstow (*–stōw* meaning a place of assembly, often a holy place, as in PADSTOW and FELIXSTOWE) may suggest a connection with the sixth-century St Augustine, who landed nearby with a mission to convert Britain to Christianity (see CANTERBURY). In those days it was presumably the beach that was broad. Steps to provide easy access to the sea were cut into the cliff in the fifteenth century, when Bradstow was a fishing village and, some say, a smugglers' haven. The modern name took a while to catch on: Daniel Defoe was still referring to Bradstow after a visit in 1723, though it was Broadstairs by the time Charles Dickens went there in the mid-nineteenth century. A Victorian tourist board's marketing wheeze, perhaps?

Canterbury

Although MAIDSTONE is now the county town, Canterbury was the principal city of a much older kingdom: its name means 'fortified town of the people of Kent'. The Celts had a fortified town here, as did the Romans, who laid it out in a grid system and built baths, temples and town houses with mosaic floors. All this was before St Augustine arrived in 597 and revived the fortunes that had flagged since the Romans departed. Augustine became the first Archbishop of Canterbury and, although his first cathedral was sacked by the Danes in the ninth century, Canterbury has remained the centre of Christian worship in England ever since. One later archbishop deserves a mention here, as he has so many places named after him. Thomas Becket was the 'turbulent priest' who fell out with Henry II and in 1170 was murdered in the cathedral by four of the king's knights. He was canonised three years later and churches dedicated to him started springing up over the country, several of them founded by the knights themselves by way of penance. Cricket St Thomas (see CREWKERNE) in Dorset and BOVEY TRACEY in Devon boast two of them, but the knights are known to have taken refuge in Knaresborough in Yorkshire and one of them is said to have founded a church called St Thomas the Martyr as far north as NEWCASTLE UPON TYNE.

Deal

This comes from the same root as the modern 'dale' and simply means 'place in the hollow or valley'. No big deal, in other words.

Dover

This means nothing more complicated than 'the waters', from an Old Celtic word. The name refers not to the Channel but to the river on which the town stands; the Dour, as it is now called, rises only about 6 km inland, but was once wide and navigable and also drove the first known corn mill in England, recorded in 762. But settlement here goes back at least 3,500 years (there is a Bronze Age ship in the museum) and it was the river Dour that carved the valley amid the cliffs that made this a sheltered place for boats and people alike.

Dungeness
'Headland near Denge Marsh'. *Denge* means 'manured land', and the name probably refers to the fertility of the area after it was reclaimed from the sea in about the fourteenth century.

Folkestone
Not, as you might be forgiven for thinking, 'town with lots of people in it' but, more probably, 'stone marking a meeting place of a man called Folca'. We know that in Anglo-Saxon times Folkestone was the most important settlement in this part of Kent, so public meetings would have been held here and it is reasonable to suppose that, as in STAINES and MAIDSTONE, the meeting place was marked with a stone.

Gravesend
Sadly, for the ghouls among us, this has nothing to do with death or graveyards. It should really be Grovesend, 'the place at the end of the grove or copse'. Cotgrave in Nottinghamshire ('grove associated with a man named Cotta') is similarly unmacabre.

Hythe
Hythe or *hithe* means 'landing place or harbour', and that is its meaning not only here but in other names such as Greenhithe ('green landing place') and ROTHERHITHE ('landing place for cattle'). See that entry for more of the cunning disguises in which this place-name element turns up.

Maidstone

This probably means 'stone of the maidens', indicating a place where maidens gathered. No one seems to know why they should have assembled here: perhaps for ritual or religious reasons. The once widely held belief that Maidstone is a corruption of 'MEDWAY town' seems to have been discredited by modern scholars.

Margate

Mar– comes from the same root as *mere*, meaning a lake, and the word is found in place names referring either to the sea or to a pool of water. Margate probably means 'gap in the cliffs, providing access to the sea'. Nearby Ramsgate is also a way through the cliffs; it may have been frequented by ravens or may be derived from a personal name; certainly it has nothing to do with rams.

Medway

The *–way* part comes from an ancient word for river, which also occurs as Wey in the names of other rivers round the country and in the self-explanatory Weymouth and Weybridge. *Med–* comes from the same source as *mead*, meaning not a meadow but the honey-flavoured drink, probably because the water was either sweet-tasting or honey-coloured. The barges carrying the products of seventeen cement works in the Rochester area in Victorian times may have changed that.

Minster

Many towns with *minster* in their name are distinguished by the name of the river on which they stand (see various examples in the box *The Place by the River*, page 210); others, such as Minster Lovell in Oxfordshire, were originally called Minster but had the name of the lord of the manor added in Norman times. Yet there are two places in Kent – admittedly about 50 km apart, but still in the same county – that are both marked on the map as plain Minster. You can call them Minster-in-THANET and Minster-in-SHEPPEY to distinguish them if you like, but very few people do. Both take their names from nunneries founded in the seventh century, making them some of the earliest places of Christian worship in this part of the country.

Queenborough

The queen in question is Philippa, wife of Edward III. He built a castle here in 1361, founded a town around it and named it in her honour. Despite investigations by the television programme *Time Team* it remains unclear what the castle's purpose was. Conceived during the Hundred Years' War and sited near the mouth of the THAMES, it may have been intended to prevent the French from sneaking up the river and attacking LONDON; alternatively, given that the Black Death had ravaged England as recently as 1348–9, it may have been a place where the king and queen could take refuge in case of plague.

Rochester

The reason for the siting of this ancient town causes no problems: it sits in a strategic position near the mouth of the MEDWAY, and the Roman road Watling Street, now cunningly disguised as the A2, runs through it. But its name has some unexplained elements. First, the Romans called it Durobrivae, which most experts say comes from the Old Celtic for 'stronghold by the bridge(s)'. The *duro* element is OK – it is from the Celtic for 'strength' or 'stronghold' and frequently appears in Roman names for settlements they had taken over. The problem is that at the time the Romans arrived, there was no bridge here: they built the first one. So only *after* the Roman invasion would it have been sensible to call this a settlement 'by the bridges'. Had the Celts built a bridge which lasted long enough for them to name a place after it but which had disappeared without trace by AD 43? It seems unlikely. Second, Bede, writing in the eighth century, calls the place Hrofaesceastre, suggesting a Roman fortified town based on an earlier Celtic settlement called Hrofi. Hrofi we can just about accept as a clipped form of Duro-brivae, but there is no archaeological evidence of the typical Roman fort that led to a town's being called *ceaster* (see the Introduction, page 11). Nevertheless, Bede's version took root and similar spellings are found in other pre-Norman documents. However, the initial *hr* was just the sort of sound the Normans couldn't pronounce, so that by the time of the Domesday Book we find Rovecestre, and by 1610 it is Rochester − a fortified town that didn't exist by a bridge of which there is no record. Rochester in Northumberland has a much less chequered history − its name means 'rough earthwork or fort', and some impressive remains of the Roman fort are still there to be visited.

Romney

The *−ey* ending is from the Old English for 'river' and the name may have meant 'broad river' because the many rivulets that ran across Romney Marsh gave the impression of one broad stretch of water.

Sandwich

'Sandy harbour or trading centre'. Like RYE, Sandwich was a medieval port but is now inland. The Earl of Sandwich, who famously gave his name to a fast food brought to him so that he wouldn't have to stop gambling to eat, took his title from this town. For the various meanings of *−wich*, see the box *Farming Country 2*, page 139.

Sheppey

'Island where sheep are kept'. The modern usage 'Isle of Sheppey' duplicates the original meaning of *−ey*.

Swanley

Related to swains rather than swans (see SWANAGE), this means 'herdsmen's woodland clearing'. Swanscombe, also in Kent, comes from the same word and means 'herdsmen's enclosed land'. Various places in Norfolk called Swanton, and Swanwick in Derbyshire, also take their names from herdsmen; on the other hand, Swanbourne in Buckinghamshire and Swanmere in Hampshire, whose endings are both associated with water, were places frequented by swans.

Thanet

Old Celtic for 'bright island', possibly with reference to a beacon positioned on what is now Telegraph Hill. What we these days – unnecessarily – call the *Isle* of Thanet was indeed once an island, separated from the rest of Kent by a now-vanished stretch of water called the Wantsum Channel. An alternative explanation for Thanet links the name with the ancient Greek word for death, *thanatos*. Thanet has more Bronze Age burial mounds than anywhere else in Britain, but to make a connection between this and a Greek legend that Britain was the home of the dead, who were rowed here in the middle of the night in boats that returned empty before dawn, ready for the next consignment, seems a touch fanciful. However, the island appears in Ptolemy's *Geographia*: he called it Toliatis, usually regarded as an error for Tanatus, which might – just might – make the *thanatos* story more probable.

Tonbridge/(Royal) Tunbridge Wells

Tonbridge probably means 'bridge belonging to the estate or manor' and it existed at the time of the Domesday Book. Tunbridge Wells ('wells near Tonbridge'), an offshoot of the older town, came into existence only in the seventeenth century, when medicinal waters were discovered here. The spelling Tunbridge is older and was used for Tonbridge until the eighteenth century, when it was deliberately changed to distinguish it from 'the Wells', which by that time was the more famous of the two (note that it was the successful parvenu, not the venerable 'parent', that got to hold on to its original name). Over the years Tunbridge Wells had many royal visitors – Queen Anne, Queen Victoria, Prince Albert and Victoria's mother the Duchess of Kent were among those who drank the waters – and it was in recognition of this that in 1909 Victoria's son, by then King Edward VII, gave it the right to use 'royal' in its name. ROYAL LEAMINGTON SPA is the only other town in England with this privilege, though Latin scholars may claim that BOGNOR and various other places that tack 'Regis' on to their names sneak in under the wire.

4

LONDON AND SURROUNDS

Would you believe that no one is sure what London means? We know that there was no settlement of any substance here before the Romans; that the Roman general Aulus Plautius built a bridge across the THAMES shortly after he landed in Kent in 43 AD, so that his men could get to the important town of COLCH-ESTER; and that the Roman historian Tacitus was writing about Londinium in the second century. But the name is certainly older than any of this. One early twentieth-century writer believed that it came from the Celtic lon din *meaning 'marsh or pool with a fort', which would be fine if there were any evidence of a fort. The same source quotes a contemporary as maintaining that it meant 'green or wet place' and came from the same root as Lutetia, the Roman name for Paris. The idea that both Paris and London mean the same thing is immensely appealing, but sadly there seems to be no basis for it. A later possibility was that London meant 'wild' or 'bold' and was named after a person who had earned this nickname. All this would suggest that it derived from Old Celtic, but modern scholars have moved on from there. The most recent theory is that it comes from a pre-Celtic language and means 'place at the unfordable part of the river'. This makes geographic sense: that early Roman bridge was close to the site of the present London Bridge, the better part of 3 km downriver from the lowest fordable point, at Westminster, and all the early settlements were centred there. Under the Romans London became an important trading centre and after they had gone it became the capital of the kingdom of the East Saxons – ESSEX. But no one ever bothered to change its name to something they could understand.*

Acton

Read *ac* as 'oak' and you are there: 'farmstead by the oak trees' or 'farmstead where oak timber is produced'. There are Actons all over the country whose names have the same meaning. Iron Acton in Gloucestershire was Actune in the Domesday Book, but over the next 150 years or so acquired the now-defunct iron works that gave it its modern name (the local oaks were used to fuel the forges during the smelting process). The village of Acton Round in Shropshire belonged in Norman times to the Earls of ARUNDEL and got its name either from its shape or from a mistaken belief that the Earl's name had originally been Aroundel.

Barnet

'Land cleared by burning', because the area was once covered by dense forest and fire was the easiest way to clear it. The name Friern Barnet derives from 'brothers or friars', meaning the Knights of St John of Jerusalem, also known as the Knights Hospitaller, who owned a manor here in the thirteenth century and probably ran a hospital or refuge for weary travellers. The name of Brentwood in Essex indicates that it too was cleared by burning.

Brent

The name tells us that the Celts thought the river Brent was holy and suggests a connection with Brigantia, a Celtic water goddess worshipped by the Brigantes tribe in northern Britain, but also connected with the Irish St Bridget. Although there is no hard evidence for this, enthusiasts maintain that if she could extend her sphere of influence across the Irish Sea to modern Yorkshire, she shouldn't have had a problem making herself known in north-west London. The river Brent gave its name to Brentford, the place where you could cross it, and, rather later, to the London Borough of Brent, which is a 1960s invention.

Bromley

'Glade where broom grows'. The Brompton area of London also takes its name from the plant, though Bromsgrove in the West Midlands is 'grove belonging to a man named Breme'. The ending *–ley* almost always signifies a glade or wood, as does *leigh*, as either part or the whole of a word. Leigh in Lancashire and Leigh-on-Sea and Great and Little Leighs in Essex all mean 'wood or woodland clearing', while Eastleigh in Hampshire was once 'east wood' and Rayleigh in Essex was 'wood frequented by female roe-deer or she-goats'. Surprisingly enough, Leighton means something completely different – see LEIGHTON BUZZARD. For places whose former woodiness is commemorated in a more obviously recognisable form, see the box *Not Rocket Science*, page 286.

Croydon

This may come as a surprise to those who live here, but the name means 'valley where wild saffron grows'. The ending *–don* comes from the same root as *–dene* ('valley') and the Old English *crog* is connected with the modern plant name *crocus*, to which saffron is related. Saffron – valued since earliest times for its wide-ranging medicinal uses, and as a dye and a food flavouring – is known to have been cultivated in ancient Crete and Persia, and was presumably well established in Croydon by AD 809, when the name was first recorded. See also SAFFRON WALDEN.

Dulwich

Another name taken from a medicinal plant (see previous entry), this means 'marshy area where dill grows'. If your kids suffered from colic and you wanted to make your own gripe water, this was the place to live.

Finchley

'Woodland clearing frequented by finches'. Well, maybe if you put some seeds out in the back garden…

Harrow

In AD 767 this was called Gumeningae hergae, which translates as 'heathen shrine(s) or temple(s) of a tribe called the Gumeningas [probably followers of a man named Guma]'. A hilltop position was always popular for places of worship and Gumeningae hergae is believed to have been one of the most important religious centres in England in pre-Christian times. By the time of the Domesday Book the Gumeningas had been consigned to oblivion (where they have remained ever since), the place name had become Herges and the original pagan shrine had given way to the eleventh-century church of St Mary. At some stage Herges evolved into Hareways and thence to Harrow, where it had settled by the time the school was founded in 1572.

Hornsey

Most settlements whose names begin with *horn* were founded on a horn-shaped piece of land (see HORLEY), but not this one. It comes from the same root as nearby Haringey and means either 'enclosure in the grey wood' or 'enclosure belonging to a man named Haring'. The earliest recorded spelling (1201) is Haringeie; Haringay alias Hornesey is found in 1580. Haringay then gradually gave way to Hornsey, but was revived as Harringay in the nostalgic name of a house built in the area in the eighteenth century. From here Harringay became the name of a neighbourhood adjacent to Hornsey, and the spelling of Haringey was adopted for the London Borough when it was created in 1965 – a pleasing instance of a name coming more or less full circle within a mere 764 years.

Kew

The meaning of Kew is debated, but whichever option you choose it is connected with a modern word. It is found in the fourteenth century as Cayho, the *–ho* meaning a projecting piece of land. Then, depending on whether you think the piece of land in question is key-shaped or prefer to believe that it was important as a landing place, you can link the first part of the name to *key* or *quay*.

Kingston

No prizes for this one: almost everywhere in England called Kingston started out as 'the king's manor or estate'. The royalness of 'the Royal Borough of Kingston upon Thames' dates back to at least the ninth century, making it the oldest Kingston – and oldest royal borough – in the country. Edward the Elder, son of Alfred the Great, was crowned here in 900, as were most of his successors for the next hundred years. Various other places called Kingston acquired the names of their Norman overlords after the Conquest, giving rise to Kingston Bagpuize, Kingston Blount and Kingston Lisle in Oxfordshire, Kingston Deverill in Wiltshire and Kingston Lacy in Dorset. See also KINGSTON-UPON-HULL.

London

See the introduction to this chapter, page 91.

Mitcham

'Large place or homestead'. The Old English *micel*, meaning 'great, large', also crops up in Mickleham in Surrey (another large place or homestead), Michelmersh in Hampshire ('large marsh'), Mitcheldean in Gloucestershire ('large place in the valley'), Mickfield in Suffolk, Mickleby in Yorkshire ('large farmstead'), Mickleton in Durham and Gloucestershire and Mickleover in Derbyshire ('large place at the ridge'). The word *mickle* is still in the dictionaries as Scots or northern English dialect for 'large', but the Scots, bless them, also use it for 'a small amount', hence the proverb 'Many a mickle maks a muckle' – which means, though you would be forgiven for not guessing this, 'Every little helps'.

New Malden

There was a settlement called something very like Malden near here at the time of the Domesday Book and, like MALDON in Essex, it takes its name from a cross on a hill. That is the place now known as Old Malden. In the 1840s the main LONDON and South Western Railway, which eventually ran from Waterloo to SALISBURY, SOUTHAMPTON and beyond, was built a couple of kilometres to the north and a station opened to service both Malden to the south and Coombe to the north. New Malden, therefore, is one of the few places in this book that didn't exist at all until the nineteenth century: it grew up purely and simply as a result of the railway station.

Plaistow

The first part of this is connected with 'play' and the whole means 'playground' or 'place where sport is played'. As late as 1832 Plaistow is recorded as being four and a half miles (nearly 7.5 km) from London, so there was doubtless plenty of open ground. On the other hand, by 1872 it is said to stand 'on the great N sewer of the London sewage-works', so it may have lost some of its charm by then.

Poplar

There was indeed once a poplar tree here, but exactly when and exactly where…?

Richmond

Those who are surprised to learn that Henry VII, despite being Welsh, was Earl of Richmond before he became king should remember that the seat of the Dukes of Norfolk is ARUNDEL Castle in Sussex and that the Duke of Devonshire is based at Chatsworth in Derbyshire. In other words, let us not worry about the logic of these things. In fact Henry took his title from Richmond in Yorkshire, whose name ('rich mount', more or less) comes from the Old French for 'strong hill'. When he built himself a palace by the THAMES, he called it after his own title and decreed that the surrounding area should take the same name. That area had previously been known as West Sheen, from the Old English for 'sheds or shelters'; the name survives in the south London suburbs of North and East Sheen and in the village of Sheen in Staffordshire.

Rotherhithe

'Landing place for cattle', because it was from this point on the south side of the Thames that cattle were shipped across the river to the meat market at Smithfield. Or so some say. Others point out that from at least the thirteenth to the seventeenth centuries Rotherhithe was called Redriff, which may have derived from Red Rose Hithe, after the sign of the local inn. This may, however, have been a popular name that existed alongside the official one: it turns up as Rethereth – surely linked more closely to Rotherhithe than to red roses – during the reign of Edward III (1327–77). The banks of the Thames are full of landing places whose names contain the element *hithe*, in some cases more obviously than others: they include Erith ('muddy or gravelly landing place'), Lambeth ('landing place for lambs'), Chelsea ('landing place for chalk') and Putney ('landing place of the hawk' or 'of a man named Putta'). Earlier forms of these names – Earhith, Lambehitha, Celchyth and Puttenhuthe – provide useful stepping stones along the way to the modern versions.

Thames

As befits a river sometimes known as 'Old Father Thames', this
name is an ancient one, either Celtic or pre-Celtic; its name is first
recorded as Tamesis as early as 51 BC. With origins that far back, it
is not surprising that the meaning of the name should be unclear:
it may mean 'dark' – from the look of the water – or 'flowing',
which would be a pretty basic name for a river, but reasonable
enough if it was the only river you knew. Many important rivers in
Britain come from the same root – the Tavy, the Tay, the Taff, the
Tamar and the Thame, among others – suggesting that the name
might simply originally have meant 'river'. The town of Thame in
Oxfordshire, which sits on the Thame, takes its name from this tributary of the Thames.

Tooting

Disappointing – there are no fairies playing the recorder here (see
NEMPNETT THRUBWELL), Tooting means nothing more than 'the
family or descendants of Tōta', who was presumably a Saxon chieftain. In Norman times part of Tooting became the property of the
de Gravenel family and part was granted to the abbey of Bec-
Hellouin in Normandy, hence Tooting Graveney and Tooting Bec.

Walthamstow

Waltham means 'forest estate', the *walt–* element coming from the
Old English *wald*, 'forest', which is also found in names such as
Southwold in Suffolk. The Waltham that is mentioned in the
Domesday Book is now Waltham Abbey, thanks to the church which
was founded here in 1060. Waltham Cross came into being in 1290,
when the body of Edward I's queen, Eleanor of Castile, 'rested'
there on its way back to London. (She died near LINCOLN and
Edward erected a cross at each of the resting places on the twelve-
day journey. It ended near Charing Cross, although the cross there

today is a Victorian replica.) Waltham Forest was originally a royal hunting ground, 'the forest near Waltham [Abbey]'. None of this has much to do with Walthamstow, except that it is close enough to Waltham for the former's name to have evolved to bring it into line with the latter. Walthamstow didn't start out as a forest estate; it was once Wilcumestou, probably meaning 'a (holy) place where guests are welcome'. Various other Walthams scattered around the country were also once estates in or near a forest, and Bishop's Waltham in Hampshire was owned by the Bishop of Winchester.

Wandsworth

The ending –*worth* generally means 'enclosure' (see the box *Farming Country 2*, page 139) and Wandsworth was an enclosure belonging to a man called something like Waendel. Although he has long been forgotten and his name distorted, the river Wandle – a back-formation of Wandsworth – has restored him to some of his former glory.

Whetstone

This does indeed mean 'whetstone', which on the face of it is an odd name for a place, but probably refers to the fact that stones suitable for use as whetstones could be found here.

Wimbledon

Probably 'hill belonging to a man named...' what? Winebeald? Wynnmann? The Normans didn't know and had shortened it to Wimmeldun by 1210.

5

❈

THE COTSWOLDS

The Old English wald *or* weald *originally meant 'woodland', later 'high wood-land' and later still 'high ground that has been cleared of its trees'. In this case we want the second option: the Cotswolds were a line of wooded hills belonging to a man named Cod. Much of the woodland was cleared centuries ago; on the open ground sheep provided a source of wealth and led to the growth of prosperous 'wool towns', many of which survive as places of chocolate-box prettiness.*

GLOUCESTERSHIRE
The shire based around GLOUCESTER, whose name attests to its Roman past, but whose origins are known to be Celtic. Once the Romans had subdued the locals, they found this area a convenient base from which to embark on the conquest of Wales.

Adlestrop
Yes, you remember Adlestrop – or you do if you have read the first line of the poem by Edward Thomas: not many people recall any more than that. Sadly – because the poem evokes summer warmth and willows, willowherb, grass, meadowsweet and haycocks – the name is rather prosaic: 'outlying farmstead of a man named Taetel'. The unknown Taetel suffered the same fate as Tidwulf in

ELSTREE: he lost his initial *t* because of confusion with a preceding 'at', so that 'at Taetel's place' became 'at Aetel's [and later at Adle's] place'. Although the similar Scandinavian *thorpe* is common further north and east, *–trop* comes from an Old English word found infrequently in the names of very small places in Gloucestershire and almost never anywhere else – Thrupp in Oxfordshire is probably the only example. See also THORPE.

Chipping Norton

Norton means 'northern farmstead' and is found throughout the country – see, for example, MIDSOMER NORTON and NORTON ST PHILIP. *Chipping* comes from the Old English for a market (see box on page 102). Called simply Norton in the Domesday Book, this grew into a market town in 1204, when the local lord of the manor, William Fitzalan – in common with many others of his rank – decided there was money to be made out of encouraging people to come to town to trade and charging them for the privilege.

Cirencester

The Old Celtic name of this ancient settlement was Korinion; the Romans came along, fortified it and, when it became apparent from the docility of the local people that the fort was no longer needed, turned it into the second largest town in Roman Britain, with a forum, an amphitheatre and a grid system of streets. Although the Romans called the place Corinion Dubonnorum (the Dubonni being the name of the docile Celtic tribe), modern usage combines their trademark *–cester* (see the Introduction, page 11) with a corruption of the original name. The town became less eminent in Saxon times, but later re-emerged as an important centre of the wool trade. It also boasted a fine Norman abbey, destroyed by – who else? – Henry VIII. All of which cannot disguise the fact that, although the name Korinion comes from the same Old Celtic root as the local

MARKET TOWNS

The Old English *cēap* and *cēping* (both pronounced as if they began with *ch*) meant 'market' and the words are still found in town names such as **Chipping Campden** and CHIPPING NORTON, and in **Cheapside**, a street in the City of LONDON. The adjective meaning 'low in price' can be traced to the same root (the Saxon for 'to buy'), but first appeared five hundred years after the word was established as a noun: there is no suggestion that these early markets were either *cheap and cheerful* or *cheap and nasty*.

In the case of most 'Chippings', the settlement dates back to Saxon times, the prefix having been added when the town was granted a charter permitting it to have a market. This is certainly true of Chipping Campden: Campden, meaning 'valley with enclosed cultivated land', existed as early as the seventh century; it graduated to being a market town in the thirteenth century and became an important centre of the wool trade.

Oddly, **Chippenham**, a market town whose history dates back to 600 and includes the weddings of both the sister and the daughter of Alfred the Great, seems to have had nothing to do with markets, etymologically speaking, but was originally a homestead belonging to a man called Cippa.

Going back to Cheapside, the name means 'district beside the market', although the street was pivotal to the market area, with the likes of Bread Street and Poultry running off it. In common with most of the City of London, its wooden buildings were largely destroyed by the Great Fire of 1666 and, as a trading centre, it went into the doldrums for two hundred years. At least a dozen other Cheapsides still exist in English towns from

LIVERPOOL to BRIGHTON, where pig markets were held on the beach in the fourteenth century.

There are also, of course, plenty of towns with the modern word *market* in their names – ones that have their own entries include MARKET BOSWORTH, MARKET DEEPING, MARKET HARBOROUGH, MARKET RASEN, NEEDHAM MARKET and STOW-MARKET. And there is one – BLANDFORD FORUM – which proclaims its 'market' status in Latin.

river Churn and the villages of North and South Cerney and Cerney Wick, no one knows what it meant in the first place.

Gloucester

The Old Celtic name for Gloucester was Caer-gloyw, and this time we do know what it meant – 'bright place'. The Romans translated this as Glevum. They not only built a fort here, they also had a retirement village for former legionaries, so that at one stage they knew the town as Colonia Glev (see COLCHESTER). Gloucester's importance lay in its being the southernmost fording point on the Severn, making it a handy spot for anyone who wanted to invade Wales. Like CIRENCESTER, it became less important after the Romans left but came back to prominence with the building of an abbey (which survived Henry VIII to become the basis of the existing cathedral) and the growth of the wool trade.

Minchinhampton

Minchin comes from the Old English meaning 'nuns': this place, which is simply Hantone – 'high farmstead' – in the Domesday Book, was granted to the Abbaye des Dames at Caen in Normandy by William the Conqueror. Reference to them was added to the name by the thirteenth century. William had founded the nunnery, along with the adjacent Abbaye des Hommes, as a penance for having broken the church's ruling on consanguinity by marrying his cousin Matilda. Having embarked on his penance, William was not going to do it by halves: although the Domesday Book values Minchinhampton at only 45 shillings (£2.25), it also records that William had given the nuns rights in the nearby village of Pinbury, valued at the not-insubstantial sum of four pounds.

Moreton-in-Marsh

If you know that 'Moreton' means 'a farmstead in marshy ground' (which you do if you have read the entry on MORETONHAMPSTEAD), you would be forgiven for thinking that this was a tautological name. In fact, the last word was originally 'henmarsh', because the area was frequented by moorhens, so the early name was more descriptive than the modern one.

Newent

There aren't many places in Gloucestershire whose names are entirely Celtic – that's a privilege that tends to belong to Cornwall, Wales and other places which succeeding waves of invaders failed to overwhelm. But Newent is an exception. It means 'new place', perhaps with a link to the Gaulish Latin for 'new market town'. It was important in Roman times, standing at a significant crossroads and also being a centre for iron smelting. It then grew into a manor in the possession of Edward the Confessor and by the time of the Domesday Book it was owned by the Norman church of Ste-Marie of Cormeilles: one Earl Roger 'gave it to this church for the soul of his father, with the consent of King William'. So it followed a not unusual pattern. The unusual thing is that it retained its Celtic name rather than ending up as, say, Newton St Mary. We are in 'best guess' territory here, and the best guess is that the Celts (presumably the Welsh) moved back at some point after being ousted by the Saxons.

Painswick

Originally simply Wick, 'dwelling or dairy farm' (see the box *Farming Country 2*, page 139), this later came into the possession of Pain Fitzjohn, hence its modern name. Pain was a member of the lesser Norman nobility (the 'fitz' part of his name suggests that he was illegitimate), but he did pretty well for himself. He married Sybilla, a daughter of the wealthy de Lacy family, and through her inherited some 115 manors, including 27 in Gloucestershire. He was at various times Sheriff of Shropshire and Herefordshire and a judge in Staffordshire, Gloucestershire and Northamptonshire. A loyal servant of Henry I (1100–35) and Stephen (1135–54), he was killed by an arrow in 1137, during a skirmish over the Welsh border. Just across that border, the name of the village of Painscastle and the substantial earthworks that are the only remains of its castle are further reminders of Pain's efforts to keep the Welsh firmly in Wales.

Paradise

What can I tell you? It's a nice place. And the pub is called the Adam and Eve.

Stonehouse

In the days when place names indicated distinguishing features, so that someone unfamiliar with the area would be able to identify a specific house (or farm or ford), a building made of stone rather than wattle and daub was remarkable enough to serve the purpose. There was a stone-built manor house here at the time of the Domesday Book, when the manor was owned by William d'Eu, a cousin of William the Conqueror, and valued at eight pounds. The house was rebuilt in 1601 by its then owner, was substantially rebuilt again after a fire in 1908, and is now a hotel.

Stow-on-the-Wold

Stōw, as we have seen elsewhere – in PADSTOW, FELIXSTOWE and WALTHAMSTOW, for example – frequently means a holy place and by the sixteenth century this one had been given the ending 'on the high ground that has been cleared of forest' to stop anyone confusing it with other holy places. It is recorded in the Domesday Book as *Edwardes stou* – 'Edward's holy place' – and there is mention of a church of St Edward, which still exists: the oldest surviving parts are eleventh century, but they were built on the site of an earlier, Saxon church. So who was Edward? Stow has historical links with Edward the Confessor – from medieval times to the present day a horse fair has been held around the time of his feast day, 13 October. But as he was not canonised until 1161, and indeed wasn't born until about 1003, it seems unlikely that a holy place would have been named after him as early as 1086, the date of the Domesday Book. Instead, local tradition mentions a missionary and hermit called Edward who lived outside the town in Saxon times, and it may be that the name originally came from him and was reinforced by links with the later king.

Stroud

An Old English name for 'marshy ground overgrown with brushwood'. Strood in Kent has the same meaning.

Tewkesbury

There was never any shortage of fortified places along the English/Welsh border: as we have seen (see CIRENCESTER and GLOUCESTER, above), the Romans built settlements to use as bases for their incursions into Wales and the Anglo-Saxons continued the tradition. Malmesbury and Tetbury are both examples of fortified places that grew up during the Anglo-Saxon period and were named after a local dignitary. (So, sadly, is Almondsbury – there is no connection with almonds.) Tewkesbury is said to take its name from a man called Theot or Theocalious, who founded a hermitage – presumably more like what we would now call a retreat or a centre for meditation – here in the seventh century. The hermitage was succeeded by a monastery which was expanded by the Normans to produce the basis of the existing abbey.

Thornbury

'Fortified place where thorn trees grow'. *Thorn–* is a friendly element in place names: it almost always means 'thorn'. So Thorne in Yorkshire is simply 'place by the thorn tree' and various settlements called Thornby, Thorncombe and Thorndon are, respectively, farms, valleys and hills where thorns grow. Withernsea in Yorkshire probably also has 'thorn' lurking in the middle of its name (*with* in Old English meant 'towards' or 'by', so this would be 'lake by the thorn tree'). The exception to this rule is Thornaby on Tees, which derives from a Scandinavian personal name. The best names among the thorny places are Thornfalcon in Somerset and Thorngumbald in Yorkshire, both of which commemorate thirteenth-century lords of the manor.

Wickwar

Most names that acknowledge a Norman manorial family end up being rather grandiose, like Shepton Montague or Naunton Beauchamp, but this humble-sounding name has the same sort of origin: it was simply the farm or dwelling belonging to the de Warre family.

Wotton-under-edge

Wotton means 'farmstead near a wood', and this one sits under the edge or escarpment of the Cotswold hills. The name of Wotton Underwood in Buckinghamshire indicates that it was actually *in* the wood. See also WOOTTON BASSETT.

Yate

The eighth-century name was *Geate*, meaning 'place by the gate or gap'. But the initial consonant was not a *g* as we know it but a *yogh*, pronounced like a modern *y*. Despite appearances, therefore, the name has changed very little.

WILTSHIRE

Originally Wilton-shire, Wiltshire takes its name from WILTON near Salisbury, the former county town. The home of some of England's prettiest villages, it can still boast a Roman fort or two.

Castle Combe

Combe means 'valley' and this one had a castle in it from Norman times. It had been destroyed by the middle of the nineteenth century, when a local history remarks on its 'meagre remains' and records the existence of 'a rude tower...recently built on the site, to indicate the position of the old castle'. In fact, the hill above the town was fortified long before the Normans arrived: an ancient Celtic hill fort was taken over and expanded by the Romans because of its proximity to the Fosse Way (see RADSTOCK). Today very little remains of any of this but the earthworks, and even they are confined within the grounds of a private golf club. The names of most of other Combes and Coombes throughout the country tell us who owned them in the years following the Conquest – Combe Abbas in Somerset belonged to Shaftesbury Abbey, while Combe Florey in Somerset, Combe Martin in Devon and Coombe

Bissett in Wiltshire all acknowledge the lord of the manor. Combeinteignhead in Devon is different: its name records the fact that it was in a district that contained ten hides of land – that is, about enough to support ten households.

Devizes

This name is unusual in being entirely of Old French origin. It means 'place on the borders', the borders in question being those between three ancient manors. There is known to have been a settlement here in Roman times, but Devizes became important only with the building of the Norman castle, which straddled the old boundary lines.

Lacock

This comes directly from an Old English word *lacuc*, meaning 'small stream', which is confusingly similar to, but unrelated to, the modern word *lake*.

Longleat

If you happen to know the slightly technical term *leat* for a channel that brings water to a mill, you'll be well on the way to working out what this name means. Records show that there was a mill on the property in the thirteenth century, which would make it much older than the existing house (which dates from the 1570s) but about the same age as the Augustinian priory that previously stood on the site. Both mill and leat are long gone, but place names often persist centuries after the reason for them has disappeared (see, for an extreme example, GATWICK).

Ludgershall

The ending *–hall* (from the Old English *halh*) generally means 'nook of land' and this one has a rather bloodthirsty context: it means 'nook with a trapping spear' – that is, a spear set up to gore animals that had been chased towards it. The facts that the Anglo-Saxons felt the need of a word for 'trapping spear' and that no fewer than four places (including Lurgashall in Sussex) take their name from it suggest that this unpleasant-sounding practice was widespread. Less controversially, Redenhall in Norfolk was a nook of land where reeds grew and Mildenhall in Suffolk probably means that it was the middle nook. There is another Mildenhall, though, in Wiltshire, which probably once belonged to a man called Milda or a woman called Milde. Walsall in the West Midlands may have been a nook belonging to a man named Walh, or one that housed a foreign enclave (see WALTON-ON-THAMES). See also MAGHULL and SAUGH-ALL MASSIE.

Marlborough

Borough in this instance means not a fortified place but a hill or burial mound – it comes from the same source as the Neolithic *long barrows*. This particular mound may be associated with a man named Maerla, or it may have been a place where gentians grew. Gentians were used for medicinal purposes in Saxon times (they're still recommended by some as a digestive tonic), so – as with horehound in ARUNDEL and dill in DULWICH – it would have been useful to know where they grew. On the other hand, given that this is a burial mound, it's tempting to associate it with a person – especially as a rumour based on no history at all says that Maerla was really King Arthur's magician Merlin. The mound said to have given Marlborough its name lies within the grounds of Marlborough College and is known as Merlin's Mount, but as alternative versions of the Arthurian legend suggest that Merlin was buried at Drumelzier in Scotland, at Bryn Myrddin (Merlin's Hill) near Carmarthen, on Bardsey Island or somewhere in Brittany it may be worth keeping a pinch of salt about your person just in case.

Melksham

It's unclear whether this place started life as a *–hām* or a *–hamm* (see the Introduction, page 20), so it was either a homestead or an enclosure. Either way, it is probably one where milk was produced – a dairy farm, in fact. Because public records compiled for tax purposes have survived, farming in the area is astonishingly well documented and we know that a man named Walter de Burgh took over the manor in 1236. At that time '32 oxen were delivered to him. In the ensuing year he bought 69 oxen, 1 bullock, 8 cows, 67 pigs, and 820 muttons, and sold 67 oxen, 7 cows, 154 pigs, and 820 mutton fleeces. In 1237–8 he bought 18 oxen, 38 cows, 23 heifers, 3 bullocks, 125 pigs, 60 goats, and 20 kids, and sold 14 oxen, 8 cows, 23 heifers, 3 bullocks, 128 pigs, and 46 muttons. He also sold 158 cheeses, the fleeces of 774 muttons, and the hides of 2 oxen, 2 cows, and 1 heifer.' So it is reasonable to suppose that, in among all that lot, he produced a certain amount of milk.

Salisbury

During the Iron Age, perhaps 2,500 years ago, and about 3 km from the present site of Salisbury, there was a hill fort whose remains can still be seen and which is known as Old Sarum. Salisbury itself was once known as New Sarum and to this day the Bishop of Salisbury signs himself 'Sarum'. But it is all a mistake. The name resulted from a medieval misreading of Sar', showing that then as now some people had a problem with punctuation. As in modern words such as *don't*, the apostrophe indicated that something was missing. Sar' was a shortened form of Sarisberie, the spelling which appears in the Domesday Book. So if not from Sarum, where did Sarisberie come from? Well, what happened was that the Romans discovered the hill fort and decided it would be a good place to build a defensive settlement of their own. They called it Sorviodunum, which is probably a Latinised form of the Old

Celtic name, meaning 'Sorvio's fort'. By 900 the Saxons had dropped the Romano-Celtic ending *dunum* and added their own version, *byrig*. In due course the Normans arrived, built their own castle on the site and started to pronounce the name in their own way. For the changing of *–byrig* to *–bury*, see the Introduction, page 20; changing the first *r* of Sarisberie to an *l* is the result of a phenomenon known as dissimilation, which means avoiding having two of the same consonant too close together.

Wilton

A tricky one, this, as a number of places called Wilton mean 'farmstead or village where the willows grow'. However, there are two Wiltons in Wiltshire, both with different meanings and neither anything to do with willows. The Wilton near SALISBURY – the one associated with carpets – gets its name from its situation on the river Wylye. Wylye is an Old Celtic name that probably means 'tricky stream', presumably because it was difficult to cross and/or prone to flooding. The other Wilton (further north, just south of HUNGER-FORD) probably means 'farmstead or village by the spring or stream', a derivation similar to that of WELLS.

Wootton Bassett

The fact that there are any number of places called Wootton or Wootton Something – over twenty in my road atlas – scattered throughout England should indicate that the name is associated with something commonplace. And indeed it is: it means 'farmstead or village in the wood'. For an alternative spelling of the same thing, see WOTTON-UNDER-EDGE. The Woottons with fancy names such as this one and Wootton Fitzpaine in Dorset commemorate Norman lords of the manor, while it should come as no surprise that Wootton St Lawrence in Hampshire boasts a church dedicated to St Lawrence. Most endearing of all the Woottons, though, is

Leek Wootton in Warwickshire, so called because – yes indeed – they used to grow leeks there.

OXFORDSHIRE

This is, of course, the shire around OXFORD, although it took over a certain amount of Berkshire when the boundaries were redrawn in 1974. Obviously most famous for its university, it also boasts the birthplace of Alfred the Great and an early twentieth-century attempt at self-sufficiency.

Bicester

This is another of those 'opinions vary' names. An archaeological dig about 2 km outside the modern town has found evidence of a Roman fort, so no difficulty there: *–cester* means what we expect it to mean (see the Introduction, page 11). It is the beginning that causes problems. It may come from an Old English word meaning a burial mound – there was an Iron Age settlement nearby and burial mounds tend to date from that period, so that has a ring of truth to it. Or it may come from a personal name. Or from a word for 'warriors'. This would give Bicester the slightly tautological meaning of 'warriors' fort', but as the first part of the name would have been Celtic and the *–cester* ending added in Anglo-Saxon times, this might have been an oversight. Or the name may indicate that there were two forts (with the prefix *bi–* meaning two): the Romans moved from their original encampment to the slightly higher ground on which modern Bicester sits, so again this is plausible. Don't like any of those suggestions? OK, then, Samuel Lewis's *Topographical History of England*, published in 1848, has these further offerings: 'This place…is supposed to derive its name either from its founder, Birinus, a canonised Saxon prelate; from Bernwood, a forest in Buckinghamshire, not far from which it is situated; or from the small stream of the Bure, on which it stands.' St Birinus, or Berin, was an Italian-born missionary of the seventh century, sent out into the world by the Pope to found his own diocese: history does not record what led him to plump for Dorchester-on-Thames. But he did, and his name lives on, in Berinsfield, which is only a couple of kilometres from Dorchester. It is incredibly unlikely, however, that he should have been associated with the naming of Bicester, given that he came along fully two hundred years after the Romans left. Some long-forgotten Saxon named Beorna or some unspecified group of Britannic warriors are the more likely culprits.

Brize Norton

Norton is straightforward enough – 'northern farmstead or village' (MIDSOMER NORTON, CHIPPING NORTON, we've met this before). *Brize* derives from the thirteenth-century lord of the manor, William le Brun, and the *n* of his name presumably slipped away over the years because Bruns Norton was just too difficult to pronounce.

Carterton

New towns such as LETCHWORTH and WELWYN GARDEN CITY were built on or near the sites of existing settlements and laid out according to a socially conscious plan. Carterton, on the other hand, was built in 1901 on farmland that had come into the hands of a builder named William Carter. He sold one-acre (about 0.4 hectare) plots at affordable prices, encouraging people to set up smallholdings and 'return to the land'. The modest success of this enterprise was overshadowed after 1937, when an air-force base was established at nearby BRIZE NORTON. Carterton's population thereafter grew substantially but it owes its later prosperity to the air rather than to the land.

Henley-on-Thames

If you chose to spell the first part of this 'High Leigh' you would get the meaning across: it is 'high – or chief – wood or glade'. Henley-on-Thames, home of the regatta, is the most famous of a number of places bearing this name; among others with the same meaning is Henley-in-Arden, which was in the medieval Forest of Arden (immortalised by Shakespeare and with a name that may derive from the Old Celtic for 'high district'). The Henleys in Somerset and Suffolk are also 'high woods', but the one in Shropshire is connected with hens: it used to be frequented by wild birds (see MORETON-IN-MARSH). Henley-on-Thames isn't in the Domesday Book (though some of the others are); the name isn't recorded until the twelfth century, when Henry II 'bought land for the making of buildings'. Camden describes the area thus: 'The Tamis, from hence having a great compasse about, windeth in manner backe againe into himselfe, enclosing within it the Hundred of Henley, mounting high with hilles and beset with thicke woods' – a fairly accurate explanation of the meaning of the name.

Hook Norton

It's not every town that has given its name to a brewery, so that is a good enough reason to include it here. You might expect it to be connected with a 'hook' of land, such as might be found at the bend in a river or hill, and indeed the Hooks in Hampshire and on the Greater London/Surrey border do mean this. You might also expect Hook Norton to be the northerly farmstead or village near the hook. But you would be so wrong. The Domesday Book spells it Hochenartone, which might enable you to guess (if you've been paying attention) that it was a farmstead or village connected with the Hoccenare people – a tribe associated with a man called Hocca, who settled on a hillside (*ōra*). Camden, bless him, spells the name three different ways in the space of the same paragraph: Hoche

Norton, Hoch-Norton and Hocknorton, all of them suggesting that by the 1580s people had altered the earlier name to a form that was more familiar, even if etymologically it was completely inaccurate. In those days the place had a ropy reputation: as Camden puts it, 'for the rusticall behaviour of the inhabitants in the age afore going it grew to be a proverbe, when folke would say of one rudely demeaning himselfe and unmanerly after an Hoggish kind, that he was borne at Hocknorton'. The arrival of the brewery, of course, put an end to all that.

Oxford

Those legendary dreaming spires disguise surprisingly humble origins. Oxford means nothing grander than 'ford used by oxen' (see the box *Crossing Places 1*, opposite). Remains of a Saxon bridge can be seen next to the nineteenth-century Folly Bridge and tradition has it that this was the site of the original ford. The Domesday Book records that in the time of Edward the Confessor the town paid the king a yearly rent of £20 and six sesters of honey (around 1.5–2 litres), but an extraordinary amount of the land listed under Oxford is designated as waste and paying no tax. Then someone had the bright idea of founding a university…

Wantage

'Place at the fluctuating or intermittent stream'. The stream, known in Saxon times as Wanoting, is now not so much intermittent as vanished. Birthplace of Alfred the Great and his eldest son and successor Edward the Elder, Wantage has another claim to fame from Saxon times: it was here that a witan or council met during the reign of Ethelred the Unready (978–1016) and established the Wantage Code, suggesting for the first time that a group of twelve senior men in each area of the country should swear 'never knowingly to accuse an innocent man nor conceal a guilty man'. Ethelred

CROSSING PLACES 1

Rivers were invented before roads and were crucial to transport and trade from the earliest times. Building a settlement near water made sense for other reasons, too – you and your livestock could drink it and it provided a ready source of power if the mood took you to build a mill. But getting from one side of a river to the other could be a problem, which is why so many places grew up alongside natural fords. It's an interesting reflection on river management over the last few centuries that by no means all of these places could still be forded: it would be a brave ox that tried to walk across the Thames at OXFORD in the driest of summers and only the strongest of swimmers could hope to get across the Avon at STRATFORD.

Most names connected with fords helpfully end in *–ford* or, particularly in the north, *–forth* (see HORSFORTH); a few end in *–wade*, which was another Old English word for 'ford', possibly influenced by the Scandinavian. These names can be divided into four broad categories:

1) *–ford* may simply be tacked on to the name of the river in question: **Lydford** was originally a place for crossing the river Lyd (from an Old English word meaning 'noisy stream'); **Ilford** is a ford over the Hyle (from a Celtic word for 'trickling stream'); **Sleaford** sits on the river Slea (so named because of its muddiness).

2) The name may tell us to whom the ford belonged: **Chelmsford** was associated with a man called Ceolmaer, **Biggleswade** with a man called Biccel. **Thetford**, on the other hand, was a public ford.

3) It may give a description of the ford: **Burford** was near a

fortified place, **Castleford** near a Roman fort and STAFFORD by a landing place. **Boxford** was a ford where box trees grew, **Crawford** was frequented by crows, **Buntingford** by buntings or yellow-hammers and HERTFORD by harts or stags. Anywhere called **Bradford** was broad, while **Romford** was wide or spacious (or indeed roomy – the derivation is the same). **Chingford** was shingly, **Cinderford** was cindery (built up from the cinders or slag of nearby iron-smelting works) and **Stamford** was stony – although **Stamford Hill** in LONDON was originally Saundfordhill and meant 'hill by a sandy ford'. **Guildford** was 'ford by the golden hill', the hill in question being the Hog's Back, originally called golden because of its sandy colour. The name changed in the nineteenth century because somebody decided that the long, narrow ridge reminded them of…a hog's back.

4) It may tell us what the ford was used for: coal was carried across the river at **Coleford**; OXFORD was used by oxen and **Shefford** by sheep.

Marking the ford – so that people didn't attempt to cross where the water was too deep – produced many places called **Stapleford** (with the same derivation as BARNSTAPLE).

Not all former fording places are obvious in the modern forms of their name: **Dulverton** in Somerset means, enticingly, 'farmstead by the hidden ford', the *ver* bit having been corrupted over the years from something more like *ford*. There's a bridge over the river now, so the fact that the ford is hidden doesn't matter as much as it used to.

There was also an Old English word *gelād* which is normally interpreted as 'difficult crossing' and survives in **Lechlade** (difficult because it was boggy) and **Cricklade** (possibly because it was rocky).

Further north, Scandinavian terms creep in: their word for a ford was *vath*, so **Wath** in North Yorkshire and **Wath-upon-Dearne** in South Yorkshire were both originally river-crossing places.

For other fords that have their own entry, see ASHFORD, BISHOP'S STORTFORD, BLANDFORD FORUM, CAMELFORD, HEREFORD, HUNGERFORD, NEW ALRESFORD, OXFORD, REDRUTH, STRATFORD and WATFORD; for places where you could get across the river without getting your feet wet, see the box *Crossing Places 2* on page 242.

gets a lot of bad press – his wars against the Danes are universally agreed to have been disastrous – but he can take some of the credit for introducing the jury system. Rumpole would have approved.

Waterperry/Woodperry

In the Domesday Book both these places were simply Perie, 'place at the pear trees', the name being connected to the word we still use for a pear wine. By the thirteenth century somebody had noticed that there were two of these places quite close together and added the first parts to distinguish 'the one by the water' from 'the one near the wood'.

6

❀

EAST ANGLIA

This region gets its name from the Angles who settled here from the fifth century, although Essex was always predominantly a Saxon area. East Anglia was one of the most important kingdoms of the Anglo-Saxon period and boasted some of its wealthiest kings, but that didn't stop it being overrun by the Danes in the ninth century. It was firmly on the Danish side of the line when Danelaw was established (see the Introduction, page 15) and as a result has its share of names of Scandinavian origin. Its early kings also did a lot of flirting with Christianity – marriages between pagan kings and Christian princesses from other kingdoms were commonplace, although reversion to paganism after the death of a Christian ruler was not infrequent either.

ESSEX

As with Sussex and Wessex, the ending of Essex shows that it was a Saxon kingdom, in this case belonging to the East Saxons. In the early times it seems to have been ruled from Kent, but then established itself as an independent entity and by AD 600 had taken control of Middlesex, which included LONDON.

Abbess Roding

The descendants or followers of a man called Hrotha must have been an influential lot – there is no end of places in Essex named after them. Abbess Roding was once the property of the Abbess of Barking, while Aythorpe Roding, Beauchamp Roding and Berners Roding take their affixes from thirteenth-century lords of the manor. Margaret Roding has a Norman church (on the site of an earlier Saxon one) dedicated to St Margaret; the church in White Roding is dedicated to St Martin, but someone obviously thought that its pale-coloured stone walls were more remarkable than the saint himself; more remarkably still, the church of St Michael and All Angels in Leaden Roding was the first in the area to have a lead roof, a fact recorded in the name by the middle of the thirteenth century. High Roding is on higher ground than the others – though still not very high, this being Essex; it once came under the juris-diction of ELY Abbey (as it then was), but was taken back by William the Conqueror as a punishment to the monks for having housed fugitives. The river Roding, which flows through or near all these places, is named after them.

Billericay

The most likely reason this name doesn't follow any of the recog-nisable patterns is that it comes from a medieval Latin word rather than the usual Celtic, Old English or Norman French. It may refer to a dyeing or tanning works and may be associated with the Asian fruit now known as myrobalan, whose Latin name is *Terminalia bellirica*. The fruit was imported into Britain in the Middle Ages and used in tanning and dyeing. The problems with this theory are 1) that a recognisable form of the name is recorded in 1291, long before the 'binomial' system of classifying plants with Latin names was invented and 2) that there is no evidence that a tanning or dyeing works existed here at the time. So this explanation, attractive though it may be, has to be filed under the heading of 'best guess'.

Colchester

This probably means 'Roman town on the river Colne', another river whose meaning has long been lost. If you are prepared to sacrifice probability for interest, you could plump for the alternative explanation, which is that *col* is short for *colonia* and that Colchester means 'Roman colony for retired soldiers'. To give a bit of background, in pre-Roman times Colchester (the oldest town in England) was known as Camulodunon, 'fortified place dedicated to the Celtic god of war, Camulos'. It was here that the British surrendered to the invading Emperor Claudius in AD 43. The Romans called the place Camulodunum and it became the administrative and cultural capital of the Roman province of Britannia, with its population given the honour of being Roman citizens. The historian Tacitus recorded that 'a colonia, consisting of a powerful body of veterans, was established at Camulodunum, to settle upon the conquered lands, as a resource against the rebels, and for initiating the allies in the requisitions of the laws of Rome'. Unfortunately all this alienated the locals to such an extent that an uprising led by Boudicca, queen of the Iceni people, resulted in Colchester being razed to the ground. It was then rebuilt from scratch with the first city wall in Britain. So, to cut a long story short, even if you choose to believe the *colonia* rather than the 'river Colne' derivation, you should rid yourself of the idea that you are dealing with a genteel Roman equivalent of a retirement village.

Dunmow

Dun– here comes from the same source as *–down* or *–don* at the end of a name and means 'hill', so Dunmow is 'meadow on the hill'. The place usually known as Dunmow is in fact Great Dunmow; there is a Little Dunmow not far away. Nothing very special? True, but sometimes a place manages to sneak into this book for other reasons. Dunmow is the home of the Dunmow flitch, a side of bacon reputedly awarded to any married man who would kneel on the church steps and swear that for the last year 'he has never had a household brawl nor wished himself unmarried'. Clearly husbands took the oath seriously: between 1244 and 1772 only eight flitches were awarded. This may be the origin of the expression 'to bring home the bacon' – or it may just be a good story.

Epping

The –*ing* element is from the same root as Dorking, Godalming and many other names associated with 'so-and-so's family and followers' (see the box *Whose Place Is It Anyway?*, page 181), but rather than being named after a person, Epping describes the place where they lived – 'on the ridge used as a lookout'. A nineteenth-century report describes Epping as 'a small market town, consisting chiefly of one long and wide street, upon a high ridge of table land' – from which, presumably, you could once have checked to see if any friend or foe was approaching. The famous forest is named after the town – until the seventeenth century it was WALTHAM Forest and the change presumably came about as Epping grew in importance.

Good Easter

I'll give you three guesses. No, wrong: nothing to do with Easter; nothing to do with goodness. The *Easter* element comes from the Old English for 'place at the sheep fold' – believe it or not, the derivation of the modern word *ewe* can be found in there somewhere. *Good* means that in Anglo-Saxon times the sheep fold belonged to a woman named something like Godgyth. The modern spelling – established by the middle of the nineteenth century – is another example of someone looking at the original version and thinking (wrongly), 'That can't be right.' Not very far away, High Easter sits on higher ground – quite close to High Roding, in fact (see ABBESS RODING). All the 'high' places in Essex seem to be crammed on to the same token hill.

Grays

This used to be called Grays Thurrock, the Grays bit coming from its being in the possession of the de Grai family in the twelfth century. Thurrock, now divided into West Thurrock and Little Thurrock and also the name of the borough in which Grays is located, means 'place where filthy water collects' and was originally applied to a marshy area on the north bank of the Thames. The good people of Grays understandably got shot of that part of their name as soon as they decently could.

Harlow

Although what we now call Harlow is a 'new town', founded in 1947, there has been a village here since Roman times. The name comes from Old English and means 'mound or hill associated with an army or large number of people'. The connection may be with a Viking army, or may simply reflect the fact that Moot Hill, just outside Old Harlow, was an important local meeting place. Harwich, on the Essex coast, means 'army camp', and again is likely to be associated with the Vikings. In both cases, the *har*– element comes from the Old English *here*, 'army', which reappears in HEREFORD.

Maldon

'Hill with a cross or crucifix'. The oldest part of the current church of St Peter is thirteenth century but, as the name of the settlement is at least two hundred years older than that, it seems likely that it replaced an earlier place of Christian worship. In recent years Maldon has become famous for another reason – the fact that television cooks recommend its salt. Bronze Age Essex man was way ahead of them: salt has been harvested from the marshes here for 2,500 years. See also NEW MALDEN.

Ongar

This translates simply as 'pasture land'. The place usually known as Ongar is really Chipping Ongar, which indicates that there was once an important market here (see the box on *Market Towns,* page 102). There is also a High Ongar, built on higher ground about a kilometre away. Ongar on its own strictly speaking refers to the now-defunct London Underground station which was until 1994 the north-eastern terminus of the Central Line.

Saffron Walden

Walden is Old English for 'valley of the Britons' and is a name given by the invading Anglo-Saxons to a place where the original residents still lived (see WALTON-ON-THAMES for more on the Anglo-Saxons' take on the natives). The area took to growing saffron much later than CROYDON, the longer version of the name being first recorded in 1582. Saffron was also grown in a part of London that was then owned by the Bishop of ELY (modern Holborn and Clerkenwell) and where Saffron Hill later earned notoriety as the home of Fagin's den in *Oliver Twist.*

Stansted Mountfitchet

There are various places called Stansted or Stanstead, and all mean 'stony place'. The Mountfitchet element comes from the Muntfichet family, known to have been in possession of land around here in the twelfth century. The modern airport – originally a US army base during the Second World War – took its name from the existing place. *Stan–* is a common element in other place names, notably Stanley ('woodland clearing on stony ground') and Stanton ('farmstead or village on stony ground').

Steeple Bumpstead

Nothing to do with bums or bumps, the second part of this name means 'place where reeds grow'. The 'steeple' part appears in the thirteenth century, to distinguish this village from Helions Bump-stead, property of the de Helion family. Oddly, the parish church has a tower rather than a steeple and the only explanation I can find for this anomaly is in a poem by Elizabeth Fleming, dating probably from the 1930s and suggesting that the steeple, which was fine and stately and admired greatly, was destroyed when a wizard sent a blizzard. Given that the blizzard also made folk scatter, turned the village eggs to batter and did a number of other conveni-ently rhyming things, my guess is that Elizabeth made this up. The Old English *bune*, 'reeds', is a source of confusion in another name, too: it is the origin of Bunny in Nottinghamshire, which means 'island [or dry ground in a marsh] where reeds grow' and has no connection with rabbits.

CAMBRIDGESHIRE

The shire surrounding CAMBRIDGE, this area seems to have been sparsely populated before the arrival of the Angles: there are few Celtic elements in the place names and those that do survive refer to topographical features rather than settlements.

Cambridge

You'd be forgiven for being confused if you had read about a place called Grontabricc in AD 745: the connection with Cambridge doesn't leap out at you. It becomes easier to make the link when you realise that what is now the river Cam used to be the Granta, and Grontabricc was the settlement by the bridge over it. Sadly this is another ancient river name whose meaning is not known for sure: it may be 'marshy water'. Grantchester, where Rupert Brooke wondered if there was honey still for tea, is just out of town and means 'settlers on the Granta' (the ending comes from the Old English *sæte*, as in DORSET and SOMERSET, rather than the Latin *castra*). The development of Grontabricc to Cantebrigie by the time of the Domesday Book and subsequently to Cambridge is the result of the Normans' inability to pronounce the original name. Then they realised that it was daft to have a town called Cambridge sitting on the Granta, so they high-handedly changed the name of the river to match. And if you are wondering, therefore, why Grantchester isn't called Camchester, the most likely answer is that it wasn't important enough for the Normans to bother with. I did mention that they were high-handed.

Chatteris

Chatteris is the highest point in the Fens at – don't laugh – 7.8 metres above sea level. This goes some way towards explaining the latter part of its name, *–ric* was the Old English for 'raised strip or ridge of land' and early spellings have Chatteris ending in *–ric* or *–riz*. As for the rest, it probably belonged to a man called Cetta.

Ely

It seems almost incredible that Ely should mean 'eely place, place where eels are found', but it's true. The name goes back to AD 731. The reason I express amazement is that one of the most glorious cathedrals in the country has been there since the eleventh century and in all the intervening years nobody has decreed that its little city deserved a more dignified name. However, as the original monastery on the site was founded by and dedicated to St Etheldreda or Æthelthryth, they might have thought that calling a town after a woman who couldn't decide how to spell her own name would lead to confusion. That said, Etheldreda's story is a good one. She was the daughter of a king of East Anglia and remained a virgin through two marriages. When her second husband, Egfrith of Northumbria, decided after twelve years that this wasn't what he wanted from conjugal life, Etheldreda left him – intacta – to become a nun, founded the monastery at Ely, where she lived until her death in 679. The monastery flourished for two hundred years before being destroyed by the Danes; it was then restored in 970. The present building was begun in the eleventh century and dedicated as a cathedral in 1109. In the meantime, Etheldreda's body had been exhumed seventeen years after her death and found to be undecayed, with the tumour that had killed her healed. She was reburied, but parts of her turned up as relics in various places throughout the following centuries – notably her hand in the church dedicated to her in Ely Place, London (once the London residence of the Bishop of Ely). And, lest you were wondering why the area is sometimes called the Isle of Ely, it is because it was an island in the middle of the Fens, which remained largely under water until the seventeenth century. To this day, if you approach Ely by road or rail, you are likely to be struck by the way the cathedral dominates the landscape for miles around: the hill on which it is built is 37 metres above sea level, which is high enough to be impressive in this part of the world.

Huntingdon

At first glance this seems like a name that should be easy to analyse, but it is trickier than it looks. The ending –*don* normally means a hill, but there is nothing worthy of that name within spitting distance of Huntingdon: the highest point in what used to be the county of Huntingdonshire is no more than 80 metres above sea level. (This point, by the way, rejoices in the name of Boring Field and has the distinction of being the lowest high point of any county in England.) The original settlement was probably, therefore, on a low rise or on a levee built to protect it from the floodwaters of the Great Ouse – high enough for people who lived on relentlessly flat land to call it a hill. As for the *hunting* part, it may be associated with huntsmen, or with a man called Hunta. The site was an excellent one: Huntingdon was not only at a handy river crossing; it was also the point where roads from all over the place converged on Ermine Street, the main road between London, Lincoln and York. The Danes were the first to fortify it, building their earthworks and the resultant settlement on the north side of the river. Not only was this more convenient if they needed supplies and reinforcements from their territories in the north and east; it also meant the Anglo-Saxons had somehow to make their way across the Ouse before they could even begin to think about attacking. It is significant, from this point of view, that nearby Godmanchester ('Roman camp connected with a man called Godmund'), which dates back to Roman times, is south of the river, on the 'right' side for access to the Roman bases of LONDON and COLCHESTER.

March

You might think, as this is a Fenland town, that the name would be connected with *marsh*. But no, it comes from an Old English word for 'boundary' and is more closely related to the modern *mark*. Originally two settlements – Merche and Mercheford, separated by a canal – March was practically an island in the middle of the Fens, although it is close to the old Roman road known as the Fen Causeway which permitted travel across this soggy area. Quite what it was the boundary of is unclear: the name may have had a geographical significance – marking the edge of a floodplain or the last stretch of safe, habitable land – or a political one, indicating the northern extent of the land owned by the Bishop of ELY. The old kingdom of Mercia takes its name from the same root, the traditional explanation being that its western border marked the eastern edge of the territory which the Welsh were defending. This is also how the Welsh Marches, along the English/Welsh border, got their name.

Peterborough

Peterborough started life as Medeshamstede, 'homestead of a man named Mede', and this was the original name of a monastery dedicated to St Peter, founded here in the seventh century. The Vikings destroyed both monastery and monks in the ninth century, but a hundred years later the building of a new abbey, also dedicated to St Peter, began and walls were built to protect the settlement. By the time of the Domesday Book the town was known simply as Burg ('fortified town'). But this was explicit enough, like saying, 'I'm going to town' when you live in a suburb. It was probably the only town, fortified or otherwise, for miles around; certainly in 974 there was no market town nearer than HUNTINGDON to the south or Stamford (see the box *Crossing Places 1*, page 117) to the west. In 1118 work started on the present cathedral and by 1333 'town' had come to be 'Peter's town', after its patron saint.

Quy

Properly speaking Stow cum Quy, this wonderful name is an amalgam of two earlier ones, the Latin *cum*, meaning 'with', indicating that two formerly separate manors have been joined together. *Stow* means 'place of assembly or holy place' (see PADSTOW); *Quy* (pronounced 'kwai') is 'raised area of pasturage on which cows are kept'; it is made up of the Old English word from which *cow* is derived and the ending meaning 'island' that also features in PEVENSEY, ROMSEY, RYE and many others. And see the next entry.

Ramsey

Another 'island' in the Fens, Ramsey was originally a dry patch surrounded by marsh. The *ram–* element comes from ramsons, or wild garlic, so the whole name means 'island where wild garlic grows'. Now that this part of north Cambridgeshire is drier than it used to be, a number of villages have sprung up around Ramsey:

Ramsey St Mary's is named after the parish church; Ramsey Mere-side acknowledges the presence of a pool nearby; Ramsey Heights reflects the area's obsession with anything that rises much above sea level (see HUNTINGDON for another example) and Ramsey Forty Foot is close to the Forty Foot Drain (40 feet being about 12 metres), dug in 1650 as a major contribution to the draining of the Fens.

Soham

'Homestead by a swampy pool'. There is no pool here now, but there was one in the time of the Domesday Book, in which the king's manor of Saham is recorded as rendering 3,500 eels and also having seven fishermen 'rendering to the king a gift of fish three times a year according to their ability'. (In this context it is worth noting that Soham is very close to ELY.) Over in Suffolk, Earl Soham and Monk Soham have the same derivation and were once under the jurisdiction of the Earl of Norfolk and the monks of BURY ST EDMUNDS respectively.

Wisbech

What was I saying about being obsessed with height? Here's another. The –*bech* element comes probably not from the word for stream or valley which has produced the modern *beck*, but from another Old English word meaning a ridge or raised ground. But we are still in the Fens, so we are not talking about a very high ridge. *Wis*– probably comes from the word for 'damp or marshy meadow', so – like MARCH – Wisbech was a settlement built on the only patch of dry ground around.

SUFFOLK

This means 'southern people' and distinguishes them from the 'northern people' of Norfolk. The people in question were the

Angles who, as we have seen, were the dominant tribe in this part of the world for several centuries.

Aldeburgh

This translates as 'old or disused stronghold' – as do Aldborough and Aldeby in Norfolk, Aldbury in Hertfordshire and two places called Aldbrough in Yorkshire. In the case of Aldeburgh, which has been subject to a series of floods throughout its history, the fort, presumably Roman, has long since vanished into the sea.

Bury St Edmunds

Edmund was a king of East Anglia who died in 869, killed in battle by the invading Danes. By this time, however, East Anglia was no longer an important kingdom, its rulers having been eclipsed by kings from Wessex. The thing about Edmund, though, was that he started doing great (albeit unspecified) deeds after his death: by 890 there were memorial coins proclaiming him a saint. Most of the information we have about him comes from a *Life of St Edmund* written in 985 by Abbo of Fleury, based at RAMSEY Abbey. (That is how you spell his name, by the way. Despite the fact that he was based at an abbey, he wasn't an abbot.) Abbo maintains that Edmund didn't die in battle: he was taken prisoner, whipped, tied to a tree and shot with arrows 'until he bristled with them like a hedgehog or thistle'. He was then beheaded and his head thrown into bramble thickets. The survivors searched for the head and found it guarded by a wolf and calling, 'Here, here, here.' Edmund was then buried in a small chapel built for the purpose and his remains were moved to Bedericsworth in about 906. There had been a monastery at Bedericsworth – the site of today's Bury St Edmunds – since about 630, but forty years after the arrival of Edmund's remains the then king – confusingly also called Edmund – granted it a large area of land, paving the way for it to become a wealthy and influential abbey. All this time, wars between Anglo-Saxons and Danes had been raging and in 1013 a Dane rejoicing in the name of Sweyn Forkbeard was accepted as king in the northern and eastern parts of the country, the area known as Danelaw (see the Introduction, page 15). But, the story goes, Sweyn was struck dead when he threatened to sack the town that was by this time known as St Edmunds. A lesson there: mess with the relics of saints at your peril. Over the next centuries the town was known sometimes as St Edmundsbury and sometimes as Bury St Edmunds, but the meaning is the same: it is the town associated with this otherwise little-known saint.

Clare

Opinions vary as to whether this name comes from a Celtic word meaning 'bright stream' or an Old English one referring to clay soils. Whatever the origin, the place gave its name to the Clare family. Lionel, second surviving son of Edward III, married into the family in the fourteenth century and, on being created a duke, adapted the name for his title, the first Duke of Clarence.

Felixstowe

Here's another saint who is little known outside Suffolk (see BURY ST EDMUNDS). Born in Burgundy in about AD 600, Felix became a missionary and the first Bishop of the East Angles. He founded a monastery at Dummoc and there is some dispute as to whether this was at Dunwich ('trading centre near the dunes') or at Walton, near modern Felixstowe. He also founded a monastery, later destroyed by the Danes, at SOHAM, where after his death he was buried for a while before being removed to RAMSEY Abbey. The journey from Soham to Ramsey had to be achieved by boat; when the people of ELY heard that the remains of their saint were being removed they set out in a larger number of boats to stop it. According to a contemporary chronicler, 'In order that it might be clearly seen that the removal was taking place by Divine rather than by human wishes, it came to pass that just as the ships of either party were approaching one another under a bright and cloudless sky, suddenly, to the discomfiture of the large force and the benefit of the smaller, a dense fog arose which separated the two parties. And so, while their adversaries were vainly wandering in different directions, our boat was carried onward in a straight course and safely deposited by the aiding waters on the bosom of our native shore.' Pretty tame as miracles go, you might think, but it meant that the remains of St Felix ended up in Ramsey and attracted a lucrative trade in pilgrims. Be that as it may, Walton has existed since at least Roman times; Felixstowe grew up as a fishing hamlet to service it. The name doesn't appear in the records until the mid-thirteenth century and means 'holy place associated with St Felix' – by this time the monastery at Dummoc (wherever it was) had long since been washed away and there was no evidence to stop the people of Walton laying claim to it.

Haverhill

Probably 'hill where oats are grown'. The *haver–* element shows the Scandinavian influence in this part of the world: it comes from an Old Norse word that recurs in Haverigg and Haverthwaite in Cumbria (respectively 'ridge' and 'clearing' where oats are grown).

Ipswich

'Harbour or trading centre of a man named Gip'. As in YATE, this initial wasn't a modern *g* but a *yogh*, so the name was pronounced Yip, a sound the Normans weren't familiar with. Ipswich was an influential place at the time of the Domesday Book and there are several references to it. The various different spellings – Gepeswiz and Gypeswiz are two – all still have the initial *g*, but this was lost by the fourteenth century. The nearby village and river Gipping have the same derivation as Ipswich, and provoke the same sort of speculation that arises with CAMBRIDGE and Grantchester: presumably of the three places associated with Gip, only Ipswich was important enough for the Normans to influence its pronunciation.

Lowestoft

This means 'homestead of a man named Hlothver', but it is interesting because it is another reminder of the Danish influence: in a region dominated by the Anglo-Saxons it would have ended in *−sted* or *−stead* (see the box *Farming Country 2*, page 139).

Needham Market

A rather sad name, the first part of this does indeed mean 'poor or needy homestead'. It is not mentioned in the Domesday Book, having presumably been only a small hamlet at that time, and it was plain Needham as late as the thirteenth century. Henry III granted it a market charter in 1245 (you couldn't have a market without a charter − see the box on *Market Towns*, page 102) and thereafter it grew in prosperity thanks to a thriving trade in wool combing. Badly afflicted by the Great Plague in the 1660s, it cut itself off from the outside world, lost about two-thirds of its inhabitants and went back to being needy. By the nineteenth century the author of the *Imperial Gazetteer of England and Wales* was able to say that it 'is well built, and contains several handsome houses', but it was never a great market town again.

Snape

Given that both Old English and Old Scandinavian left their mark on place names in this part of the world, this could mean either 'boggy ground' (OE) or 'poor pasture' (OS). Whichever is true, the Romans managed to extract salt from it, so it wasn't a complete write-off. There's a Snape in Yorkshire, too, which was once on the fringes of a large marshy area, so the Old English derivation is probably the one to go for there.

Stowmarket

Stow doesn't always mean a holy place, as it does in FELIXSTOWE; sometimes it is simply a meeting place, and this is probably the case with the hundred (administrative district) of Stow. Its principal town, Stowmarket, was originally called something like Thorney, or 'thorny island', but changed its name when it became the most important trading centre in the area in the thirteenth century. Stowlangtoft, also in the hundred of Stow, was once the property of the de Langetot family.

NORFOLK

The 'northern people' of the East Anglian kingdom, as opposed to the 'southern people' who lived in SUFFOLK. Its place names are a mixture of the rural, the regal and the military, with a nod – as always in East Anglia – towards the dangers of being so very flat.

Acle

One suggested meaning for this name derives from its topography. In Roman and Anglo-Saxon times, Acle was on the coast and was an important fishing port. All the area between it and GREAT YARMOUTH, which we now call The Broads, was under the sea, making it reasonable to suppose that the waters periodically 'overflowed' into the town, giving it the name 'place that overflowed'. However, most modern experts think that it is more likely to have been 'clearing in the oak trees' – think of it as 'oak ley' and check the entry on BROMLEY for more about the –*ley* ending. There were certainly once a lot of oaks here: in Elizabethan times hundreds of them were felled to provide timber with which to build warships. In further support of this theory, lots of other names beginning with *ac–* are known to derive from the Old English word for 'oak' – see ACTON.

Caister-on-Sea

The Roman fort from which this names derives (see the Introduction, page 10, for more about Roman forts) was built in the second century AD. It was originally on an island on the north side of the estuary where the Bure, the Yare and the Waveney flowed into the sea, so it occupied a strategic position; in the year 260 Burgh Castle was built on the other side of the estuary by way of reinforcement. Both were abandoned in the fourth century, when Roman forces were withdrawing from Britain, but you can still visit the ruins.

Diss

'Place at the ditch or dyke'. This was presumably a drainage ditch, as the town is built round one of the deepest natural lakes in the country: in places it is six metres deep, but boasts another fifteen metres of mud below that.

Great Yarmouth

Some time between the construction of the Roman fort at CAISTER and the compiling of the Domesday Book, the sea at the mouth of the river Yare (which probably means 'babbling stream') receded sufficiently for a town to be built on the newly emerged sandbank. Before the Norman Conquest Yarmouth was the property of King Edward the Confessor and boasted seventy burgesses – townsmen of the higher social and financial strata. This is not a very big deal – NORWICH had 1,320 – but it meant that, North Sea permitting, Yarmouth was there to stay. The 'Great' in its name appeared some time in the Middle Ages, in time for Thomas Nashe to satirise the town and its fish industry in a book called *Lenten Stuffe* published in 1599: its epigraph begins, 'Containing the description and first procreation and increase of the town of Great Yarmouth in Norfolk. With a new play never played before, of the praise of the red herring.'

Holt

Nothing to do with either a railway halt or an otter's den, this is 'place near the wood or thicket'. A number of other towns around the country bear this name and all mean the same thing. Old English had various words for 'wood' – *hurst*, which also appears frequently in place names, is derived from another. The distinguishing feature of a *holt* seems to have been that it contained a single species of tree, leading to names such as Bircholt in Kent, Buckholt ('beech') in Hampshire and Sussex, Alderholt in Dorset, Knockolt ('oak') in Kent and Wiggenholt ('wych elm') in Sussex. Eversholt in Berkshire was 'the wood of the wild boar' (see the box on *Animal Place Names*, page 78).

King's Lynn

Lynn comes from the Celtic word for a waterfall or a pool at the foot of it – *linn* is still used in this sense in Scotland. Called simply Lynn at the time of the Domesday Book, it was for a while in the possession of the see of NORWICH and was known as Bishop's Lynn. Henry VIII took over the town (and its tax revenues) at the time of the Dissolution of the Monasteries and it wasn't long before somebody had a bright idea about changing its name.

Norwich

The ending *–wick* or *–wich* can have a number of loosely related meanings (see the box *Farming Country 2*, opposite), but in this instance it is probably 'trading centre or landing place'. Norwich

FARMING COUNTRY 2

In Old English, an outlying farm was a *stoc*, which has come down to us as −*stock* or −*stoke*. **Tavistock**, 'outlying farm on the river Tavy' and **Basingstoke**, 'outlying farm associated with Basa's people', are examples of this. So, too, is STOKE-ON-TRENT, which for a long time was called simply Stoke − if it was the only outlying farm around, there was no need to be more explicit.

Less common but not to be ignored is −*worth* or −*worthy*, from another Old English word for 'enclosure': a homestead or bit of farmland surrounded by a protective fence or a ditch. MARKET BOSWORTH, KENILWORTH, LUTTERWORTH and TAMWORTH have their own entries, but other notable −*worths* around the country include **Haworth** in Yorkshire ('hedged enclosure', though presumably the hedge wasn't high enough to keep out the howling winds that gave *Wuthering Heights* its name); **Lulworth** in Dorset ('Lulla's enclosure'), **Petworth** in Sussex ('Peota's enclosure') and **Saddleworth** in Lancashire (passing over a ridge shaped like a saddle). The most interesting-sounding of the −*worthies* is **Martyr Worthy** in Hampshire, but it's a bit of a disappointment: it belonged in the later Middle Ages to a family called le Martre, and there is no evidence that anyone died for their faith here.

As time went by, farms began to specialise and were called *wīc*. This word had originally just meant 'dwelling' (which seems to be the origin of WARWICK), but it developed a range of meanings from village to town, market place to port. In the farming context, however, it came to refer most frequently to a dairy farm; this explains why there are so many places called **Butterwick** and several called **Keswick**, 'cheese farm'. But there is also GATWICK ('goat farm'), BERWICK ('barley farm'), **Hardwick** ('where the herds were'), **Swanwick** ('where the herdsmen were' – see SWAN-AGE) and others. The –*k* ending is a late variation on this theme; a *wīc* that became important before about the tenth century is nowadays generally spelt –*wich*, as in IPSWICH and NORWICH. DROITWICH and NANTWICH are two other examples of the *wīc*'s tendency to specialisation – they both refer to salt works.

Of course, the Anglo-Saxons were not the only people to farm in England. Once the Norsemen had finished their rampaging, they too settled down and brought their language with them. Thus towns that were originally farmsteads in the north and east regularly end in –*by* rather than –*ham*, as in DERBY, ASHBY and WHITBY. The Danelaw equivalent of –*stoke* or –*stock* was –*thorp(e)* or –*throp*, with modern pronunciation sometimes at variance with spelling: ALTHORP, **Scunthorpe**, **Heythrop**. And finally the Old Scandinavian for 'site of a house and its outbuildings' – 'homestead' is probably easier – survives in modern place names as *toft*. LOWESTOFT is the most famous example, but there are also **Brothertoft** and **Kettletoft**, both of which are more likely to come from personal names than to mean what they look as if they mean.

was once an important river port (and much closer to the sea than it is now); the *nor*– element of the name indicates that it was to the north of IPSWICH.

Swaffham

'Homestead of the Swabians', a tribe originally from Swabia in Germany. There are two other Swaffhams, both near CAMBRIDGE: Swaffham Prior was once in the possession of the Prior of ELY and

Swaffham Bulbeck was owned by a family named de Bolebech. As for the Swabians, nothing more specific is known of them than that they must have arrived in among the waves of Angles and Saxons from the fifth century on. The answer to the question 'What were they doing in this part of East Anglia?' can only be 'Everyone's got to be somewhere.'

Watton

One of the most frustrating things about place names is the frequency with which you come across several places with exactly the same name but entirely different meanings. Watton is a case in point. The one in Norfolk means 'farmstead belonging to a man called Wada', while Watton at Stone in Hertfordshire means 'farmstead where woad is grown; oh and by the way it's near that big stone'. Watton in Yorkshire was once Uetadun, so the ending means not 'farmstead' but 'hill', in this case a wet one.

Wells-next-the-Sea

From the same source, if you'll excuse the pun, as WELLS in Somerset – natural springs. There used to be a lot of them here, rising out of the local chalk. Wells was once an important port, but silting up of the harbour means that it is now nearly 2 km inland.

7

BERKSHIRE, BUCKINGHAMSHIRE, BEDFORDSHIRE AND HERTFORDSHIRE

In Anglo-Saxon times these four counties were a bit of a mishmash – part Outer Mercia, part Middlesex, part the territory of the East Angles with the northern portion of Wessex thrown in. Not to mention being the scene of many battles between Alfred the Great and the Danes. They are generally calmer now, but their place names reflect some of the earlier conflict.

BERKSHIRE
One of the few 'shires' not to be named after its most important town, Berkshire means 'shire centred on the hilly place'. Being Celtic in origin, this ranks alongside Kent and Cornwall as one of the oldest county names in the country.

Aldermaston

To make sense of this name, you need to divide it as *Aldermas–ton*, not, as you might be tempted to do, *Alder–maston*. Aldermaston has nothing to do with alders (see ALDERSHOT for examples of places that do); instead, it is a 'farmstead belonging to a chief or noble-man'. The Domesday Book spelling Aeldremanestone underlines the link to the modern word *alderman*.

Eton

The *e* comes from the Old English *ēa*, 'water or river', so Eton started out as a farmstead by the river, growing up – centuries before Eton College was thought of – to serve the castle at WINDSOR, across the Thames, and also the many travellers on the Windsor-to-London road.

Hungerford

The simple interpretation seems to be the accurate one in this name: it was a ford associated with hunger, because the surrounding land was infertile. Other possibilities include the suggestion that the name was originally Ingleford, 'ford of the Angles', because the river Kennet, on which Hungerford sits, divided Angle territory from Saxon, but this seems to have no basis in history. It is also said that Hingwar the Dane drowned while crossing the Kennet and that the settlement was named after him. The first record of this story appears two hundred years after Hingwar's death and is prob-ably an early form of urban myth, but it is worth mentioning here because Hingwar was the alternative name for the Viking chieftain also rejoicing in the epithet of Ivar the Boneless. The reason for this has inspired all sorts of speculation – did he suffer from a genetic disease that made his bones weak? Was he either lame or literally legless? Or perhaps impotent? We shall never know. We don't know what the name of the river Kennet means, either, but it is old and Celtic.

Maidenhead

'Landing place of the maidens', the *–head* in this instance being connected to *–hithe*, as in ROTHERHITHE. The explanation may be that the area was frequented by maidens – for some religious reason, perhaps; there were certainly nuns in the priory in nearby Cookham. Or perhaps it was a particularly easy place to land, so that if we were naming it now we might call it 'girly landing place' instead. Alternatively, it may be using 'maiden' in the sense of 'new, unspoiled', because the Danes, having travelled up the THAMES in long boats in the ninth century, disembarked here, established a settlement and built a new landing place. Cookham, sadly, probably doesn't mean 'village noted for its cooks', but rather 'village built on a hill' – from an Old English word that survives in the modern *haycock*.

Slough

Exactly what it sounds like: a boggy place. Although the name goes back to the twelfth century, Slough didn't become a substantial town until the arrival of the railways, by which time it had presumably dried out a bit. It's easy, post-John Betjeman, to be dismissive of Slough and assume that it deserves its dreary name; more disappointing is the discovery that the picture-postcard Cotswold villages of Lower and Upper Slaughter have the same derivation and were also once boggy places.

Thatcham

The *thatch* element here does indeed mean 'thatch' – it was either a settlement of thatched houses or a river meadow where materials for thatching were gathered (that *hām* or *hamm* dilemma again, see the Introduction, page 20). Thaxted in Essex was also originally a source of thatching materials.

Windsor

This means 'bank or slope with a windlass', presumably because the Anglo-Saxons who first settled here built a winch or windlass to help lift goods out of boats and into the village – the THAMES was, after all, a main thoroughfare between LONDON and points west, so a good place to have a settlement. The Anglo-Saxon king Edward the Confessor held court in what is now Old Windsor, but it must already have been a reasonably civilised place before he contemplated moving there. All this pre-dates the existing castle, so the timeline is: the Anglo-Saxons found a settlement beside the river and install a windlass to make it run more efficiently; Edward the Confessor takes a liking to the place; William the Conqueror takes over and decides it will be a powerful statement if he builds a castle on the nearest hill. Result, New Windsor – a title it was given as recently as 1070 – home of the oldest and largest inhabited castle in the world.

BUCKINGHAMSHIRE

Back to counties that are named after their principal town. Church and state, woods and water all feature in Buckinghamshire place names.

Beaconsfield

There are two schools of thought about this name: most modern reference books interpret it as 'open land near a beacon or signal-fire', but some go for 'open space surrounded by beech trees'. Beaconsfield is on the fringes of the Chiltern Hills but, at an elevation of only 114 metres, is hardly the highest point around. Nor, therefore, is it the most obvious location for a beacon, whose purpose is to be visible from a long way away. In favour of the other suggestion is the fact that as late as the 1920s almost a quarter of the parish of 4,504 acres (1,740 hectares) was planted with beech trees: there were almost certainly more in earlier times. The nineteenth-century prime minister Benjamin Disraeli was MP for Buckinghamshire from 1847 to 1876, after which he was ennobled as the first Earl of Beaconsfield. The title died with him in 1881 and has not been used since.

Buckingham

This –*ham* was originally a –*hamm* (see Introduction, page 20), so the full name is 'land in a bend in the river, belonging to the family or followers of a man called Bucca'. The river in question is the Great Ouse, whose name comes from yet another Celtic or pre-Celtic word for water and is called 'Great' to distinguish it from the Little Ouse in Suffolk and Norfolk, and from various other Ouses across the country. You have to be quite a linguist – and prepared to dig a fair way back into Indo-European roots – to recognise that Ouse comes from the same source as *wet* and *water*, but it's true nevertheless.

Chalfont St Peter/Chalfont St Giles

The entry for 'Chalfont' in the Domesday Book almost certainly refers to St Peter, but there are references to Chalfont St Giles by the thirteenth century. So even in these early days there were two communities, distinguished by their proximity to one church or the other. Opinions vary as to what Chalfont means – the 'font' bit is certainly a fountain or spring, but the original settlement may have been at a cold spring, a spring frequented by calves or a spring belonging to a man named Ceadel. As for the saints, Peter was the apostle, Giles was a Greek-born monk of the seventh century whose fame spread across Europe as the patron saint of lepers and crip-ples, with the result that he has many churches named after him, notably the cathedral in Edinburgh. Ayot St Lawrence and Ayot St Peter in Hertfordshire tell a similar tale: first there was a place called Ayot, deriving from the same Old English word as the modern *gate* and meaning 'gap or pass belonging to a man called Aega'; later the community boasted two churches dedicated to different saints, Lawrence being an early Christian martyr.

Chesham

'Heap of stones by the water meadow' (making this another *hamm*: see previous entry). The stones were the local 'pudding stones', used in prehistoric times to mark roadways and meeting places. Pudding stone is a conglomerate containing pebbles of a different colour and composition from the main body of the rock, so it would have been easy for passers-by to spot. Although the area still has its fair share of woods, the name of nearby Chesham Bois comes not directly from the French for *wood* but from the name of the Norman lords of the manor, the de Bois family (whose name did, however, mean wood).

High Wycombe

This and neighbouring West Wycombe derive from a dative plural form of $w\bar{\imath}c$ meaning 'farm, dwelling' (see the box *Farming Country 2*, page 139), so the name means nothing more than 'place where the dwellings are'. It is not connected with the river Wye which flows through it — in this instance the name of the river is a back-formation. Nor is there any link with *combe*, meaning 'valley'. In fact, if the powers that be had spelt the name Wicken, as they did with places from the same source in Cambridgeshire and Northamptonshire, it would have been altogether clearer.

Marlow

As in MARGATE, the *mar-* element here is related to *mere* and means 'lake or pool'; Marlow is 'land remaining after the draining of a pool'. It seems likely that — for some reason and at some time before the early eleventh century, when a form of this name is first recorded – the THAMES changed its course at this point, leaving a piece of land that eventually dried out and became fit to live on.

Milton Keynes

Although the town now known as Milton Keynes is one of the youngest in this book – it came into being in 1967 – the name is as old as most of the others. Like other Miltons (and there are many of them – Milton Abbas in Dorset, Milton Clevedon in Somerset, Milton Ernest in Bedfordshire, Great and Little Milton in Oxford-shire, Milton under Wychwood in Oxfordshire, to name but a few), the first part of its name means 'middle farmstead or estate': such a place might once have stood between a Sutton and a Norton. Milton Keynes appears as Middeltone in the Domesday Book; by 1227 it has become Middeltone Kaynes, because of its association with the family of de Cahaignes.

Newport Pagnell

What's a 'new port' doing in the middle of Buckinghamshire, you may ask. Well, like LANGPORT, it isn't a port so much as a market town, and it has been 'new' since the time of the Domesday Book: the Normans built a number of market towns shortly after the Conquest and this was one of them. Pagnell (or Paynel or Paynelle in its earlier forms), the name of the local lord of the manor, was added in the thirteenth century.

Princes Risborough

This and neighbouring Monks Risborough started life as 'hills where brushwood grows': in this instance, as in MARLBOROUGH, the –*borough* comes not from the word for a fortified town but from *beorg*, 'hill'. *Ris* for brushwood recurs in Risbury in Herefordshire and two places called Risby, one in Suffolk and one in Lincolnshire. Monks Risborough was in late medieval times under the control of the monks of Christchurch, CANTERBURY; the prince of Princes Risborough was Edward the Black Prince, son of Edward III (he was a great warrior and allegedly earned his nickname because he wore black armour in battle). Edward had custody of the manor in 1343 and is said to have had a palace here (an area surrounded by a moat can still be seen to the west of the churchyard). After he died in 1376 it remained a royal possession, being granted to Catherine of Valois, wife of Henry V (1413–22), as part of her dowry and to Margaret of Anjou, wife of Henry VI (1422–61), as part of hers. Around 1630 Charles I sold it to the City of London to help pay his debts – one of the people who subsequently acquired it was Sir Peter Lely, the painter. It was never in royal hands again, but the princely affix remains.

BEDFORDSHIRE

A county that seems to have been on the border between warring parties throughout its history. Saxons versus Danes, Norman king versus Norman pretender to the throne – all found something to bicker about.

Ampthill

This has the unappetising meaning of 'anthill' or 'hill infested with ants'. The Domesday Book spelling *Ammetelle* shows the link with *emmet*, an archaic or dialect word for 'ant'. Domesday also tells us that there was woodland for three hundred pigs, but commenting on the ants was outside its remit. We know that Henry III granted Ampthill a charter – and with it permission to hold a market – in 1219 and that Catherine of Aragon lived here when she and Henry VIII separated in 1531 (it was after the divorce two years later that she moved to the better-known Kimbolton in Cambridgeshire, 'farmstead of a man named Cynebald'). William Camden, writing in the 1580s, says that there had been until recently 'a stately house, resembling a castle and environed with Parks', built in the reign of Henry VI (1422–61) by Sir John Cornwal Baron Fanhop (Camden's spelling) and financed by spoils won from the French. Bartholomew's *Gazetteer* (1887) tells us that it is a town and parish with a population of 2,257, that it has a railway station, a telegraph office, a post office and one bank, and that market day is Thursday. All immensely useful and interesting, but the ants remain a mystery.

Bedford

Nothing very earth-shattering here (in terms of the name, that is – no disrespect to the town). The second part refers to a ford; the first part could be a personal name or it could mean a deep valley. The river that needed to be forded was the Great Ouse (see BUCK-INGHAM). Historically, Bedford is more exciting, because it sits on the border between Wessex and Danelaw (see the Introduction, page 15). Before that it was in Mercia, whose great king Offa is said to have been buried here in 796. The Danes occupied the town in 899 after the death of Alfred the Great. It was reclaimed in 915 by Alfred's son, Edward the Elder, who was the first to fortify it. A hundred years later the Danes were back, sailing up the Ouse and burning everything in sight. Nor did things calm down after the Norman Conquest. The land around Bedford was granted to a Norman called Ralf de Tallebosc, who built the first castle here. This was besieged by King Stephen in 1137, during his war with his cousin Matilda over who should be on the throne. It later became the focal point for barons rebelling first against King John (1199–1216) and then against his son, Henry III (1216–72). The latter successfully besieged it in 1224, hanging eighty of the rebels and destroying the castle in the process. Wander round this pleasant town today and your most likely reaction is, 'Who'd have thought it?'

Houghton Conquest

There are many places in England called Houghton and they mean 'farmstead on a ridge or hill spur' – the Old English *hōh* also meant 'heel' and indirectly produced the modern 'hock'. I include this one because it ought to be more interesting than it is: 'Conquest' here refers not to the Norman Conquest, but to the family who lived here in the thirteenth century.

Leighton Buzzard

Unlike many names containing *leigh*, this is connected not with woodland but with leeks – the Old English is *lēac*. The word evolved to mean vegetables generally, so the distinguishing feature of the original settlement was a vegetable or herb garden. Presumably the Normans didn't know this – in the Domesday Book the name is recorded as Leston. One of the town's websites makes the proud boast that over the centuries Leighton has been subject to sixty different spellings, 'depending on the fancy of the writer'. In the thirteenth century – when it is found as Letton – a man named Theobold de Busar was an important local clergyman and left his mark on the town's name (the same website tells us that over the years a mere forty variations in the spelling of Buzzard have been found).

Luton

'Farmstead on the river Lea', a definition which is found as Leyton in east London with reference to the other end of the same river. *Lea* probably means 'bright river', but may be associated with the Celtic god Lug or Lugh, regarded as a trickster but also as a master of all sorts of arts and skills, from poetry to smithery to warfare.

Potton

'Farmstead where pots are made', or so it was in the tenth century. A gazetteer of the 1870s lists its principal industry as straw-plaiting. Times change and we must change with them.

Sandy

Most place names beginning with 'sand' refer to sand: anywhere called Sandhurst means 'sandy wooded hill'; Sandgate in Kent was originally 'gap leading to a sandy shore'; Sandwell in the West Midlands was 'sandy spring'; the various Sandfords were all 'sandy fords' and so on. Sandwith in Cumbria might also have been called Sandford had it been further south – the *–with* element shows a Scandinavian influence. Sandy itself wasn't just sandy, it was a sandy island, the *–y* coming from the same root as the *–ey* ending in, for example, SELSEY and SHEPPEY.

Woburn

Burn or *bourne* means a stream and Woburn is 'crooked or winding stream'. On the face of it this is odd, as it isn't built on a river, but it may be that the name originally referred to a district rather than a village and certainly the Ouzel – a tributary of the Ouse a few kilometres to the west – is very sinuous at this point. Nearby Woburn Sands does have sandy soil; it was once called Hogsty End, but when its particularly salubrious microclimate gained fame and people started to come here to 'take the air', it may have been felt that something a little less earthy was required.

HERTFORDSHIRE

Also on the Wessex/Danelaw border, Hertfordshire saw its share of action before settling down to be full of commuter towns. But the unashamed eccentricity of having a place named after Baghdad (see BALDOCK) must acquit it of any accusation of boringness.

Baldock

Surely the only place in England named after a place in Iraq. People lived here in the Iron Age and during the Roman period, when it was an important crossroads, but the settlement fell into disuse after the Romans left. The present town was founded by the Knights Templar in about 1148. The knights encouraged prosperous merchants to settle here and used their rents to help finance Crusades. And, showing off their knowledge of the Middle East, they called it Baldac, the Old French for Baghdad. Today Baldock is twinned with Eisenberg in Germany and Sanvignes-les-Mines in France, but not with its namesake.

Berkhamsted

Just when you thought you were getting the hang of this place-naming business, here is something to wipe the smirk off your face. The town most of us think of as Berkhamsted is sometimes known as Great Berkhamsted; about 30 km to the east is a (smaller) place called Little Berkhamsted. There is no argument about the ending – like most other *–hamsteds* or *–hampsteads*, it means 'homestead'. But there the certainty ends. The first part may come from an Old Celtic word meaning 'hill' (as in BERKSHIRE) or from an Old English one meaning 'birch'. Some authorities maintain that (Great) Berkhamsted was on a hill and that Little Berkhamsted was covered with birches. But there is no shortage of birches near Berkhamsted, and Little Berkhamsted is hilly too. Pay your money… And why 'hamsted' is spelt like this when HEMEL HEMPSTEAD – with an *e* and a *p* and an *a* – is just down the road is, frankly, anybody's guess.

Bishop's Stortford

Stortford is 'ford by the tongues of land', and this is the name that appears in the Domesday Book. Its origins are Old English, but there is reason to believe that there was a Roman settlement here – it sits near a Roman road, in a convenient position to have been a stopping-off point between St Albans (see the box on *Saints*, page 33) and COLCHESTER. William the Conqueror built a castle at

Stortford and donated it to the Bishops of London in perpetuity, whence the rest of the modern name; the castle was razed by King John not much more than a century later as part of a battle with the Pope, but the connection between town and bishops remained. The name of the meandering river Stort, which produced the 'tongues of land', is a back-formation from Stortford, first recorded in the sixteenth century.

Bushey
This doesn't *exactly* mean 'bushy', but it's not far off: it is either an enclosure near a thicket, or one enclosed by box trees.

Cheshunt
Perhaps surprisingly, this has nothing to do with the pudding stones of CHESHAM. Instead *ches–* refers to a Roman fort (see the Introduction, page 11) and *–hunt* comes from *funta* meaning 'fountain or spring'. So Cheshunt was originally a Roman fort by a spring.

Chorleywood
Chorley, as it was known in the thirteenth century, means 'clearing of the free peasants'; the *–wood* is a later addition. There are Chorleys in Cheshire, Staffordshire and Lancashire that have the same origin; most Charltons are also 'free peasants' farmsteads', often with the addition of a Norman manorial name, as in Charlton Mackrell in Somerset, or one reflecting church influence, as in Charlton Abbots in Gloucestershire. In Anglo-Saxon times, ceorls – independent peasant landowners – were men of a certain substance; after the Norman Conquest their status was gradually whittled away until they became little more than villeins, tied to a feudal landlord. This diminution in status is reflected in the pejorative modern words *churl* and *churlish*, which derive from *ceorl*.

Elstree

A fine example of how names evolve through mumbling and confusion. In the eleventh century this was *Tithulfes treow* – 'tree [probably marking a boundary] belonging to a man named Tidwulf'. Over time people came to assume that the initial *t* belonged to the word *at*, so *at Tidwulf's tree* became *at Idwulf's tree*. In the thirteenth century the spellings *Idulvestre* and *Idulfestre* are recorded, in the fourteenth *Idelstre* and *Adulvestre*, with *Ilstrey* and finally *Elstree* emerging in the sixteenth. So 'El' is all that remains of poor old Tidwulf, whoever he was.

Harpenden

This probably means 'valley of the harp', but the explanation is likely to be the slightly disappointing one that the valley is harp-shaped, rather than the more romantic suggestion that the river bubbled through it in a melodious way reminiscent of the sound of a harp.

Hatfield

There are a number of towns in England with this name and most boast an earlier spelling along the lines of Haethfelth, which gives a clearer indication of their origins: 'open ground where heather grows'.

Hemel Hempstead

Hempstead is one of many spellings for the Old English word meaning 'homestead' (see MORETONHAMPSTEAD and BERKHAMSTED). Hemel means 'broken, undulating', presumably a description of the surrounding countryside.

Hertford

This was originally a ford across the river Lea (see LUTON) where harts or stags could be seen: I doubt if that is the case nowadays.

Like BEDFORD, Hertford sat on the boundary between Wessex and Danelaw and was important as a place where the river could be crossed. Also like Bedford, it was fortified by Edward the Elder. Doubly so, in fact, because there had been a village on either side of the river and Edward turned both of them into strongholds. Which may have kept the Danes out, but probably also had the effect of scaring the deer away.

Letchworth

The oldest 'garden city' in the world, Letchworth was founded by Ebenezer Howard in 1903. His plan, a reaction against the hellish urban conditions of the late nineteenth century, was to create towns surrounded by countryside and with wide roads, comfortable houses, adequate facilities and recreational space. Rather than start from scratch, Howard built round a much older village – it appears in the Domesday Book and the name probably means 'enclosure that can be locked'.

Royston

In the twelfth century this was called Crux Roaisie, 'cross belonging to a woman called Roisia', which in the fullness of time was shortened to Cruceroys and then to Roys; –ton meaning 'village' was added later. The story goes that a settlement here grew up in Roman times because it was a junction of two major roads: Ermine Street, which connected LONDON, LINCOLN and YORK, and the Icknield Way, a highway that ran along a ridge from SALISBURY Plain over into East Anglia. Shortly after the Norman Conquest the Lady Roisia (pious wife of the local lord of the manor?) erected a cross at the crossroads – the stone which formed its base can still be seen.

Stevenage

The name probably means 'place by the strong oak tree', which makes you wonder how many weak oak trees there were in eleventh-century Hertfordshire.

Tring

In the Domesday Book this was Treunge. Split it into *Tre* and *unge* and you have a tiny bit more of a clue to its probable meaning of 'wooded slope'. If this is right, the first part comes from the Old English *trēow* , meaning 'trees', and the second from *hangra*, 'slope', a word which turns up in more recognisable form in various places called Clayhanger, 'clayey slope'.

Watford

'Ford used when hunting'. The ford was used in pre-Roman times and later lay on a route that took travellers from the Roman road Watling Street across the Chilterns near TRING and on into the Midlands. The modern High Street follows this route and the original settlement was probably built on the first dry ground above the river banks. Watford in Northamptonshire has the same derivation and Watford Gap – now best known as a service station on the M1 – is a valley that allows road, rail and canal routes to cut through the northern end of the COTSWOLD hills.

Welwyn Garden City

For the concept of a garden city, see LETCHWORTH. Welwyn was the second of them, founded in 1920. Unlike Letchworth it was not built around an existing village, but was named after a small town just to the north of it. There has been a settlement here since pre-Roman times; the name dates back to at least the tenth century and means 'place by the willow trees'.

8

EAST MIDLANDS

Much of this area was once in the middle-England kingdom of Mercia, the most influential in the country in the eighth century, when King Offa held on to power for a remarkable forty years. He came as close as anyone before Alfred the Great, who was born fifty years after Offa's death, to creating a united England. He took over Kent and Sussex and even briefly dominated Wessex. But after his death Wessex soon bounced back – and then there were the Vikings to contend with.

NORTHAMPTONSHIRE

An undemanding county name, but a county with some appealing names in it for all that. The ones chosen to appear here show little sign of the strife that was a constant feature in most other counties. A 1907 encyclopaedia describes Northamptonshire as 'pleasantly diversified by low hills, beautiful vales, extensive woodlands copiously watered by numerous rivers and streams' and this topographic gentleness seems to be reflected in the place names.

Althorp

This once belonged to a Saxon named Olla and is recorded as Olletorp in the Domesday Book, by which time it was owned partly by a man named Humphrey and partly by William Peverel, a knight said to have fought at the battle of Hastings. They had both moved on by 1486, when the Spencer family took possession. For the *–thorp* element of the name, see THORPE.

Irthlingborough

Oh joy! This *almost* means 'fortified manor belonging to the earth-lings', making you hope there might be a Martianborough down the road. It actually means 'fortified manor belonging to the ploughmen', but it's surely near enough to cause a little merriment.

Nobottle

Speaking of merriment, here's a place name that makes you want to laugh out loud. And do you know what? It means 'new building'. How disappointing is that? But there is nevertheless something interesting about it, etymologically speaking. The first syllable was originally spelt Neu, from *nīwe*, the Old English for 'new'. This is one of only two places in England where that prefix morphed into *No–*, and the other is the now-abandoned village of Nobold (which comes from exactly the same source and also means 'new building'), about 30 km away. Some feature of the medieval Northampton-shire accent, perhaps? For some other silly-sounding names, see the box *You Cannot Be Serious* overleaf.

Northampton

Camden tells us that 'the very navill, heart and middle of England' is near Northampton. He may be right but is is still a nice straight-forward name that means what it ought to mean: 'northern home-stead'. Originally just Hamtun, by the time of the Domesday Book it had acquired the 'north' to distinguish it from SOUTHAMPTON, despite the fact that Southampton derived from *hamm* rather than *ham* and meant something completely different.

YOU CANNOT BE SERIOUS

This book is full of interesting-sounding names that have disappointing meanings and ordinary-sounding names that turn out to be fascinating. But there is a third category – those, like NOBOTTLE, that have perfectly sensible derivations but whose modern names make us laugh – or in some cases snigger. For example:

Badgers Mount, Kent. Surely an argument in favour of the use of the apostrophe. If this is written Badger's Mount, as it is on some maps, we have a chance of realising that it means a hill frequented by a badger, rather than being a statement about its sexual activity.

Fryup, Yorkshire. *–up* comes from the same root as in BACUP and means 'valley'. Probably, in this instance, dedicated to the Norse goddess Friga rather than to bacon, eggs and a fried slice.

Goonbell, Cornwall. 'Distant open pasture' – one of those odd Cornish names whose elements occur nowhere else and leave most of us clutching empty air when we try to guess their meaning.

Great Snoring, Norfolk. Less cute than it appears, this is merely 'associated with a man named Snear'. There is a Little Snoring, too.

Loggerheads, Staffordshire. This is cheating a bit, because it is easy to be funny if you name a place after the local pub. The pub in question was once called the Three Loggerheads, using the word in the old-fashioned sense of a blockhead or fool.

Loose, Kent. Not what you might expect, but still not very elegant: it means 'place by the pig sty'.

Nasty, Hertfordshire. The *n* is a mistake here, in more ways than one – the name should be Asty, which means 'eastern enclosure'.

But the Middle English for 'at the eastern enclosure' was *atten Asty*, and over time the *n* was separated from the first word and tacked on to the second, in a reversal of what happened at ADLE-STROP and ELSTREE.

Ogle, Northumberland. This was probably once 'Ocga's hill', but is surely more fun the way it is.

Pratts Bottom, Kent. 'Bottom' in place names refers to the bottom of a valley, and this one was associated with a family called Pratt as far back as the fourteenth century. Six Mile Bottom in Cambridgeshire is six miles (10 km) from Newmarket.

Seething, Norfolk. As the *–ing* suggests (see the box *Whose Place Is It Anyway?*, page 189), this comes from a personal name and means 'Sitha's followers' place'.

Ugley, Hertfordshire. The butt of many feeble jokes about its Women's Institute, this actually means 'Ugga's woodland clearing'. As with Ogle, above, you can't help feeling that the modern version is an improvement.

Wigglesworth, Yorkshire. 'Enclosure [see the box *Farming Country 2*, page 139] belonging to a man named Wincel'. The thirteenth-century spelling Wicleswrthe, showing the loss of the 'liquid' *n* (see DURHAM), gives a hint as to how the modern spelling developed.

Paulerspury/Potterspury

The story here is similar to that of WATERPERRY and WOODPERRY. These villages were both originally just Pirie – 'place at the pear tree' – but, being very close to each other, were given distinguishing names in the thirteenth century. The longer versions acknowledge the de Pavelli family's ownership of one manor and the presence of a pottery in the other. Potterne in Wiltshire, Potterhanworth in

Lincolnshire and POTTON in Bedfordshire all also commemorate the fact that pots were once made in these places; Potters Bar in Hertfordshire is later (1509) and is named after a family called Potter (some of whose ancestors would, however, have been potters).

Rushden

'Valley where rushes grow'. Most places whose names begin with *Rush–* have this meaning: there is another Rushden, in Hertfordshire; a Rushbrooke in Suffolk; a Rushford in Norfolk (not a ford, however: it was originally Rushworth, meaning 'enclosure where rushes grow'); a Rushock ('rushy place') and a Rushwick ('dairy farm among the rushes') in Worcestershire; and various Rushtons. Rushes were an immensely useful commodity – they were used as floor coverings, either woven into mats or just strewn about; they were a raw material for thatch; and they could be dipped in animal fat to make a cheap substitute for candles – so it is no surprise that so many place names indicate where they could be found.

Silverstone

Not a silver stone, sadly, but the rather less picturesque 'Saewulf's farmstead'. The name of Silverdale in Lancashire means 'silver valley', but only because of its grey limestone, rather than because it is worth digging for buried treasure in the area.

Yardley Gobion

Yardley means 'wood or clearing where yards are cut'. The obsolete meaning of a yard as 'a straight slender shoot or branch of a tree; a twig, stick' is the one that is relevant here. The word appears in the Anglo-Saxon translation of the Lindisfarne Gospels (c. 970), where it is described as being 'shaken by the wind'; the Authorised Version of the Bible renders it 'reed' – so as with RUSHDEN, we are probably talking about a roofing material rather than anything

more substantial. As for Gobion, the manor here was in the possession of the Gubyun family in the thirteenth century. Another family
with a similar name owned the 'high or chief homestead' that
we now know as Higham Gobion in Bedfordshire, while the de
Hastinges are commemorated in Yardley Hastings.

LEICESTERSHIRE

Its name remembers the presence of Roman forts, its history the
rebellion of barons against weak Norman kings and there was
plenty of conflict between Anglo-Saxons and Danes in between.

Appleby Magna/Appleby Parva

Appleby means 'farmstead or village where apple trees grow'. The
−by element is the Old Scandinavian equivalent of the Old English
−ham and is common in this part of the country (see the box *Farming Country 2*, page 139). The second words of the names are Latin
for 'large' and 'small' respectively. They indicate that at some point
in the Middle Ages a village called Appleby grew too large to be
self-supporting and sent out a few families to establish a new settlement nearby, probably clearing more woodland to produce fields
in which crops could be planted. The two villages, still closely
allied, had to have distinguishing names and so Appleby Magna
and Appleby Parva were born. This system − known as 'mother
and daughter' villages − explains the names of Peatling Magna
and Parva and Ashby Magna and Parva, all in Leicestershire, and
also of Great and Little Missenden in Buckinghamshire, Much
and Little Wenlock in Shropshire and many others. The use of
the Latin endings seems to have been particularly popular in
Leicestershire, but wasn't always logical. The village now known
as Great Glen was variously Magna Glen or Glen Magna in the
thirteenth century but had dropped the Latin in favour of the

English name by 1766. Yet its 'daughter' remains Glen Parva to this day.

Ashby de la Zouch

Almost everyone's favourite place name, particularly if they read Walter Scott's *Ivanhoe* at school and remember the jousting contest held here, Ashby means 'farmstead or village where ash trees grow'. The twelfth-century de la Zuche family added their name to the existing one, as did the de Folevilles in Ashby Foleville, also in Leicestershire, and the de Mares in Mears Ashby in Northampton-shire. Canons Ashby, Ashby St Ledgers (both Northamptonshire) and Ashby St Mary in Norfolk all reveal church allegiances, while Cold Ashby in Northamptonshire really is in a cold, exposed place and Ashby cum Fenby in Lincolnshire was in a marsh or fen. See also ASHBY PUERORUM for a way-out variation on this theme.

Earl Shilton

The other two places called Shilton – there is one in Oxfordshire and another in Warwickshire – appear in the Domesday Book as Scylftune and Scelftone respectively, and these spellings give a clue to the meaning of all three places: 'farmstead on a shelf or ledge' (see the Introduction, page 20, for another example of the Old English *sc* softening to *sh*). The earl commemorated in Earl Shilton was Simon de Montfort, Earl of Leicester in the early part of the thirteenth century and notorious for his cruelty during the Albigensian Crusade against the supposedly heretical Cathar sect in the south of France: when thousands of Cathars took sanctuary in a cathedral in Béziers, he is said to have given the order, 'Kill the lot of them – God will recognise his own.' Despite this, his exploits – if that is the word – were overshadowed by those of his son, also called Simon, who led the revolt of the barons against Henry III in the 1260s, convened the first vaguely democratic Parliament in

English history and now has a university named after him, whereas his father has only a village. Serves him right, you might say.

Leicester

This goes back to an ancient river name, Legra or Ligor, as a result of which the local people were called Ligoran – 'people dwelling near the river Ligor'. Add a Roman settlement and you produce the Old English Ligera ceastre, 'Roman town in Ligoran country'. Remind yourself about the Saxon *yogh* (see YATE) and you'll see that the Domesday Book's Ledecestre is a logical development; add a few centuries of sloppy pronunciation and, hey presto...

Loughborough

Irish names beginning with *lough–* tend to be connected with a lake; in England they are mostly derived from personal names. Thus Loughborough is a fortified place connected with a man called Luhhede and the Loughtons in Essex and in Buckinghamshire are Luhha or Luca's farmsteads. Loughton in Shropshire is the exception – it means 'farmstead by a pool'.

Lutterworth

The ending *–worth* (or, less commonly *–worthy*) comes from the Old English for 'enclosure' or 'enclosed settlement' (see the box *Farming Country 2*, page 139). Lutterworth was the enclosed settlement on what was then the river Lutter, meaning 'bright stream', but is now called the Swift. Faster but not as clean as it used to be? It's difficult to be sure, but the name change had happened by William Camden's day, so whatever physical attributes the river had then are probably long gone. Camden is at his best on the subject of Lutterworth. John Wycliffe, the religious reformer who made the first translation of the Bible into English and generally fell foul of the church hierarchy, was once rector here, and Camden reports that 'one and forty yeeres after his death his dead corps was cruelly handled, being by warrant from the Councell of Siena turned out of his grave and openly burned'. He goes on to remind us: 'Neither is it to be forgotten that neere to this towne is a spring so cold that within a short time it turneth strawes and stickes into stones.' There are certainly springs just outside the town: legend has it that they sprang up where some of Wycliffe's ashes were spilled as they were being carried to the river to be disposed of unceremoniously. Why they should be so cold is another matter, but it is tempting to believe that Wycliffe is having some strange posthumous revenge.

Market Bosworth

This is another 'enclosure' designated by the ending –*worth* (see previous entry). Originally connected with a man named Bosa, it became an important market town late enough – possibly as late as the 1530s – to have the modern word, rather than the earlier Chipping, affixed to its name (see the box on *Market Towns*, page 102). It achieved notoriety from 1485 – or perhaps more accurately from the 1590s, when Shakespeare's *Richard III* was first performed – as the scene of the final battle of the Wars of the Roses, when the about-to-be-defeated king almost certainly did not cry out, 'A horse, a horse, my kingdom for a horse.' Some 50 km away, on the other side of Leicestershire, Husbands Bosworth never attained the commercial importance of Market Bosworth, so when the need to differentiate between the two arose it was given the rather more humble name of 'farmers' or husbandmen's Bosworth'.

Market Harborough

Probably 'hill where oats are grown', although it is also possible that it was 'hill frequented by he-goats'. The importance of the medieval market can still be seen in the modern town: the main square was formerly the sheep market, and the seventeenth-century grammar school had to be built on arches to make room for the butter market beneath. There also used to be a market for cattle and other live-stock, but this has now moved out of town and a supermarket and car park have been built on the site.

Melton Mowbray

Here and in most other places where the name occurs, Melton is simply a corruption of Middleton or 'middle farmstead', which has more frequently evolved into Milton (see MILTON KEYNES). Mowbray is the mark of yet another Norman lord of the manor.

Oakham

Like OKEHAMPTON, this is an exception to the general rule that place names beginning with *oak–* or *oke–* have something to do with oak trees. The rule holds true with Oake in Somerset, Oaken in Staffordshire, Oakengates in Shropshire, Oakford in Devon, Oakhanger in Hampshire, Oakmere in Cheshire and many more. But not Oakham – it is simply the homestead of a long-forgotten man named Occa.

RUTLAND

What has been, on and off, for many years the smallest county in England has a rather ordinary name: 'estate of a man called Rota'. Camden makes it sounds more interesting, however. He reports a local legend that some king or other granted to a man named Rut the amount of land he could ride round in a day; that area of land became the county, which Rut duly named after himself. Camden will have none of this, however: 'Let such fables be packing,' he scoffs, 'I would not have the truth prejudiced with an extravagant tale.' He prefers a more prosaic approach, 'And whereas the earth in this shire is every where red, and so red that even the sheepes fleeces are thereby coloured red, whereas also the English-Saxons called red in their tongue roet and rud, may wee not suppose that this Country was named Rutland, as one would say a redland?' He's wrong, but we can't blame him for trying.

Uppingham

The presence of 'up' in a name is often comforting. Upton almost always means 'higher farmstead'; places with *up–* prefixed to the name of a river, such as Uplyme in Devon and Upwey in Dorset, indicate that they are upriver from – well, from somewhere further downriver; and Upchurch in Kent and Upminster in Greater London indicate the presence of a church on higher ground. Uppingham obliging falls into step with this generalisation: it is 'homestead or village of the hill dwellers'.

NOTTINGHAMSHIRE

Inextricably linked in most people's minds with the bad guy from Robin Hood, Nottinghamshire – as its first entry shows – has a history going back to Druidic (that is, Celtic) times, but had plenty of activity throughout the Roman, Anglo-Saxon and Danish periods too.

Blidworth

Not an earth-shattering name in itself – 'enclosure belonging to a man named Blitha' – but it has an intriguing street name. Just outside the village, reached via Rickett Lane, is the so-called Druid Stone. Some five metres tall with a girth of thirteen metres, this has a hole through its base large enough to crawl through. Legend has it that passing a child through the hole would cure it of rickets, a once common disease caused by a lack of vitamin D and resulting in malformation of the bones. Vitamin D deficiency is less common in Middle England than it used to be, so modern evidence to back up this story is lacking, but this may well be where Rickett Lane got its name. While you are here investigating old legends, you might like to visit the church of St Mary of the Purification, where Robin Hood's companion Will Scarlet is said to be buried. (Little John's impressively long grave can be seen in the churchyard in Hathersage in Derbyshire; that name means a ridge that is associated either with he-goats or with a man called Haefer. And see ROBIN HOOD'S BAY.)

Boughton

This is one of those tricky names that could mean any one of a number of things and the Domesday spellings don't pin them down. This town and the Boughton in Northamptonshire were both recorded as Buchetone, which could mean either 'Bucca's farmstead' or 'farmstead where male goats or deer are kept'; in the latter case the first syllable comes from the same source as the modern word *buck*. Several other Boughtons were once Boltone or Boltune, which also has two possible interpretations: they could be 'farmsteads where beech trees grow' or 'farmsteads held by charter'. This applies to Boughtons Aluph, Malherbe and Monchelsea in Kent, all of whose second words derive from the names of manorial families. Edward Hasted's *History and Topographical Survey of the County of Kent*, published in 1798, makes no mention of beech trees, but does give some background to the idea of being held by charter, 'In the time of the Saxons this place [Boughton Aluph] was in the possession of earl Godwin, who was succeeded in it by his eldest son earl Harold, afterwards king of England, on whose death in the fatal battle of Hastings, William the Conqueror having obtained the crown, seized on all the late king's estates, and gave this of Boughton to Eustance, earl of Bologne, who had followed him over hither, as a reward for his services.'

Kirkby-in-Ashfield

Kirkby is an Old Scandinavian name for 'village with a church' and you can imagine that there were quite a few of those, so they needed to be distinguished. This one had some open ground where ashes grew; Kirkby Lonsdale in Cumbria is in the valley of the river Lune; the second half of Kirkby Malzeard in Yorkshire means 'poor clearing' and comes from Old French; and Kirkby Overblow, also in Yorkshire, should really be Oreblow, because it is a reference to iron smelting. Most places called Kirby were also originally 'villages with a church' – Kirby Bedon in Norfolk and Kirby Bellars in Leicestershire have added the names of manorial families, and Kirby Grindalythe in Yorkshire began life 'on the slope of a valley frequented by cranes'. Kirby le Soken in Essex had a special juris-diction or *soke*, which meant it had privileges over and above those of owning a manor. Various places called Kirton mean the same as Kirkby, with the Old English ending having prevailed over the Scandinavian. The modern word *kirk*, commonly used in Scotland for a church, comes from the same Scandinavian root; for more about the ending *–by*, see APPLEBY MAGNA/APPLEBY PARVA and the box *Farming Country 2* on page 139.

Mansfield

This means 'open ground on the river Maun', the open ground being of particular interest because it was on the fringes of the vast Sherwood Forest. The Maun was originally known as the Mamm, from an Old Celtic word meaning 'breast', suggesting that it was a place of worship associated with a Celtic mother goddess. Mam Tor in Derbyshire, 'breast-shaped hill', derives its name from the same source.

Newark

Dismiss the thought that this must have something to do with Noah, or at least with escaping from a flood: it means 'new fortification' or 'new building', the ending being connected with *work*. Newark has an ancient history: tools from the Neolithic period (as much as six thousand years ago) have been found in the area, as have the remains of Roman villas. The town sits very close to the old Roman road known as the Fosse Way (see RADSTOCK), which in this part of the country masquerades as the A46. The name Newark, however, is Old English and the fortifications it refers to probably reflect the fact that the settlement was much fought over, first between the Angles and the Saxons and, once that conflict had been resolved, between the victorious Saxons and the invading Danes. Newark fell under Danish rule for a while, but not for long enough for anyone to bother to change the Saxon name. As a foot-note, the first person known to have been lady of the manor in Newark was Godiva, who owned about 335 hectares of land in the vicinity and was the only Anglo-Saxon woman to remain a major landowner after the Norman Conquest. (She was married to Earl Leofric of Mercia, whose territory encompassed most of central England, which is how she came to be in COVENTRY when the urge to ride naked through its streets came upon her.)

Nottingham

The *–ingham* ending tells us that this was originally a homestead associated with the followers of someone (see the box *Whose Place Is It Anyway?* on page 189); the beginning hints that that someone was a man called Snot. Poor fellow. His descendants must have been grateful that the Normans had trouble pronouncing the *sn* sound and allowed the name to evolve to its current form. A more interesting explanation – discounted by modern scholars, but worth throwing in anyway – comes from a Welsh monk called Asser, who wrote a contemporary biography of Alfred the Great. He maintained that Snottingham meant 'home of the children of the excavations', or cave-dwellers, and that the Old Celtic name for the place was Tyogofawg, which meant the same thing (*ogof* is still the Welsh word for 'cave' and *ty*, 'house', is found in many modern place names). One nineteenth-century writer claims that 'in my girlhood I used to see the rock-houses in which many families dwelt, but which are now built over. The sand rocks on which Nottingham is built are easily perforated; and under the garden of my father's house a large vault was discovered, from which openings appeared to have led towards St Mary's Church on one side, and an old priory on the other.' One place where you can still see evidence of Nottingham's cave system is in the cellars of the oldest pub in England. Ye Olde Trip to Jerusalem traces its history back to 1189, the year that Richard I (the Lionheart) came to the throne. One of Richard's first acts as king was to launch the Third Crusade, to recapture Jerusalem from the Muslims, and the knights about to set off for the Holy Land foregathered in Nottingham Castle, a favoured royal stronghold at the time. Add to this the fact that in those days *trip* meant a resting place rather than a short journey, and that the knights would doubtless have fancied some refreshment before setting off, and you have an explanation for the name of the pub.

Ollerton

I mentioned under ALDERSHOT that some places beginning with *alder*– were associated with alder trees and some weren't. Well, here is a third category: a place associated with alder trees that looks nothing like it. *Oller*, both here and in the town of the same name in Cheshire, derives from the same word as Aldershot and both mean 'farmstead where alders grow'. The different ways the names have developed must just be set down to regional variations in pronunciation.

Trent

The principal river of the area has, like most rivers, an ancient name, but it is more picturesque than many: it comes from Old Celtic words meaning 'crossing many roads' and, by extension, 'trespassing on land where it had no right to be'. In other words, it was prone to flooding.

Worksop

The ending *–op*, also found in Glossop in Derbyshire, comes from the Old English for a narrow valley, as anyone who has driven the Glossop Road out of Sheffield can testify. It is possible that the *works–* part of Worksop means a fortification (see NEWARK), but more likely that it derives from a personal name.

DERBYSHIRE

Under Danelaw, Derby was one of the 'Five Boroughs', the principal fortified towns of the Danish territory, the others being LEICESTER, LINCOLN, NOTTINGHAM and Stamford (see the box **Crossing Places 1***, page 117). The Danes seem to have built Derby from scratch, rather than taking over an existing settlement, hence the complete Scandinavianness of its name.*

Ashbourne

Another name that means what it ought to mean: 'stream where the ash trees grow'. The commercially produced Ashbourne water is pumped from springs near the town.

Bakewell

Famous worldwide for what it calls puddings and everyone else calls tarts, this pretty town has a plain name: 'spring or stream associated with a man called Badeca'. Nearby Tideswell similarly just means

'Tidi's spring or stream', but then you could hardly expect a village in the middle of the Peak District to have much to do with tides.

Belper

There is evidence of an Anglo-Saxon settlement here, but the name first appears in Norman times and comes from the Old French meaning 'beautiful retreat' (*beau repaire*, in the sense of a place you might repair to). In the thirteenth century it boasted a handsome deer park, which probably explains the name. Bizarre, then, that it should have become famous for something as unromantic as nail-making. The manorial family was called de Ferrers and, as their name will suggest if you happen to know French or Latin, they were ironworkers; they are credited with introducing the concept of the blacksmith's forge to England and certainly established a thriving nail-making business. For centuries Belper nails were considered the best in the country. The industry survived the introduction of cotton mills, which gave employment to women and children but allowed the menfolk to carry on making nails. In 1846, Belper was producing two million nails a week and business fell away only when mass production came in around 1900. Which proves nothing much except that a place name can stick around long after the reason for it has died away.

Bolsover

The first part of this is a personal name; the second is worth a mention because it does indeed mean 'over'. At least it is connected with 'over' – this ending tends to mean a place on high ground, usually a flat-topped ridge. Southover in Sussex and Birchover in Derbyshire are other examples. The contraction *-or* often has the same meaning, giving rise to names such as Heanor, also in Derbyshire and meaning simply 'place at the high ridge'; English and Welsh Bicknor (which sit on either side of the river Wye, hence their distinguishing affixes; Bicknor means 'pointed ridge'); and Wentnor in Shropshire (derived from a personal name).

Buxton

The famous spring waters (which emerge from the ground at a cosy 28°C) attracted the Romans, who built baths here, turned the place into a thriving civilian settlement and called it Aquae Arnemetiae, after a local water goddess. After the Romans left and the baths fell into disrepair, Aquae Arnemetiae seems to have become associated with a rocking stone or logan stone – one that is balanced on top of a smaller one so that it rocks when it is pushed. No one has ever identified this stone, but early spellings of Buxton tell us that the ending means 'stone' rather than 'farmstead'; experts prefer this explanation to the alternative that it was a place where bucks were seen. Believing the 'rocking stone' story also allows you to trace a connection with the modern *buxom*, though following this word's evolutionary path from 'flexible, yielding to the touch' to its current suggestion of an ample bosom is – sadly – beyond the scope of this book.

Chapel-en-le-Frith

Yes, there was a chapel here – the present church sits on the same site. It was and is dedicated to Thomas Becket (I mentioned in the entry for CANTERBURY that he got everywhere in the years following his martyrdom in 1170). *Frith* is Old English for 'sparse woodland, roughly cleared land on the edge of a forest' and is also found in Firbank in Westmoreland and Frithville in Lincolnshire, among others. The mishmash of languages in Chapel-en-le-Frith probably comes about because the Normans who built the chapel 'christened' it in their own language – indeed, the earliest recorded use of the name has the Latin *capella*, perhaps because Latin was the language of scholarship and of the church. But the Normans would have retained an existing, Old English word to describe the location. The survival of the Old French 'en le' is an oddity, like ASHBY DE LA ZOUCH.

Chesterfield

'Open land near a Roman fort'. There was an Iron Age fort here before Roman times and it was probably the site of frequent inter-tribal conflicts. In the first century AD the Romans took over, built the place up and used it as a base for their campaign to suppress the Brigantes tribe. The surviving Brigantes having been enslaved and put to work on the land to grow grain for the increasing population, the Roman army worked its way north but probably continued to use Chesterfield as a supply depot. Between the years AD 69 and 117 it housed a cohort of 480 men. Once you include the wives and families of the senior officers (the only ones allowed to marry) and the girlfriends of the others, this probably added up to a population of about a thousand, quite substantial for an outpost of the empire in those days.

Derby

This is an Old Scandinavian name meaning 'farmstead or village where deer are kept' (for more about the –by ending, see APPLEBY MAGNA/APPLEBY PARVA and the box *Farming Country 2* on page 139). Unusually, settlements on this site seem to have undergone complete changes of name, rather than having one group of residents adapt what was used by the previous incumbents. The Romans called their fort here Derventia, because it was on the Derwent (see MATLOCK). Subsequently there was an Anglo-Saxon village called Northworthy, 'northern enclosure'. Then the Danes came along and created Derby. The Normans for once seem to have had no problem with the name: it appears in the Domesday Book with its modern spelling. Street names in Derby reflect a long and varied history: there is still a Caesar Street, while in 2010 the city hit the headlines because a new road was named after the computer-game action hero Lara Croft, who was designed by a local software company. It is tempting to imagine future authors of books on place names scouring websites and muttering, 'Now who on earth was she?'

Dronfield

'Open land infested with drones': as with AMPTHILL, you might have thought this was somewhere not to built your home. Nevertheless, Dronfield was here at the time of the Domesday Book, though it was not substantial: it is recorded as having land for only one plough.

Eyam

This is the 'plague village' that in 1665 isolated itself so that the infection wouldn't spread across the countryside. The plague, which had been rampaging through London, arrived in this isolated spot courtesy of a parcel of cloth delivered from the capital to the local tailor, George Vicars. The cloth was damp, so George hung it in front of the fire to dry, thus releasing the fleas that bore the disease and signing his own death warrant and that of many of his neighbours. As more and more people succumbed, the rector William Mompesson and his predecessor Thomas Stanley persuaded their flock that they should stay within the confines of the village until the danger had passed. Food and supplies were left at an agreed spot above the village; coins to pay for them was either washed in the well or soaked in vinegar to purify them. Nevertheless, Eyam lost three-quarters of its inhabitants in the space of sixteen months. It had its name hundreds of years before that, though. Eyam derives from *egum*, a dative form of *ēg*, meaning 'island' or, in this case 'piece of land between streams' – the same word that gave us the ending of SELSEY, RAMSEY and many others scattered through the book.

Matlock

Today Matlock is the county town of Derbyshire and the name tells us that its importance as an administrative centre goes back a long way. But just as you might not recognise OLLERTON as being connected with alder trees, so could you be forgiven for not realising that Matlock had anything to do with oaks. The −*ock* ending comes from Old English *āc* , meaning 'oak', and the rest is from *mæthel*, 'meeting place'. This is related to the old word *moot*, meaning something like a local council meeting, from which we get the modern adjective *moot*, 'debatable', as in *a moot point*. So the whole name means 'meeting place by the oaks'. And speaking of things that don't look as if they have anything to do with oaks, Matlock stands on the river Derwent, whose name derives from the Old Celtic for 'river with an abundance of oak trees'.

Ripley

The −*ley* is the same 'woodland clearing' that we have seen elsewhere and *rip* tells us that it was 'strip-shaped'. So we are probably talking about a strip of land that cut a path through the wood − the Domesday Book records that Ripley has 'woodland pasture two leagues long and one broad', a league being about five kilometres. The Ripleys in Surrey and Hampshire and Ripe ('place by the strip of land') in Sussex have the same derivation. Ripley in Yorkshire is more likely to be derived from an ancient tribal name, as is Ripon ('place in the territory of the Hrype people').

Sandiacre

The imperial system of measurement has its roots in practical applications and comparisons − a inch was the width of a man's thumb, a yard the distance from his nose to the tip of his outstretched arm – and so it is with the acre. Originally merely an area of ploughed land, it came to mean the area that a yoke of oxen could plough in a day, reckoned as 4,840 square yards (just over 4,000 square metres or 0.4 hectare in today's parlance). So Sandiacre started life as a sandy area (not necessarily an acre) of ploughed land.

Shirebrook

In the names of counties *shire* means 'district' (see the box *Shires and Counties*, page 62). One explanation for the name of this town says that the first half comes from the same word, only here it means 'boundary' – specifically the county boundary between Derbyshire and Nottinghamshire. So Shirebrook would have begun life as 'place on the brook on the county boundary'. Shireoaks, fractionally over the border into Nottinghamshire, was 'place on the boundary where oak trees grow'. Confusingly the Old English *scīr* , which evolved into 'shire', also meant 'bright' or 'clear', so it is possible that Shirebrook was a brook with bright, clear water. This would link it with various places called Shirley ('bright clearing'), Shirburn in Oxfordshire ('clear stream'), Shirwell in Devon ('clear spring or stream'), Sheerness in Kent ('bright headland') and SHERBORNE in Dorset.

LINCOLNSHIRE

Lincolnshire is perhaps the county that shows most evidence of long-term Danish settlement, witness the number of names ending in –by. But in this sparsely settled area, what this probably shows is that, although the Normans were nominally in charge – here as elsewhere – from 1066, they did not move in in great numbers and the Old Scandinavian names were allowed to remain.

Aby

We're firmly into Old Scandinavian territory here – *á* means 'river' or 'stream', so it is a common element of place names in the north of England. The rivers Brathay, Greta and Rothay (respectively 'broad river', 'stony river' and 'trout river') are all examples, as are AMBLESIDE in Cumbria and Ayresom in Yorkshire ('place by the river houses'). Aby, brief and to the point, means 'farmstead or village on the river'.

Ashby Puerorum

For other places named Ashby see ASHBY DE LA ZOUCH, but this one is enough of an oddity to deserve its own entry. *Puerorum* is Latin for 'of the boys' and the story goes that a thirteenth-century Bishop of LINCOLN, one Oliver Sutton, decided that all profits of the living of the parish of Ashby should go to support the choirboys of Lincoln Cathedral. The living would normally have been what the local clergyman lived on, and we don't know what happened to him, but at least the choirboys didn't go hungry. He was quite something, was Oliver: when someone set fire to a church within his jurisdiction, he issued an injunction insisting that the culprits be excommunicated, which was strong stuff in 1299.

Barton-upon-Humber

Barton – 'grain farm or store' – is a common name throughout the country, used anywhere that grain was grown or stored (the modern word *barley* comes from the same root). Many Bartons have posh-sounding additions because of their Norman lords of the manor: Barton Seagrave in Northamptonshire and Barton Stacey in Hampshire are examples. Barton le Clay in Bedfordshire boasts clay soil, while Barton in Fabis in Nottinghamshire takes its name from the Latin for beans, as it was originally a place where beans were grown. (It is recorded as Barton in le Benes in the fourteenth century, but somewhere along the line someone opted in favour of the Latin.) Barton-upon-Humber, of course, takes its name from the river on which it sits, and that name is so old that no one has a confident suggestion as to what it means. Well, Geoffrey of Monmouth did – he suggested that it was named after Humber the Hun, who drowned here while trying to invade Britain in days of yore – but I have mentioned elsewhere that, fun though he is, Geoffrey is not the most rigorous of sources.

Boston

This *may* mean 'marker stone of a man called Bōtwulf'; if it does, the Bōtwulf in question may or may not be the saint better known as St Botolph, a seventh-century missionary who has churches dedicated to him up and down the country. The most notable of these include two in the City of London and, more relevantly, one in Boston. St Botolph is known to have established a Benedictine monastery, long since destroyed, at a place called Ikenhoe, and Lincolnshire tradition has it that Ikenhoe is Boston. Most scholars now think this is unlikely and place Ikenhoe somewhere in Suffolk, in which case Boston was probably named after a Lincolnshire chieftain called Bōtwulf who had nothing to do with the saint. Tradition persists, however, even across the Atlantic: Boston in Massachusetts is named after Boston in Lincolnshire and has a St Botolph's district and an Inn @ St Botolph.

Brigg

Brigg is a variant of 'bridge', which wouldn't earn it a place in this book were it not for the fact that its thirteenth-century name was Glanford Brigg. The ending *–ford* obviously means 'ford' and the chronology is likely to have been:

1 Find a natural place to cross the river (i.e., a ford)
2 Establish a settlement there

3   Build a bridge for the convenience of the growing settlement.

So far, so mundane. The interest starts with *Glan*, which comes from the Old English *glēam* and means 'revelry'. It suggests that step 2 of the above was actually 'establish a settlement there and start partying'. No more details are available, perhaps because nobody could remember them very clearly the next day. Glandford in Norfolk has the same derivation and a certain amount of merriment also took place at Playford in Suffolk, Playden in Sussex and PLAISTOW in Greater London.

Cleethorpes

As with other *–thorpes* (see THORPE), these were outlying farmsteads. In this case they lay outside a place called Clee, named after its clay soil. Over time these outlying settlements grew large enough to become a town and to subsume the original village into little more than a suburb, now known as Old Clee. By place-name standards, then, Cleethorpes is comparatively recent: Clee (that is, Old Clee) is in the Domesday Book, but something recognisable as the modern name does not appear until 1552.

Grantham

This was probably 'homestead or village of a man named Granta' long before it was the home of Isaac Newton or Margaret Thatcher. An alternative explanation is that it was built on gravel – Old English *grand*. Either way, it is the source of both the surname Graham and the personal name that derives from it. And before you say, 'But surely Graham is a Scottish name?' let me remind you about the twelfth-century baron William de Graham. William's name indicates that he was from the Grantham area, but the Foundation Charter of Holyrood Abbey tells us that he was in Edinburgh in the service of the Scottish King David I in 1127. This is the first known appearance of the name, and most people who today have the surname Graham (however they choose to spell it) are believed to be descended from William.

Grimsby

The name Grimesbi appears in the Domesday Book and means 'farmstead or village belonging to Grimr'. Local legend relates that Grimr was a merchant who rescued and brought up a Danish prince named Havelok after the latter had, according to William Camden, 'beene cast forth to perish, or to take his lucke'. Havelok started his career as a scullery boy in the king's kitchen but, thanks to 'his heroycall valour in feats of arms', ended up marrying the king's daughter. Camden regards this story as most suitable 'for them that take pleasure to passe out the long nights with telling of old wives tales'. It is based on a Middle English romance called *The Lay of Havelok the Dane*, probably composed around 1280. Given that, if the events have any basis in history, they took place in about the sixth century, *The Lay* is hardly an eyewitness report and the chances are that Camden is right to be scathing.

Holbeach

Lots of places whose name begins with *hol–* mean something to do with 'hollow', and this is no exception. But the *–beach* element doesn't mean 'beach'; it probably means 'ridge' (see WISBECH), so this was 'place on a concave ridge'. The lie of the land makes this translation more likely than another suggesting that it was a hollow brook. Other 'hollow' places include various Holcombes ('hollow or deep valley'), a couple of Holbrooks (either 'hollow – that is, "deep" – brook' or 'brook in a hollow') and Holborn in central LONDON ('hollow stream' or 'stream in a hollow').

Lincoln

This was originally Lindon, from an Old Celtic name meaning 'place by the broad pool'. The city sits on the river Witham, which does broaden into a pool at this point. The Romans then came along and established a *colonia*, a place for retired legionaries (see COLCHESTER). Turning Lindon colonia into Lincoln was the matter of only a few centuries of abbreviating and/or mumbling.

Louth

This features in the Domesday Book as Lude, from the Old English for 'noisy stream'; the river on which it stands is still called the Lud and at one time it powered a dozen watermills, so must have been strong and might well have been noisy. The Lincolnshire Louth is not to be confused with the place of the same name in Ireland, which may refer to the phallic nature of a standing stone dedicated to the god Lugh.

Market Deeping

Calling your settlement 'deep or low-lying place' is not exactly helpful when you live in Lincolnshire, so the group of villages now known as The Deepings soon used other features to distinguish them. In the Domesday Book there was a Deeping, an East Deeping and a West Deeping, but only the last of these survives under that name. Thanks to the advent of markets and churches, in addition to Market Deeping we now have a Deeping St James and a Deeping St Nicholas.

Market Rasen

Like other places with a 'market' element in their name, Market Rasen gained that status in the late Middle Ages (1358 in this case). Before that it was merely Rasen, meaning 'place at the plank bridge'. The surviving packhorse bridge built in the early fourteenth century – across the river Rase, near the village that is now West Rasen – is made of stone, not planks, but records indicate the existence of an earlier, presumably wooden, structure. In the days when carts were a rarity, packhorses carried goods from one market town to another, and also to the coast for export, returning with salt and imported merchandise; bridges allowing them to cross rivers were essential to efficient trading. However, when carts became the transport method of choice, bridges needed to be wider and the narrow packhorse bridges fell into disuse. The one at West Rasen is one of the finest surviving examples.

Norton Disney

You just long for Mickey Mouse to be living here, but in fact it was a family called d'Isney or d'Isigny, whose ancestors had come to England with William the Conqueror. There is a tenuous connection with Mickey Mouse, though: Walt Disney's father claimed to be descended from the Lincolnshire d'Isneys.

Skegness

Ness, meaning 'promontory', is found in a number of names such as Neston ('farmstead on a promontory') and Widnes ('wide promontory') in Cheshire, Totnes in Devon ('belonging to a man named Tota'), Great and Little Ness in Shropshire and Nesbit in Northumberland ('promontory on the river bend'). Skeg may be a personal name, but it is more interesting to believe that it means 'beard-shaped' and refers to the beard-shaped promontory eroded by the sea to the south of the town.

Twenty

In the middle of the nineteenth century, several different companies built connecting stretches of railway across northern Lincolnshire and it fell to the Bourne-Spalding Railway Company to construct the 15 km or so link between – oddly enough – Bourne and Spalding. Although this was a sparsely populated piece of fenland, it was decided to have three intermediate stations on the line in order to transport farm produce. The first station after Bourne had no obvious village to which to attach itself, so a new name was needed. At this point the story acquires alternative punchlines: either the surveyor, looking at his OS map, found that he was at Plot Number Twenty; or a nearby milestone announced that it was twenty miles (32 km) to Colsterworth. Whichever is the truth, the station was called Twenty and a village grew up around it. This effort clearly exhausted the surveyor's ingenuity. The next designated station was to serve the hamlet of Tongue End, but for some reason this didn't appeal. Then the surveyor noticed that the railway line crossed a drainage ditch called Counter Drain, so that became the station's name. The railway was closed in 1959, but both Tongue End and Twenty are still on the map.

Wainfleet All Saints

Places where a river could be crossed were so important in earlier times that they have been given two boxes to themselves (see *Crossing Places*, pages 117 and 242). But here is a variation on the usual *–ford* or *–bridge* theme. *Fleet* is an Old English word for 'creek' or 'stream' (see FLEET). The importance of Wainfleet was that the stream was either shallow enough and/or had a solid enough bottom that it could be crossed by a wagon: *wain* is still a poetic word for a wagon and survives, for example, in the name of Constable's painting *The Haywain*. The ending All Saints derives from the local church and distinguishes this village from Wainfleet St Mary and Wainfleet Tofts, the second part of whose name is Old Scandinavian for a homestead (see the box *Farming Country 2* on page 139).

9

WEST MIDLANDS

The term West Midlands has a number of different official meanings: it is a county, a region and a conurbation. For the purposes of this chapter it is a bit of all three and, like its eastern sister of the previous chapter, was once mostly part of the kingdom of Mercia. It extends far enough north to have had conflicts with the Danes, far enough west to have waged war against the Welsh and far enough south to have interested a daughter of Alfred the Great. The first entries here are in the modern county of West Midlands which, having come into being in 1974, is too recent for its name to be much of a puzzle.

Bilston

Bil– is one of the most confusing of openings to a place name, because it may come from one of several personal names (Billings-hurst in Sussex, 'wooded hill of a man named Billing'; Bilsthorpe in Nottinghamshire, 'outlying farmstead of a man named Bildr'; Bilsby in Lincolnshire, 'farmstead or village of a man named Billi'); it may refer to a promontory as in Portland Bill or Bilsborrow in Lancashire ('stronghold on the promontory') or it may, as in this case, refer to a sharp ridge. So Bilston – a contraction of the Old English Bilsetnatum – means 'farmstead or village of the people living near the sharp ridge'. If you are on the ball, you will have spotted the *set* in the middle of that longer name and realised that it is the same as the endings of SOMERSET and DORSET.

Birmingham

'Homestead of Beorma's family or followers'. There is evidence of settlement in pre-Roman times, but most of the local names are Old English and suggest that the Saxons cleared a lot of forest and established farms or villages in the space they created: the endings of Selly, Yardley, Moseley and Warley all indicate 'clearings in woodland'. Nevertheless, Birmingham hadn't achieved 'second city' status – or anything like it – by the time of the Domesday Book: it is valued at one pound, having land for a mere six ploughs. It started to come into its own in 1166, when local noble Peter de Birmingham, the first person recorded as using that name, was granted (doubtless with some cash changing hands) the right to hold a weekly market. Becoming a market town in those days meant you had set your toe on the bottom rung of the ladder to growth and prosperity and Birmingham, once the smaller neighbour of Aston ('eastern farmstead'), had soon outstripped it. After that, there was no stopping it.

Bournville

Which came first, the town or the chocolate? Answer: the town, in 1893. In 1878 the chocolate-making firm of Cadbury, based in BIRMINGHAM, needed larger premises and moved to an area to the south-west of the city. The local river, the Bourn, and a nearby mansion called Bournbrook were initially the inspiration for the name of the new factory; the *–brook* ending was changed to the French-sounding *–ville* to suggest that the chocolate had a certain *je ne sais quoi*. George Cadbury wanted his workers to be healthy and happy without, presumably, relying too heavily on consumption of his products. So in addition to decent pay and working

WHOSE PLACE IS IT ANYWAY?

As I have said elsewhere, contemporary records of the early Anglo-Saxon period are thin on the ground. The original settlers were illiterate, so would not have kept records at a local level. Many of those that gave a bigger picture were compiled by and kept in monasteries and were destroyed either by the Vikings or by Henry VIII. The result is that England has a plethora of places named presumably after a local chieftain about whom we know nothing.

One key to such place names is the letter *s* or *n* before a common ending such as *–ham, –ton* or *–bury*. Both were indications of 'possession', as an *'s* still is in Modern English. Thus **Aylesbury** is 'Aegel's fortified town' (remembering that the *g* was pronounced as *y* – see IPSWICH – makes this clearer). **Huddersfield** may be 'Hudraed's field' and Ormskirk is 'Ormr's church'. **Banbury** is 'Banna's fortified town', **Braintree** is 'Branca's tree' and **Fakenham** is 'Facca's homestead'. Very often the place name is literally the only indication we have that the man (it was usually but not always a man) existed; scholars can do no more than assume that the unknown element was a personal name. This is also the reason why it is impossible to be certain about the meaning of so many places. **Cheltenham**, for example, may be 'homestead of a man called Celta'; it may equally be 'enclosure by a hill called Celte'. There is nothing to tell us for sure – and in this instance the uncertainty over the Old English *hām* and *hamm* (see the Introduction, page 20) adds to the confusion.

Another clue to a connection with a personal name is the syllable *–ing*, either at the end of the word or in combinations such as *–ington* and *–ingham*. This indicates that the place was associated either with the man himself or with his followers or descendants. Thus **Bridlington** was associated with someone named Berhtel, while **Hastings**, **Godalming** and **Reading** were settled by the followers or descendants of Haesta, Godhelm and Reada respectively. Occasionally these personal names are really nicknames and tell us something about the man: we can guess that Haesta was quick-tempered or violent and that Reada had red hair, but for the most part we don't even know that.

A third possibility with –*ing* names is that the association is not with a person but with a characteristic: **Withington**, for example, is 'homestead with willows' and **Clavering** is 'place where clover grows'. The earliest recorded spellings normally tell us (if we have sufficient grasp of Old English grammar) which of these options is most likely; if not, we are thrown back, as so often, on educated guesses.

Other places less obviously named after people include:

Basildon 'Beorhtel's hill'
Bletchley 'Blaecca's clearing'
Didcot 'Dudda's cottage'
Ilkley 'Yllica's clearing'
Sizewell 'Sigehere's stream or well'
Tilbury 'Tila's fortified place'
Ullswater 'Ulfr's lake'
Wembley 'Wemba's clearing'
Worksop 'Weorc's enclosure'

And there are many, many more – far too many to list here. If the place you are looking for doesn't feature anywhere in the book, this could well be the heading it comes under.

conditions, he created a model town, providing not only housing but schools, pension schemes, medical services and sports facilities. At that time, Cadbury specialised in cocoa and drinking chocolate – the concept of a bar of chocolate came later, with the dark chocolate brand-named Bournville appearing in 1908, three years after Dairy Milk. Port Sunlight on Merseyside is a similarly employee-oriented model town: it was founded in 1888 by the future Lord Leverhulme of Unilever fame. He did the opposite of what Cadbury had done: where the chocolatier named a product after the town, Leverhulme named his village after his most famous product, Sunlight soap. Also deserving of a mention in the 'benevolent employer' stakes is woollen-mill owner Titus Salt of Yorkshire who, in 1853, moved his operations out of Bradford (see the box *Crossing Places 1*, page 117) and provided comfortable accommodation and amenities for his workers. Titus named his village Saltaire, after himself and the river on which it sits.

Coventry

Place names ending in *–try* tend to mean 'tree associated with so-and-so' and this is the case with Daventry in Northamptonshire, with OSWESTRY in Shropshire and with Coventry (not to mention Braintree and Manningtree in Essex and ELSTREE in Hertfordshire, among many others). Exceptions to this rule are names that describe the tree. Appletree in Northamptonshire and Plumtree in Nottinghamshire are among the more self-explanatory examples, but this category also includes several places called Langtree ('tall tree'), Rattery in Devon ('red tree'), Faintree in Shropshire ('variegated tree') and WARTER in Yorkshire ('gallows tree'). It is likely that the trees in question marked boundaries between two or more estates, where meetings of local councils typically took place. So the men after whom Coventry and Daventry are named would have been Saxon landowners, the edge of whose property had a tree imposing enough to act as a landmark.

Dudley

Another of the woodland clearings alluded to under BIRMINGHAM, this one belonged to an Anglo-Saxon called Duda. He was long gone by the time the Normans came along, but they instantly recognised the strategic importance of the site and had begun building a castle within five years of landing at Hastings. Town, castle and local nobility all grew in prominence until they hit a bad patch in the sixteenth century. Edmund Dudley was executed by Henry VIII on a trumped-up charge of treason. His son John, Duke of Northumberland, was beheaded for his part in trying to put his daughter-in-law, the Protestant Lady Jane Grey, on the throne instead of the Catholic Mary Tudor. John's son Robert, first Earl of Leicester, was the favourite of Elizabeth I but was associated with all sorts of political and amorous scandals (see KENILWORTH). A couple of generations later, the Dudleys took the Royalist side in the Civil War, adding up to over a century of bad political choices. The family survived and continued to rule the town until 1791, but the castle crumbled away and its remains are now – how are the mighty fallen – in the grounds of the local zoo.

Halesowen

Hales are nooks or corners of land (like the *–halls* discussed under LUDGERSHALL and elsewhere), and these particular nooks have passed from one noble owner to another over the centuries. Owen was the son of Henry II's half-sister Emma, who had married David, Prince of Gwynedd, in 1174. Henry gifted the manor to David; after her husband's death, Emma restored it to Henry's son and successor, Richard I, but Owen remained Lord of Hales. The town of Hales must have been called Halesowen, at least in popular parlance, by then, but the longer name is not recorded until the 1270s. This was well after Owen's death and after Richard's successor, King John, had granted the manor to the Bishop of Winchester so that he could found an abbey here. The abbey became very prosperous, but was suppressed during the Dissolution of the Monasteries. Its lands were granted to one John Dudley, Duke of Northumberland, about whom we read under DUDLEY and who wasted no time in squandering his good fortune and having his head cut off.

Rowley Regis

Rowley was another of the many clearings mentioned under BIRMINGHAM; the *row–* part means 'rough'. The addition of *regis* (Latin for 'of the king') is much older than in BOGNOR REGIS: it goes back to at least the fourteenth century, probably much earlier, and indicates that the land belonged to the king.

Smethwick

The ending *–wick* frequently denotes a farm or dwelling that had some sort of speciality (see the box on *Farming Country 2*, page 139), and the most common explanation for this name is that Smethwick was connected with smiths. It was certainly renowned for its metalwork by the sixteenth century, but the name pre-dates that by five hundred years. This adds grist to the argument for the other interpretation, in which *Smeth–* means not 'smith' but 'smooth' and the name becomes 'farm on a level plain'.

Solihull

Not the most glamorous name in the book, this means 'muddy hill' or possibly 'hill where the pig sties are'. Shall we move on?

Sutton Coldfield

Here as elsewhere, Sutton means 'southern farmstead or village'. Coldfield was once spelt *Colefeud*, which gives us the clue that it refers not to temperature but to the fact that charcoal – an important fuel – was produced there.

Wednesbury

Like any other invaders, the Saxons brought their gods with them and it is thought that there was a temple to the god Woden, after whom Wednesday is named, here; *–bury* tells us that it was a fortified place. The name of nearby Wednesfield, from the same source, indicates that it was once open land.

West Bromwich

Bromwich is 'dwelling or farm where broom grows', and this one is to the west of Castle Bromwich. There was a castle in Castle Bromwich in the twelfth century, but there isn't a lot left of it now. What does remain is in the undignified-sounding location of Pimple Hill.

WARWICKSHIRE

To many people this is Shakespeare country, but it also has echoes of other phases of history: KENILWORTH was the home of an Elizabethan romance made famous in Sir Walter Scott's novel; WARWICK was an intermittent battleground for five hundred years; and RUGBY inspired an international sport and the **Flashman** *novels. Something for everyone, you might say.*

Kenilworth

'Enclosure belonging to a woman called Cynehild', whose name suggests that she was a warrior. More than that, we don't know. But the story of Kenilworth gives an idea of just how incestuous history was in this part of the world. One of the earliest recorded events is Lady Godiva (see NEWARK) founding a monastery here – her husband was Earl of Mercia and this was very much his heartland. Perhaps the most famous episode in the castle's history is that recounted by Sir Walter Scott in *Kenilworth*: it revolves round the life and tragic death of Amy Robsart, secretly married to Elizabeth I's favourite, the Earl of LEICESTER. The Earl of Leicester was a member of the DUDLEY family – and we know what happened to them.

(Royal) Leamington Spa

The name Leamington is mundane enough: it means 'farmstead on the river Leam', which in turn means either 'marshy river' or 'river where elms grow'. The interest comes with the royalty and the spa. The discovery of a mineral spring is first recorded in 1480, the second in 1784 and the establishment of a commercial spa hard on its heels, in 1786. Thereafter springs continued to be discovered and baths to open. Leamington soon came almost to rival BATH as a mecca for valetudinarians: it boasted elegant architecture, pump rooms, assembly rooms and disgusting-tasting water, all that one could ask of a spa town. Queen Victoria obviously thought so. She visited in 1830, when she was a mere princess, and shortly after her accession to the throne she granted Leamington what was at the time the unique privilege of calling itself 'Royal'. TUNBRIDGE WELLS now has the same honour, but that came later.

Nuneaton

Eaton is a common name, meaning 'farmstead or village on the river' – *ēa*, the Old English for 'stream', is still found in modern dictionaries, but is probably most familiar to those who solve crosswords or play Scrabble. As a place name, Eaton may be found on its own (most famously as ETON, but also as Eaton in various places across the country) or qualified by some descriptive or manorial name. Long Eaton and Little Eaton, both in Derbyshire, fall into the first category, Eaton Bishop in Herefordshire and Eaton Constantine in Shropshire into the second. Nuneaton was merely Eaton at the time of the Domesday Book; in 1150 a Benedictine priory was founded here and the distinctive feature of having a houseful of nuns in the vicinity was added to the town's name.

Rugby

Long before there was a school whose pupils had a creative attitude to the rules of football, this was Rocheberie, 'fortified place of a man named Hrōca'. There was a small Roman fort here in the fourth and fifth centuries, but there is little evidence of what the Saxons did with the place after that. The treaty that gave a substantial part of northern and central England to the Danes in 886 had Rugby just inside English territory, but the Danish influence was significant enough for the Old English ending to have been changed to the Scandinavian –*by* by 1200. It may be that a Danish civilian population moved in and remained after the war was over.

Shipston-on-Stour

Early spellings of Shipston – Scepuuaeisctune is one – are long and complicated enough to indicate that this wasn't just a village where there were sheep, but one where sheep were brought to be washed in the river. The ancient lie of the land – and of the water – made it ideal for the purpose. There were droving roads along which the sheep could be herded. Access to the river was steep on one side, for encouraging the animals into the water, and shallow on the other, for ease of emerging. And the flow of water was steady but not so fast that the sheep were washed away. Perfect. For the meaning of Stour, see the box *The Place by the River*, page 210.

Stratford-upon-Avon

Stratford means, more or less, 'street ford'. The Old English word *stræt* came from the Latin *via strata*, 'paved road', so any settlement called Stratford grew up by a ford near a Roman road, as did Strefford in Shropshire and Stretford and Trafford in Manchester

– Trafford was Stratford in the thirteenth century and was probably subject to the sort of confusion that beset ELSTREE. The ford near Stony Stratford in Buckinghamshire was indeed stony, while its neighbour Fenny Stratford was marshy. From its obscure Anglo-Saxon origins, Stratford-upon-Avon (for more about Avon, see the box *The Place by the River*, page 210) grew into a modestly prosperous market town until a chap called Shakespeare really put it on the map.

Warwick

The first syllable comes from the same root as the modern *weir* (see WAREHAM), so this means 'dwellings by the weir or river-dam'. Fortified by Æthelflæd (see STAFFORD) in the tenth century, the town went on to feature in the Wars of the Roses in the fifteenth, being the home of the earl known as Warwick the Kingmaker. The Norman castle subsequently went through a number of incarnations, falling into ruin in the sixteenth century when Ambrose Dudley was Earl of Warwick (what was it about that family? See DUDLEY, HALE-SOWEN and KENILWORTH), being extensively (and expensively) restored in the seventeenth, having its grounds laid out by Capability Brown and its portrait painted by Canaletto in the eighteenth and converted to a tourist attraction in the twentieth.

Whitnash

'Place by the white ash'. What today we call the white ash is *Fraxinus americana*, not common in Europe. Our common ash is *Fraxinus excelsior*, and it doesn't have white undersides to its leaves, as the American species does. So a white ash tree – probably marking a boundary, as in COVENTRY – must have been eye-catching. Ashes were also sacred to the pre-Christian Celts. Whitnash sits on a number of ancient leylines and once boasted a holy well (long since dried up), so there may be a religious significance to the name.

STAFFORDSHIRE

One of Staffordshire's most famous sons, the novelist Arnold Bennett, summed up his county thus, 'England can show nothing more beautiful and nothing uglier that the works of nature and the works of man to be seen within the limits of the county. It is England in little, lost in the midst of England, unsung by searchers after the extreme.' A little unfair, perhaps: it has beer, pottery and pigs, all of which raise considerable enthusiasm in some quarters.

Biddulph

'Place by the pit or quarry'. There are neolithic remains aplenty around Biddulph, most notably the standing stones known as the Bride Stones. These are the remains of an ancient burial mound and, if they are local, would confirm the existence of an important quarry.

Burton-upon-Trent

Burton combines two common elements – *bury*, meaning a fortified place, and *tūn*, a farmstead. Any farmstead established near a forti-fied town could therefore have been given this name, which explains why there are so many Burtons scattered across the country. It's not clear who originally fortified a precursor of Burton-upon-Trent: probably not the Romans, although there is evidence that they had civilian settlements in the area. Wilfrid, a seventh-century Bishop of York, built at least one monastery here, but it is unlikely that this justified the description 'fortified'. Nor could it have been to guard against the Danes, as the name pre-dates their invasion by a hundred years. So that remains a mystery. But it raises a diversion, which is, that it is extraordinary how much the modern alcohol trade owes to the early church: it was Wilfrid's monks who discov-ered the peculiar properties of Burton water – gypsum has some-thing to do with it – that made it particularly good for brewing beer. Once William Worthington in the 1760s and William Bass in 1777 established the breweries that bore their names here they ensured the town's international fame among beer drinkers for ever more, but the monks were ahead of them by about a thousand years.

Cannock

This simply means 'small hill' and describes Cannock's setting precisely. The 'chase' in Cannock Chase refers to a hunting forest that covered much of the area in the Middle Ages.

Coven

'Place where there are huts or shelters'. In this context *coven* is related to the modern word *cove* in the sense of a sheltered bay and has nothing to do with witches.

Eccleshall

This name combines the nook of land discussed under LUDGER-SHALL with the Romano-British church discussed under ECCLES. The current church dates back to 1189, but an earlier wooden one is known to have been burned down by the Vikings in the eighth century. A nineteenth-century source suggests that the Roman general (and future emperor) Vespasian founded a town here in AD 60 and that the temple he dedicated to Jupiter later became a Christian church. However, this source also claims that the town's name means 'eagles hall', after the eagle-headed standards carried by Roman legionaries, so it is not entirely to be trusted.

Keele

Say 'cow hill' fast enough and this is what you get. That is the origin of the name – 'place where cows graze'.

Leek

Nothing to do with vegetables, this is an Old Scandinavian name meaning 'place at the brook'. Further south a place in a similar situation would probably have been called Beck, the Old English equivalent.

Lichfield

It used to be believed that this name meant 'field of corpses', a reference to a bloody battle between the invading Angles and the resident Britons. This would have made the derivation Old English and linked it with the modern 'lich gate', under which funeral biers used to find temporary shelter. However, modern scholars have discovered that both the settlement and the name are older than that. The Old Celtic name was Letoceto, meaning 'grey wood'; the Saxons converted this to Liccidd and added 'field' in the eighth century. So it translates as the less evocative but still quite attractive 'field near the grey wood'.

Penkridge

To find the meaning of this name you need to divide it *pen–kridge*, so that the second element is not a ridge but a tumulus or burial mound (it comes from an Old Celtic word that is also found in CREWKERNE). *Pen* comes from the ancient word for 'chief' or 'hill' discussed under PENRYN. A tumulus that could be the one referred to in the town's name has been identified just outside the modern town. There is not much left of it now, but it would have been prominent two thousand years ago.

Rugeley

Now here, by contrast with the previous entry, is something that doesn't look much like ridge and yet means precisely that. This is a purely descriptive name for the site: 'woodland clearing on a ridge'.

Stafford

This is 'ford by a landing place'. Evidence of a settlement goes back to pre-Roman times, but Stafford came to prominence when

Æthelflæd, daughter of Alfred the Great, was fighting the Danes in the tenth century. The area around Stafford was marshy and prone to flooding, so she fortified a piece of reliably dry land. On such terrain, local knowledge as to where to land your boats and get across the river would have been vital information for any general.

Stone

What you see is what you get here – this is 'place by the stones'. Legend has it that the original stones were placed on the graves of the two sons of King Wulfhere of Mercia, murdered by their father in 665 because they had converted to Christianity. He repented, however, and built a church over the stones. It has been through various incarnations – Norman priory, destruction by Henry VIII, the usual sort of thing – but the present church of St Michael occupies the same site as the Saxon one. An alternative explanation of the name is that there was a prominent stone building in the area at a time when stone was an unusual building material, but that isn't nearly such an appealing story.

Stoke-on-Trent

Stoke here means, as it generally does, an outlying farm or settlement (see the box *Farming Country 2*, page 139). There are no further details about the origin of this particular Stoke, but it remained a small village until the growth of the pottery industry in the eighteenth century. The addition of the river name distinguished it from other Stokes, many of which have a second part derived from manorial families: Stoke d'Abernon in Surrey, Stoke Mandeville and Stoke Poges, both in Buckinghamshire, and Stoke Gifford in Gloucestershire are all examples of this. Stoke Ferry in Norfolk sits at the place where a ferry used to cross the river.

Tamworth

Now better known for its pigs, this was once the most important city in Staffordshire – Æthelflæd (see STAFFORD) built a castle and defeated the Danes here. But the name is a comparatively ordinary one. It simply means 'enclosure on the river Tame', with Tame having the same derivation as THAMES.

Uttoxeter

Worth a mention if only to differentiate it from EXETER and other places with a similar ending. This is nothing to do with Roman fortifications; in the Domesday Book it is Wotocheshede, which means 'heath associated with a man named Wuttuc'. The thirteenth-century spelling Wittokeshather makes the connection with heath-land and heather clearer and also evokes sympathy for the 'let's shorten names whenever we can' school of thought. Camden in the sixteenth century spells it Utcester, suggesting a confusion with the 'Roman fort' ending (see the Introduction, page 11), but also giving an idea of how it evolved towards the modern spelling and pronunciation.

Wolverhampton

Sadly, apart from the nickname of the football team, there is no connection with wolves. This was originally Heantune, 'high farm-stead', and evolved into Hampton by analogy with all the other places called Hampton. The first part derives from the name of the lady who owned the manor in the tenth century. Wolvercote in Oxfordshire, Wolverley in Worcestershire and Wolverton in Buck-inghamshire all similarly come from personal names. But see the box on *Animal Place Names*, page 78, for a couple of places that really are named after wolves.

10

❧

WESTERN ENGLAND

The recurring theme of this chapter is conflict with the Welsh, from Roman times until at least the thirteenth century. King Offa of Mercia fortified his western boundary in the eighth century and his famous dyke still marks part of the border between England and Wales, the area known as the Welsh Marches (see MARCH). William the Conqueror's efforts to subdue the Welsh led him to create a number of 'Marcher Lords' – Norman barons ostensibly loyal to William but in fact having almost complete autonomy over their own mini-kingdoms. And still the Welsh held out. All of which explains why there are so many fortified towns and the remains of so many castles in this part of England.

HEREFORDSHIRE

One of the most sparsely populated counties in England, Herefordshire has still seen plenty of action over the centuries. Its place names include the usual assortment of Old English, Old Scandinavian and Norman French, with the proximity of Wales adding a substantial smattering of Celtic to the mix.

Edvin Loach

A tiny place with a great name. The *–vin* part comes from the same root as the modern *fen* and means marshland; this particular fen once belonged to a man named Gedda (pronounced Yedda), producing the Domesday Book entry of Gedeuen. Later a family called de Loges moved in, giving the thirteenth-century Yedfen Loges and, eventually, the modern form. Just up the road from Edvin Loach is Edwyn Ralph, whose first part is from the same root – it seems to have been confused with the name Edwin somewhere along the line. Ralph was the name of the manorial family in Norman times. Also nearby are Tedstone Wafre and Tedstone Delamere, commemorating two late medieval landowners. Tedstone was originally Teddesthorne, meaning 'thorn tree of a man named Teod'. Herefordshire doesn't have a monopoly on weird and wonderful names, as a glance at a map of Dorset will tell you, but it certainly has its fair share.

Hereford

A ford, obviously, but an important one: the *here–* part means that it was suitable for an army to cross. For a lot of its length the Wye forms the border between England and Wales and reliable crossing places were at a premium. In the seventh century the Anglo-Saxons fortified a gravel mound on the north bank of the river as a way of keeping out the marauding Welsh. (History books often describe the Welsh of this period as marauding, presumably because the books were written by the English.) Thereafter Hereford grew rapidly and remained an important stronghold until Edward I finally subdued Wales in the dying years of the thirteenth century.

Ledbury

A fortified town on the river Leadon, whose name means 'broad stream'. Camden gives a bit of background: he describes it as 'a towne well knowne, which Edwin the Saxon, a man of great powre, gave unto the church of HEREFORD, being assuredly perswaded that by Saint Ethelberts intercession he was delivered from the palsey. Touching the militare fort on the next hill I need not speake, seeing that in this tract, which was in the marches and the ordinary fighting ground plot, first betweene the Romans and Britons, afterwards between the Britons and the English, such holds and entrenchments are to be seene in many places.' In other words, it was another place whose purpose was to keep the Welsh from marauding (see previous entry).

Leominster

Leon – Old Celtic for 'at the streams' – was the ancient name for this district. St Edfrith of LINDISFARNE came here in about the year 660 and converted the local king, Merewald, to Christianity; thereafter a priory was built and gave its name to the settlement around it. Nothing remains of the Saxon priory, but its twelfth-century replacement is a remarkable building with two naves, well worth having a town named after it.

Much Marcle

This is another name that becomes less cute when you analyse it. 'Much' is a way of saying 'large' or 'great', to distinguish the 'mother' village from a smaller related one – there is a village called Little Marcle a couple of kilometres away (see APPLEBY MAGNA/ APPLEBY PARVA for more about this). The original name of Marcle or Merchelai divides into 'mark' and 'leigh' – 'woodland clearing on a boundary'.

Ross-on-Wye

Ross comes from a Celtic word meaning either 'promontory' or 'upland heath or moor' and both would be accurate descriptions of the town's situation above the Wye valley. The name of the river, to distinguish this Ross from other places with a similar name, was officially added only in 1931.

Symonds Yat

Yat comes from the Old English *geat* meaning 'gate' or 'gap'; this particular gap – in the hills above the river Wye – was once associated with a man named Sigemund.

Yazor

A corruption of the earlier Iavesovre, in which the *–ovre* means 'high ground' or 'ridge' (see BOLSOVER), this was once a ridge associated with a man named Iago. In this context it is a Welsh name and probably has nothing to do with Shakespeare's choice of it for the villain in *Othello*. On the other hand, it means 'supplanter', so it isn't a nice name to give to anybody.

WORCESTERSHIRE

Not strictly a border territory, but Worcestershire was for a short while in the late twentieth century part of the same county as Herefordshire, so it seems wrong to separate them. Plus the Romans stopped off here on their way to invade Wales, so that fits the general theme of 'border conflict'.

Bewdley

This comes from the Old French *beau lieu*, meaning 'beautiful place', and its current spelling helps to explain why Beaulieu in Hampshire, home of the National Motor Museum, is pronounced 'bew-lee'.

Childswickham

An old name – the full form is recorded in 706, although the Domesday Book has only the curtailed Wicvene. The origins of Wickham are, in this case, Celtic rather than Old English, so it has nothing to do with homesteads, but means 'wood near a moor or upland pasture'. Childs probably *is* Old English, though, and comes from a now archaic meaning of *child*, 'young man of noble birth': more recent writers using the word in this sense usually spell it *childe*, as in Byron's *Childe Harold's Pilgrimage*. So the name could refer to an area owned by the local chieftain's son – Young Master Ethelred, perhaps, said with suitable tugging of forelock.

Droitwich Spa

Droitwich has a bizarre claim to fame: it is one of the few places in England where brine – naturally occurring salt water – comes out of the ground. Not only that, but the water has a salinity that rivals that of the Dead Sea, ten times saltier than normal sea water. The Romans called the settlement here Salinae, 'place of the salts', but salt extraction goes back before that, to at least the second or third century BC – salt, of course, having been an important preservative for many centuries until the invention of refrigeration (see BUDLEIGH SALTERTON). The *–wich* of the modern name comes from *wīc* (see the box *Farming Country 2*, page 139) meaning a specialist farm – in this case specifically a salt works. Droitwich appears in the Domesday Book as Wich; by the thirteenth century the works were being described as 'dirty' or 'muddy' – *drit* being the Middle English word that has evolved into *dirt*. Confusion is added at this point by Edward III (1327–77), who would have spoken a form of French: he granted the town the right (*droit*) to manufacture salt. One way or another, from one language or another, Droitwich was born. Exploiting the waters to create a spa town didn't happen until the nineteenth century, well after BATH, LEAMINGTON SPA and HARROGATE had become popular. The difference with Droitwich was that you didn't have to force yourself to drink the waters (you would have been sick). Instead you bathed in them, enjoying their therapeutic effects and feeling practically weightless because of the buoyancy of the salt.

Kidderminster

Ethelbald, King of Mercia, granted land for the building of a monastery not far from here in 736, but nothing more is known about it. However, the fact that the place is recorded as Chide-minstre in the Domesday Book indicates that there was – or had been – some large religious establishment nearby. (Sacked by the Danes? Always a reasonable guess.) The name means 'Cydela's church or monastery', but no one knows who Cydela was: perhaps an earlier chieftain whose name was already attached to the area when the church was built. The present church of St Mary and All Saints, known to be on the site of an earlier one, dates mainly from the fifteenth and sixteenth centuries but the chances are that Cydela's minster was here or hereabouts.

Malvern

This is an ancient – Old Celtic – name meaning 'bare hill'. Excavations of the fort on Midsummer Hill in Malvern suggest that it was occupied by civilians as well as soldiers for a period of four or five hundred years before the Romans arrived. The popular legend that the British leader Caratacus (sometimes spelt Caractacus) fought his final battle against the Romans here is unlikely to be true: Tacitus, one of the principal sources for this period, describes a site that doesn't fit the facts and modern scholars think that the action probably took place near CHURCH STRETTON.

Mamble

The ancient Britons seem often to have had women – possibly in the voluptuous form of mother goddesses – on their minds when describing features of the landscape; they thought that this one was a breast-shaped hill. See also MANSFIELD.

Pershore

As with a lot of places ending in *–nor*, the *–ore* here means 'slope or bank' (see BOLSOVER). The first half of Pershore comes from an uncommon, dialect word meaning osiers or willow twigs. So the settlement was on a slope where you could gather osiers, a useful commodity for such activities as basket-making, fencing and the construction of weirs.

Redditch

It's not clear whether this means a red ditch or a reedy ditch – modern names beginning with *Red–* might have evolved from the Old English for either, and in the absence of early documentation it is impossible to be sure. The Latin form Rubeo Fossato, which an eighteenth-century source claims to have found in the year 1200, means 'red ditch'. But if the name had evolved from 'reed' to 'red' by that time, which it could easily have done, the person translating it into Latin may have made a false assumption about its origins. The experts seem to be clearer about Reddish in Greater Manchester, though: it was definitely reedy.

Tenbury Wells

The first part tells us that this was a fortification on the river Teme (one of many rivers whose name comes from the same root as THAMES). The Normans built a castle here to defend the river crossing, but the name is Old English, suggesting that the Anglo-Saxons had been there ahead of them, presumably defending themselves against the Danes. The Wells element recalls a brief period in the nineteenth century when Tenbury flourished as a spa. Certainly Queen Victoria liked it, but she was a sucker for spa towns (see LEAMINGTON SPA).

THE PLACE BY THE RIVER

When the ancient Celts first started to give features in the landscape descriptive names, they came up with 'sparkling water' (tone – see TAUNTON), 'dark stream' (**Dawlish**) and the like. But their basic word for 'river' or 'water' was *aesc*. Incomers – Romans, Anglo-Saxons or Vikings – not being fluent in Old Celtic assumed that this was a proper name, so they referred tautologically to 'the river Aesc'. This has found its way into modern English as Axe, Exe and Esk, and given its name to many of the places that sit on the various rivers.

Thus **Axminster** began life as 'place with a large church on the river Axe'. That river, which flows south into Lyme Bay near **Axmouth**, is one of two with the same name in the West Country: the other flows west into the Bristol Channel and has an **Axbridge** along its course. Along the Exe, which rises on **Exmoor**, grew the settlements of EXETER, **Exebridge**, **Exford** and **Exmouth**. In Cumbria, we find **Eskdale**. In that small handful of names we have a moor named after the river, a fortified town on the river, places built by a bridge or a ford, a place at the mouth of the river and a place in a valley that the river ran through. These endings crop up again and again to describe places near rivers all over the country.

The meanings of many ancient river names have been lost in the mists of time. The Wye is one: no one can even be definite about which language it comes from. Its age, coupled with the fact that there is more than one river named Wye or Wey, makes it likely that it too means 'river' or 'water', but it is impossible to be sure.

Other rivers whose meanings have been lost include the Severn, first mentioned by the Roman historian Tacitus in the second century AD. He calls it Sabrina, but this is almost certainly a Latin take on an existing name. Then there are the Humber, the Fal in Cornwall, the Isle in Somerset and many more. But even if we don't know what the river's name means, we can spot it in places such as **Weybridge**, **Severn Stoke**, **Humberston**, **Falmouth** and **Ilminster**, recognise the familiar endings and draw our own conclusions.

Of course there are many river names whose meanings we do know. Creedy means 'dwindling' or 'weakly flowing', but it provided a sufficiently reliable supply of water for the Saxons to build a settlement here. Indeed, **Crediton** was the cathedral city of Devon for a hundred years until it was superseded by EXETER in 1050. More fiercely flowing rivers were obviously more common – 'strong, fiercely flowing' is probably what Stour meant and there are five rivers with that name in England. Thus we have places called **Stourbridge**, **Stourton**, **Stourmouth** and, with reference to the families or churches who owned them in the later Middle Ages, **Stourpaine** and **Stour Provost**. Teign means 'sweeper, flooder' and gives rise to **Teignmouth**, **Teignbridge**, **Teign-combe** ('narrow valley on the Teign') and **Teigngrace**, Grace having been at one time the name of the local lord of the manor.

And so it goes on. There is barely a river in the country that doesn't have a town at its mouth, flow through a valley or across a moor or commemorate the place where the first bridge or ford was. It isn't surprising. Rivers were important. People lived close to them.

Worcester

We don't know much about the Weogora people, except that they lived here in pre-Roman times, choosing the site because it was somewhere you could cross the Severn (see the box *The Place by the River*, page 210). The Romans certainly passed through on their way to invade Wales, but it is unlikely that they built a garrison here: an ancient road leading north-east to DROITWICH may indicate that Worcester, conveniently placed on the river, was an early salt-trading centre. It was also religiously important: a cathedral church was built here in the seventh century and Worcester became the centre of the new diocese; at the beginning of the ninth century its name is recorded as Wigornensis ecclesia ('church of the Weogora'). Two hundred years later the more familiar *–cester* ending – indicating a former Roman settlement – had prevailed and the Domesday Book records a recognisable form of the modern name.

SHROPSHIRE

At last, you might be thinking, a county name that isn't simply shire *tacked on to the end of the main city. Sadly, you would be celebrating prematurely. The spelling may have altered a touch over the years, but this is, essentially 'Shrewsbury-shire' (see the entry for that city for more details). The county name has for many centuries been abbreviated – when abbreviation was required – to 'Salop', from its Anglo-Norman form, but when it was officially changed to Salop in the 1970s it lasted a mere eight years before a local protest made the powers that be change it back again.*

Bishop's Castle

The bishop commemorated here was the Bishop of Hereford, who owned vast tracts of land in this part of the world from AD 792. The story is that one Egwin Shakehead, so called because he was afflicted by a 'trembling palsy', had been cured of the disease in Hereford Cathedral and gave his considerable estates to the bishop in gratitude. The downside was, of course, their proximity to Wales (see HEREFORD). William the Conqueror put the Bishops of Hereford in charge of defending their local stretch of the border and the castle at Bishop's Castle, probably built in the 1080s, was an early contribution to the cause.

Church Stretton

Another name derived from the proximity of a Roman road (see STRATFORD), Stretton grew up alongside a road that ran from Viriconium, northern terminus of Watling Street (see WROXETER), roughly south towards Caerleon in Monmouthshire. The presence of a church dates back to Saxon times, although the name is not recorded until the thirteenth century. Nearby All Stretton, whose name dates from about the same time, commemorates an early owner called Alfred; Little Stretton is a later 'spin-off' from the larger town. The Stretton Hills are named after the villages.

Cleobury Mortimer

Another fortified town along the Welsh border, this once boasted two castles, at least one of which pre-dated the Norman Conquest. The first part of the name derives from the Clee Hills, whose name probably means 'rounded, ball-shaped hill'. At the time of the Conquest, Cleobury was in the possession of Edith, widow of Edward the Confessor; she was soon evicted and the manor given to Ralph de Mortimer, who had fought on the winning side at the Battle of Hastings. It was one of the last good political moves the family made for three hundred years. Hugh Mortimer, Ralph's son, refused to pay homage to Henry II (1154–89) and had the castle at Cleobury sacked for his presumption. His grandson, another Hugh, went against family tradition by siding with the king. Unfortunately he chose to champion King John (1199–1216) against the barons at the time of Magna Carta – not the strongest royal cause in the history books. A few generations later, Roger Mortimer got involved with Queen Isabella in a revolt against her husband, Edward II (1307–27), and was hanged for treason. Before that, however, he had, through a prudent marriage, acquired LUDLOW Castle and made Ludlow his family headquarters, leaving only his name to remind people that there was never a dull moment when the Mortimers were in charge at Cleobury.

Craven Arms

This is one of the smattering of English towns named after an inn (see INDIAN QUEENS, WATERLOOVILLE and NELSON for some others). There was a village here in the seventeenth century, but it started to grow only when the road junction on which it stood and later the railway became important. The inn itself was named after the Earls of Craven, who owned nearby Stokesay Castle. Craven probably comes from the name of a district in Yorkshire, which in turn probably means 'place where garlic grew'. Stokesay was an 'outlying village or hamlet' (see STOKE-ON-TRENT) belonging to the de Say family. But when all is said and done it's a pub by a railway station.

Ironbridge

No prizes for guessing what the name means, but the bridge is important because it was the first to be built of cast iron. That's the first ever. Anywhere. In the world. It was the work of Abraham Darby III (1750–1791), grandson of the pioneering industrialist who first successfully used coke in the smelting of iron. Abraham I established a foundry at Coalbrookdale, in what is now Ironbridge Gorge, and produced the finest quality iron there had ever been. His son was responsible for manufacturing cast-iron cylinders used in early steam engines and steam boilers. In short, these guys came pretty close to inventing the Industrial Revolution – or, if that is an overstatement, it is at least true to say that without them it wouldn't have happened when it did and as quickly as it did. Abraham III was able to build his iron bridge – which enabled you to cross the Severn (see the box *The Place by the River*, page 210) without using a ferry – because his father and grandfather had improved the quality of the material and made it cheap enough to be used in such huge structures. Sadly, as with many pioneering feats, the iron bridge had a few technical flaws: it was opened in 1781 and by 1802 was already in need of repair and restoration. That said, it is still there, albeit in an open-air museum.

Ludlow

Although Ludlow grew up in late medieval 'let's not trust those Welshmen an inch' days (see frequent references throughout this chapter), its name is older than that and refers to its location – 'mound above the noisy stream'. Anyone who has been here when the river Teme is in full spate will acknowledge that the Anglo-Saxons had a point.

Market Drayton

The common place name Drayton means 'farmstead at or near a portage or slope used for dragging' and is related to the modern words *drag* and *dray*. Sometimes this indicated that boats had to be dragged over an obstacle; given the site of Market Drayton, in this case it is more likely to mean that carts had to be dragged uphill. The town grew up round the church of St Mary, built in about 950 on an escarpment above the river Tern. It became an important market town – and added that fact to its name – in the thirteenth century. Various other places called Drayton distinguished themselves from each other by the addition of a manorial name (Drayton Bassett in Staffordshire, Drayton Beauchamp and Drayton Parslow, both in Buckinghamshire) or by a practical description – Dry Drayton in Cambridgeshire was on less marshy ground than nearby Fen Drayton, or indeed than Fenny Drayton in Leicestershire.

Oswestry

This translates as 'Oswald's tree'. Oswald, seventh-century king of Northumbria, was killed fighting the Mercians and the Welsh at the battle of Maserfeld, somewhere near the Welsh border. That much is history. After that it becomes a little more – shall we say open to question? Some versions of the story say that he was crucified, in which case 'Oswald's tree' would have been the cross on which he died. Others have it that his body was hacked to pieces on the battlefield and an arm carried to a sacred ash tree by a pet raven; at the point where it fell to the ground, a holy well sprang up. Either way, Oswald had been instrumental in the spread of Christianity in the north of England; he was also killed fighting pagans, so very soon after his death he came to be regarded as a saint. Bits of him turned up in various places around the country, notably at Bardney in Lincolnshire, and were treated as holy relics (see also BAMBURGH). Camden is scathing about the 'ridiculous miracles' that Oswald is believed to have performed posthumously; and particularly dismissive of the legend that one of his hands had failed to decay along with the rest of his body, but Camden was a sceptic in a credulous world. The real problem with associating all this with Oswestry is that there is no convincing proof that Oswestry and Maserfeld were the same place. Tradition has it that it is so, but tradition may be wrong. The town is named after a tree associated with someone called Oswald. Feel free to leave it at that if you like.

Shrewsbury

You mightn't think it from the spelling, but the name of Shrewsbury is closely linked with that of Shropshire. It means 'fortified place of the Shrob district', *shrob* meaning brushwood or scrubland – both *scrub* and *shrub* in Modern English come from the same source. As for the long-running difference of opinion over the pronunciation, Camden has this to say,

> 'We at this day call [this city] Shrewsbury and Shrowsbury, having mollified the name, whereas our Ancestours called it Scrobbes-byrig for that it was anciently a very thickete of shrubs upon an hill. But whence it is that it is now called in the British tongue Ymwithig, and by the Normans Scripesbery, Slopesbery, and Salop, and in the Latin tongue Salopia, I am altogether ignorant unlesse it should bee the ancient name Scrobbes-berig diversely distorted and disjointed.'

'Diversely distorted and disjointed' pretty much sums it up. Salop, the old alternative for Shropshire, is certainly an example of the Normans not being able to get their tongues round the Old English name.

Telford

Now here's a thing – a name ending in *–ford* that didn't start life as a place where you could cross a river (see the box *Crossing Places 1*, page 117). Telford is a new town, named after the engineer Thomas Telford (1757–1834), Surveyor of Public Works in Shropshire from 1787 and responsible for a remarkable number of feats of engineering in the area. His achievements included forty bridges: not all of them are still with us, but it was Telford who, more or less single-handedly, put a stop to the practice of bridges being washed away every time the Severn flooded. He had the wit to see that Abraham Darby's iron bridge (see IRONBRIDGE) was too fancy by half and badly constructed to boot; his own first iron bridge, at Buildwas, was much simpler, broader and lighter. (It survived until 1903 without anything like the amount of shoring up that Darby's needed.) Telford then moved on to construct the Ellesmere Canal. This entailed finding a way of carrying water across the Vale of Llangollen and led him not only to come up with the *idea* of the stupendous Pontcysyllte Aqueduct but to *make it work* – and continue to work two hundred years later. He was a great man and deserves to have any number of towns named after him. He had to wait a while, though: the new town, formed from the merger of a number of smaller and older places, wasn't designated as such until 1963.

Wem

There are two unfortunate aspects to Wem: its name means 'dirty or muddy place' and its most famous son is the notorious 'hanging' Judge Jeffreys. The judge was created First Baron Jeffreys of Wem in 1685, following his contribution towards preventing a recurrence of the Monmouth Rebellion against James II (1685–88) – he had adopted the simple measure of condemning to death or transportation practically everyone involved. With these two blots on Wem's escutcheon, it's no wonder that the Shropshire Tourist Board concentrates on its other claim to fame – to have invented the sweet pea: much more appropriate for such a pretty little town.

Wroxeter

This isn't a huge place today, but in Roman times it was the fourth largest city in Britain with a population of about five thousand. One of the most famous Roman roads, Watling Street, ended here, indicating that it was of great strategic importance – there were a number of places nearby where the Severn could be forded. Discarded as a fortress when the army moved north to CHESTER, it remained a civilian city after the Romans had left Britain and was finally abandoned when the Angles moved in. The Romans had adapted the local Celtic name, Wrekin, to produce Viroconium (pronounce the *v* as a *w*, as they did, and this becomes less random than it might at first appear). Wrekin, though its meaning has been lost, is still the name of a nearby hill. In due course the Anglo-Saxons added their word for a Roman settlement to the Celtic base and came up with something like Wreken-Ceaseter. This was altogether too much for the Normans, who put it in the Domesday Book as Rochecestre, but a spelling that was more faithful to the original emerged by the thirteenth century and duly evolved into the modern name. Camden, visiting Wroxeter in the sixteenth century, knew all about the Roman city but recorded that there was little to be seen of it. However, nineteenth-century excavations uncovered some of the best Roman remains in the country, with the result that we know now that there were about 3 km of walls surrounding an area of 70 hectares and with magnificent public baths.

CHESHIRE

You remember we got a bit excited about the meaning of Shropshire? Well, let us hope we have learned our lesson and that we recognise, resignedly, that this name is just a garbled form of CHESTER-shire.

Alderley Edge

This is an *alder*– name that has nothing to do with alder trees (see ALDERSHOT). Although *–ley* means 'woodland clearing', the surviving woodland is primarily oak and beech and it was once connected with an otherwise unknown woman named Althryth. The settlement was known as Alderley for many centuries; it was the steep escarpment nearby that was Alderley Edge. The town, growing fast after the arrival of the railways encouraged wealthy Manchester businessmen to settle here, officially adopted the longer name in 1864. The local legends, made famous in the novels of Alan Garner, of wizards, white horses and knights who will awake to defend the country in its darkest hour are associated with the escarpment rather than the town. The only wizards known to be living here today are of the 'footballing legend' type, but the town's proximity to the home of Manchester United ensures a plentiful supply of them.

Alsager

The meaning of this odd-looking name would be clearer if anyone had thought to hang on to the thirteenth-century spelling, Alle-sacher. Well, OK, not much clearer… The point is that the ending was originally the same as in SANDIACRE, and therefore indicated an area of ploughed land, in this case belonging to a man called Aelle. The fact that the modern pronunciation uses a soft *g* (as in *wager*) further distances the name from its linguistic origins.

Chester

This straightforward name went through a surprising number of changes before settling down. In ancient Celtic it was Deoua, either because it was on the Dee or because it was dedicated to the river's goddess. The Romans Latinised this to Deva and their fort later became known as Deva Victrix ('victorious Deva'), because the 'valiant and victorious' twentieth legion was stationed there. As a strategic base on the border with Wales Deva became one of the most important towns in Roman Britain. It retained its status after the Romans left, when the Anglo-Saxons added to its fortifications to help keep out the Danes and called it 'the fort where the legions used to be' – Legacaestir. The Welsh, to confuse the issue, persisted with Deverdoeu, a variation on the original Deoua, but also adopted Caerleon, a translation of Legacaestir. It didn't seem to bother them that this was identical to the name they gave (and still give) to a town at the southern end of the same border. The modern Welsh for Chester is still Caer. By the time of the Domesday Book the English name had been shortened to a recognisable ancestor of Chester: it was the most important place around, so no one was going to ask, 'Which Chester do you mean?' Over the centuries, however, as Chester became less dominant and other places called *–chester* or *–cester* grew, it became necessary to be able tell them apart: thus from the fourteenth to the eighteenth century Chester was commonly known as Westchester. Camden, listing the various names it has taken over the years, records the contemporary (1580s) usage as an either/or: 'West-Chester of the West situation, and simply Chester'. Daniel Defoe, writing in the 1720s, uses the longer form, but by the time of Bartholomew's 1887 gazetteer it is back to plain Chester – and there it has remained. Unless you are Welsh.

Congleton

The history of Congleton is such that although it is most likely that its name is Old English in origin, it is also possible that it had Danish influence. If the former, then Congleton means 'farmstead or village on a rounded hill'; if the latter, it is 'farmstead or village on a bend in the river' – either of which fits the bill geographically. Confusingly, the town stands on the river Dane, which has nothing to do with the invading Danes but comes from an Old Celtic word meaning 'trickling stream'. More fun than all this, however, is the tale associated with Congleton's nickname of Beartown. The town used to be famous for its cock-fighting and bear-baiting in the days when these were popular sports. One year, in the 1620s or so, the local bear died just before Wakes Week, the time of the annual fair when the bear would have been a major attraction and money-spinner. The story goes that the town had been saving for a new Bible and diverted the princely sum of 16 shillings (80p in today's money) to buy a new bear. They were then able to replenish the Bible fund with the takings from the bear-baiting.

Crewe

Perhaps surprisingly for a place inextricably associated with railways, this name has a watery origin. It is from an Old Celtic word for a weir or fish trap, which itself derives from a word for a crossing point or ford (in the case of Crewe, it would have been over marshy ground rather than a river). The suggestion is that a wicker net was stretched across the ford to catch fish, hence the two interlinked meanings. Although Crewe appears in the Domesday Book, it didn't become substantial until the 1830s, when the Grand Junction Railway Company established its locomotive works here and established rail links between London, Birmingham, Liverpool and Manchester. For many years thereafter, if you were going by rail anywhere north of Clapham Junction, you were likely to have to change at Crewe and to this day it remains an important railway junction for the north-west and North Wales. Interestingly, this happened because of that much more modern concept, nimbyism: when the works and the station were first proposed, the citizens of NANTWICH and Winsford protested successfully against something so noisy and dirty happening in their back yard.

Knutsford

An old rumour connected with this name needs to be debunked. Yes, it means 'ford associated with a man named Knut', but there is no hard evidence to show that he was the Danish king otherwise known as Canute, the one whose royal power was not great enough to prevent the tide coming in. It could have been any other guy called Knut who needed to get across the river.

Nantwich

As in DROITWICH, the –*wich* element refers to the local salt works, and the twelfth-century addition of *namet* means that they were 'named' – that is, famous. The briny spring by the river was probably discovered in pre-Roman times and the business of extracting salt from it was important enough for a settlement to grow up around it. At one time there were over two hundred salt houses in the area and the local museum exhibits part of a 7.5-metre-long, 700-year-old 'salt ship' carved out of oak. It isn't a ship in the sailing sense, but rather a storage vessel in which brine was kept before being transferred to a lead container for boiling. The importance of salt is reflected in the names of other nearby towns, including Middlewich and Northwich, both of which derive from the fact that they are north of Nantwich. The oldest working salt mine in England is, however, at Winsford – the deposits here were discovered by prospectors looking for coal in 1844, long after the name of the town had been established as 'ford associated with a man called Wine'.

Sandbach

The ending *–bach* comes from the same source as *beck*, meaning a stream flowing through a valley, and this, as the name suggests, was a sandy one.

Warrington

'Farmstead or village by the weir or river dam'. Throughout history, Warrington owed its importance to its being a safe place to cross the Mersey (see MERSEYSIDE): there has been a settlement here since at least 1000 BC. Bronze Age Celts, Romans, Anglo-Saxons and Normans all took advantage of the crossing place, and even after the first stone bridge was built in 1495 the town retained its strategic importance. During the Civil War the Royalist Lord Derby set up his headquarters here, inflicting heavy losses on the Round-heads at the battle of Stockton Heath and forcing them to retreat by setting fire to the centre of the town. Later centuries saw the building of a new bridge and the arrival of the railways and the Manchester Ship Canal, all helping to attract trade and industry and proving that being in the right place at the right time is as crucial to the prosperity of a town as it is to anything else.

11

LIVERPOOL, MANCHESTER AND SURROUNDS

Two cities that grew up because of industries: Liverpool as a port, Manchester as a centre for the world's clothing industry. But there are still place names based on the lie of the land and on the distrust of foreigners…

MERSEYSIDE

Considering the size and importance of the river, Mersey is a surprisingly recent name, first recorded in 1002 and meaning 'river on the boundary'. The boundary was the one between the old kingdoms of Northumbria and Mercia, although the river also later formed part of the border between the historic counties of LANCASHIRE and CHESHIRE. Merseyside has been an official administrative entity in one form or another since the 1970s, but we all know what it means – 'LIVERPOOL and places round there'.

Aintree

An ancient and diseased oak felled in Bull Bridge Lane, Aintree, in 2004, may have been the 'one tree' of the place name, but if so it would have to have been the better part of eight hundred years old: the name is first recorded in 1220. However, in olden times the landscape was known to be flat and featureless, so it is perfectly possible that there was only one tree in sight, whichever way you looked. The famous racecourse took its name from the village, staging its first flat races in 1829 and the first Grand National in 1839. A piece of pub-quiz trivia: what was the name of the first horse to win the National? Answer (and I promise I am not making this up): Lottery.

Birkenhead

'Headland where birch trees grow'. That may have been true in the thirteenth century, but it is hardly a distinguishing feature of the landscape nowadays.

Bootle

This is a tantalising name: it means 'large or important building' but no one knows what the building was. There's also a Bootle in Cumbria and we don't know what that building was either.

Crosby

This means 'village where there is a cross or crosses', and indeed there are two crosses in Crosby. But then there were once two villages, Great Crosby and Little Crosby, each of which had an ancient well surmounted by a cross. There are a number of places called Crosby around the country, all with the same derivation; sadly Crosby Ravensworth in Cumbria, which sounds as if it should be haunted by ravens, is merely named after a family of that name that used to live here.

Fazakerley

Another of those names whose whole is greater than the sum of its parts. Break it down and you have the prosaic 'woodland clearing [*ley*] by the ploughed land [*acre*] on the border [*faes*]'. Add it together and, hey presto, you have the off-the-wall, tongue-twisting, one-of-a-kind Fazakerley. It's a shame they didn't achieve the same magic when they named Newport or Redhill.

Haydock

This is probably a Welsh name meaning 'grain farm', so although both the look and the meaning of the word are agricultural, there is no connection with *hay*, nor with any of the modern senses of *dock*.

Knotty Ash

Fans of the comedian Ken Dodd will be pleased to know that this Liverpool suburb does indeed exist. Although there is no evidence that it ever had jam butty mines, it did once have an ancient, gnarled ash tree in its centre. In fact the place was called simply Ash in the early eighteenth century and extended its name as the tree grew older and knottier.

Liverpool

Let's dispose of –*pool* first. It means 'pool'. Probably in this case a tidal creek that no longer exists. And, believe it or not, the *Liver*– part is connected with 'liver'. The normal explanation is that the water in the pool was dirty and muddy, clogged up with reeds, looking a bit like liver. A bit far-fetched, you might think, but it is hardly the only entry in this book of which that could be said. The name is not mentioned in the Domesday Book; it first appears at the end of the twelfth century, when Liverpool was no more than a hamlet. Credit for its growth into a substantial port can be given to King John, who in 1207 needed a port from which to send troops to Ireland, to quell some disturbance or other. He didn't trust the Earl of CHESTER, so that ruled out the obvious choice. Instead, he granted Liverpool borough status and gave people tax incentives and gifts of land to come and live here. The Port of Liverpool took off. As a sideline to the name itself, the adjective 'Liverpudlian' is first recorded in 1833 and started life as a joke because of the connection between 'pool' and 'puddle'. And the city's symbol, the Liver Bird, first appeared on a seal dated 1350. It was probably originally based on an eagle, a symbol used by King John because it was sacred to his namesake, St John the Evangelist. But over the centuries this was forgotten as linguists and heraldry experts conspired to cause confusion: the upshot of it all is that the symbol is now officially a cormorant, and the most famous of all Liver Birds, the statues on the top of the Liver Building, which date from the early part of the twentieth century, are vaguely cormorant-like.

Maghull

Hull here means 'nook of land'; it comes from the same Old English root as *–hall* in LUDGERSHALL and the other places discussed under that entry. *Mag* means 'mayweed', so this was 'nook of land where mayweed grows'. The odd thing about mayweed is that the *may*– element comes from the Old English *maegtha* and originally had nothing to do with the may that is a synonym for hawthorn and is named after the month of May. So mayweed started life as something like magweed and changed its name in the sixteenth century, presumably because of a confusion with may. Or May. The spelling of Maghull is therefore much closer to the original Old English than the modern term for the plant it is named after.

Meols

There has been a settlement here since Neolithic times and the Romans, Anglo-Saxons and Vikings all left their mark: archaeological findings suggest that this was an important port long before King John bribed people to move to LIVERPOOL. The name, however, is Scandinavian, meaning, appropriately 'sand hills'.

Saughall Massie

The ending of Saughall is related to that of MAGHULL, and why one of them should have ended up as –*hall* and the other as –*hull* is a mystery. The distinction had already taken hold by the time of the Domesday Book, where they appear as Salhale and Magele, so perhaps the explanation is merely that two different Norman scribes wrote down unfamiliar names in the way that seemed best to them. Anyway, the first part of Saughall comes from 'sallow tree' – a type of willow – so it is 'nook of land where sallows grow'. Massie, like so many apparently random additions that make place names sound posher, derives from a family who owned land here in Norman times.

Southport

Self-explanatory; interesting because it sounds as if it ought to have evolved over the centuries but in fact emerged fully fledged from an entrepreneur's brain. There has been a settlement here since before the Domesday Book and until the eighteenth century it was called South Hawes, probably from the Old English for 'neck of land'. Until the 1790s it had few inhabitants and lots of sand dunes. Then one William Sutton, landlord of a pub in the next village, decided that it would be an ideal spot for sea-bathing (the new 'big thing' – see BLACKBURN/BLACKPOOL). He built a hotel which he called the South Port, supplied conveyances to take people to and from the canal 6 km away (the nearest form of public transport until the railways arrived fifty years later) and watched a town grow up around him.

Speke

A dictionary of place names published in 1915 maintains that this name derives from Walter l'Espec, who founded Kirkham, RIEVAULX and Warden Abbeys in the early part of the twelfth century. Although Warden Abbey is in Bedfordshire, the other two are in North Yorkshire and Walter seems to have focused his activities on this part of the world, even leading the Yorkshire barons in a battle against the Scots in 1138. He was an itinerant justice of the north, responsible for enforcing the king's rights, but there is no record of his having spent much time in Merseyside. More recent scholars have taken note of this; they have also realised that Speke appears in the Domesday Book (valued at 64 old pence – a little under 27p), which almost certainly appeared before Walter was born. Modern opinion is that Speke probably comes from the Old English for 'branches' or 'brushwood', but I mention Walter because I like the fact that his name comes from the French for 'woodpecker' and because he generally makes a better story.

Wallasey

The Domesday name is Walea, 'island of the Britons': the first part comes from the Old English *walh*, whose genitive plural is *walas* and whose close resemblance to the name of a nearby principality is no coincidence. In fact, *walh* wasn't specifically a Briton or a Welsh person. It meant a stranger or a foreigner, so, as far as the Anglo-Saxons were concerned, Wales – and indeed Wallasey – was simply a place where foreigners lived (see WALTON-ON-THAMES for others). The 'island' part comes from the fact that that northern part of the Wirral was once frequently cut off by high tides. So far so good, and if people had remembered the origins of the name it would probably have appeared on modern maps as Walsey. However, they obviously *didn't* remember, because in 1351 it suddenly turns up as Waleyesegh. The new Anglo-Saxon ending is an entirely

THE BOOK OF ENGLISH PLACE NAMES

superfluous duplication of…the existing Anglo-Saxon ending. So it's 'the island of the island of the Britons' – or the Welsh or the foreigners, whichever you prefer.

Wirral

Another place whose name is based on the Old English for 'nook' (see MAGHULL and SAUGHALL MASSIE above). This is 'place at the nook where bog-myrtle grows'. Bog myrtle isn't found there nowadays, but then there are fewer bogs on the peninsula than there used to be.

GREATER MANCHESTER

Like Merseyside, Greater Manchester is an official name for an area whose boundaries may be a bit vague in people's minds but whose general meaning is entirely self-explanatory.

Blackrod

Now why would you build a settlement here? It means a dark or gloomy clearing in a forest. Well, it is near an old Roman road (good for communications) and on high ground (good for defence), but surely there must have been other, less gloomy places around? Or they could have cut down a few more trees to brighten it up? An enigma. Anyway, a gloomy clearing it once was. The ending *–rod* is Old English, but is much less common than *–ley* or *–leigh*, which also mean 'clearing'; it is found, more frequently as *–royd*, almost exclusively in Yorkshire and Lincolnshire. The wonderfully named Mytholmroyd in West Yorkshire means 'clearing at the river mouths', because it started life on marshy ground where two rivers met.

Bolton

Bolton is related to BOOTLE in that it means 'settlement with a special building' and also in that no one seems clear what the special building was. The suggestion that it was a church is a bit of a cop-out, as there was no shortage of churches in Anglo-Saxon and Norman England. More likely, if not very exciting, is that it was the central part of a settlement, as opposed to outlying farms. A similar problem applies to other Boltons around the country. There is no way that the 'special building' in Bolton Abbey was the abbey, as it was built forty years after the name Bolton was first recorded there. A more forceful version of the same argument applies to Castle Bolton in Yorkshire, whose castle is fully three hundred years younger than the name.

Dukinfield

'Open land where ducks are found'. Sweet. But not entirely uncontroversial. The town's coat of arms features a raven, because this also appears in the arms of the Dukinfield family and it has been suggested that the name derives from the Old Norse *doken*, 'raven'. However, the seventeenth-century Lieutenant Colonel Robert Duckenfield, who distinguished himself fighting on the Parliamentarian side in the Civil War, spelt his name thus, so it looks as if he had come down on the side of the ducks.

Eccles

The Latin word for church is *ecclesia* and, as the Romans were among those who brought Christianity to Britain, it makes sense that they should bring their vocabulary with them. As the pagan Celts had no buildings that we would think of as churches, they had no word to describe them and therefore used their own version of the Latin one when the need arose. Thus, when the Anglo-Saxons arrived, they found buildings called something like *egles*. They adopted the word in their turn to refer specifically to early Romano-Celtic Christian churches and, in due course, to the communities living around them. Hence Eccles. Or so it is assumed:

there is evidence of a settlement here in Romano-Celtic times, but no specific remains of an early church.

Horwich

The ending of this name comes not from *wīc*, meaning a farm (as in NORWICH, DROITWICH, GATWICK and many more), but from *wice* meaning a wych-elm. And it wasn't any old wych-elm, but a 'hoary' or grey one. It must have been substantial in 1221 when the name is first recorded; there's no evidence of it now.

Hyde

'Hide' is one of the Domesday Book's favourite words. It was the standard unit of assessment for tax purposes: not a specific measurement, but an area of land deemed capable of supporting a family. It varied from place to place depending on climate, fertility of the soil, that sort of thing. So an area assessed at 'one hide' could, in the absence of any more imaginative name, come to be known as Hyde. That's what happened here, and also in Hyde Park in London.

Manchester

In Roman times Manchester was known as Mamucio or Mamucium, possibly because the original settlement was built on a rounded or breast-shaped hill (see MANSFIELD and, for the *−chester* ending, the Introduction, page 11). Roman occupation dates from the first century AD, when Julius Agricola, the general in charge of the invading forces, decided that this high ground, overlooking a point where two rivers joined and conveniently situated on the main road between CHESTER and YORK, would be just the place for another defensive garrison. The usefully named Camp Street, in modern SALFORD, marks the site of the first, wooden fortress; a larger, stone one was later built a few kilometres away at Castlefield. There was never a castle at Castlefield − the name derives from the presence of the Roman fort.

Mossley

The modern word *moss* comes from the Old English for 'swamp' or 'bog', and that is the origin of this name – 'woodland clearing by a swamp'.

Oldham

You'd think this would be an easy one, wouldn't you? Obviously it is a homestead or village that had been in existence longer than, say, Newham. But no. The second half is definitely Scandinavian rather than Old English and means 'island or promontory' – it's the same root as a number of places called Holme (if their origins are Danish) or Hulme (if they are Norwegian). And the *Old–* part probably doesn't mean 'old'. It is more likely to be from the Celtic for 'slope' or 'cliff', or may just possibly be from a personal name. So this could be 'promontory on a slope', 'Alda's promontory' or, at a pinch, 'old promontory'. There's no way of knowing for sure.

Ramsbottom

Although it has been suggested that the *rams–* element of this name is connected with rams – either the animals themselves or a ram-shaped rock – it is now considered more likely that it is to do with wild garlic or ransoms, which could easily have flourished in the damp forest that once lined the river Irwell here. *Bottom* in this context means not just a valley but a broad river valley – thus a reliable source of water. A good place to build a settlement, therefore, and also an ideal place for a small settlement to develop into a thriving mill town when the Industrial Revolution came along.

Rochdale

In the Domesday Book this appears as Recedham, 'homestead with a manor house'. This evolved into Rachedham and then, by the end of the twelfth century, into Rachedal, having had the Old

Scandinavian word for 'valley' appended to it. The name of the river, initially Rached and now Roch, is a back-formation. So Rochdale doesn't mean 'valley of the river Roch'; it means 'homestead with a manor house in a valley [through which the river Roch happens to run]'.

Sale/Salford

Sale is not somewhere that is up for auction, but 'place by the sallow-tree'. The sallow must have been a popular tree in this part of the world, because Salford means 'ford where sallow-trees grow'. (It means that in Salford in Bedfordshire, as well, but Salford in Oxfordshire was connected with salt.) Sallows obviously extended over on to the Wirral, too: see SAUGHALL MASSIE. In fact, they feature in place names all over the country: Selby in Yorkshire, Selborne in Hampshire and Selham in Sussex are respectively the farm, the stream and the homestead where sallows grow. Sellafield in Cumbria is 'open ground by a mound where sallows grow', the middle bit coming from an Old Scandinavian word for a burial mound.

Stockport

Another name whose meaning is less obvious than it looks (see OLDHAM for another example). *Stock* is nothing to do with livestock, but means 'outlying farm or hamlet' (see the box *Farming Country 2*, page 139); *port* is not a port but a market place, as in LANGPORT. So this adds up to 'market place at an outlying hamlet'.

Westhoughton

'Westerly farmstead or village on a nook of land'. There isn't an Easthoughton, but there may once have been. The hamlet that we know used to lie to the east of Westhoughton was the alluringly named Chequerbent, which probably meant that bent-grass grew there and was either variegated or planted in a chequerboard pattern. Sadly, most of Chequerbent is now buried under the M61; with a name like that it surely deserved a better fate.

Wigan

This was very probably the Roman town of Coccium, but arguments still rage: some claim that Coccium derives from a Latin word for scarlet and is a reference to the clay soils of the area; others use the same argument to site the Roman town somewhere where iron deposits make the soil appreciably redder than it is at Wigan. It's even been suggested (surely fancifully) that the 'scarlet' reference is to a brothel. There is also debate about the name Wigan, which may derive from a Welsh personal name or may mean 'little settlement'. The latter might link Wigan more closely with Coccium, as the Roman town probably wasn't a very substantial one.

12

YORKSHIRE

This is, obviously, the shire based round YORK and it used to be divided into three ridings. 'Riding' comes from the Old Scandinavian for 'a third', so all this means is that the Vikings split the county into three for administrative purposes. There was never a South Riding – the East Riding was bordered to the south by the Humber, but the West Riding continued a good bit further down, to encompass ROTHERHAM and SHEFFIELD. In 1974 the county boundaries were redrawn and four administrative units emerged: West, North and South Yorkshire and the East Riding of Yorkshire. Some people still stubbornly refused to acknowledge these changes (this is Yorkshire, after all), but the 1970s divisions are clear enough for the purposes of this chapter.

WEST YORKSHIRE

This was once an industrial centre, with towns growing up round mills and mines. In the early twentieth century, according to a contemporary encyclopaedia, 'the great coal-field of the West Riding yields not only the Silkstone bituminous coal, most valuable as a house coal, but also the Barnsley thick coal, semi-anthracitic, and therefore admirably fitted for iron-smelting and for use in engine furnaces'. So now we know. As for the manufacturing, 'Leeds

produces every variety of woollen goods; Bradford, mixed worsted fabrics and yarns; Dewsbury, Batley and adjoining districts, shoddy.' All of which is just an excuse to tell you that shoddy *was 'a yarn or fabric made from wool waste or clippings' – a generally inferior material that is the source of the modern adjective.*

Ackton/Ackworth

It's 'keep you on your toes' time again. These two places are within 10 km of each other, yet have different derivations: Ackton is 'farmstead where oaks grow', while Ackworth is 'enclosure of a man called Acca'. In the Domesday Book they were quite distinct – Aitone and Aceuurde respectively – but over the years they have drifted towards each other. Acklam in North Yorkshire is another oaky place; the ending is from a dative plural form of the more common *–ley*, so the result is 'place at the clearing in the oak woods'.

Brighouse

Stick a *d* in the middle and your problem is solved: 'houses by the bridge'.

Dewsbury

This was probably once a stronghold connected with a man named Dewi, which is mildly interesting because Dewi is a Welsh name and you wonder what he was doing here. Parish information dating from 1837 tells us that 'antiquarians supposed the name, Dewsbury, to be derived from the original planter of the village, Dui or Dew, who, previous to the arrival of Paulinus, had fixed his abode and fortified his "Bury".' It has been suggested that the reference is to St David; certainly Dewsbury was a local centre for Christianity, having two churches perhaps as early as the seventh century. But this idea may have arisen from a confusion between two different saints called Paulinus: St David's Welsh tutor was not the same person as the seventh-century first Archbishop of York referred to here. The same account continues, 'Another conjecture holds, that the original name is Dewsborough, or God's Town. A superstitious practice of considerable antiquity still exists here, which consists in ringing the large bell of the church at midnight on Christmas eve, and this knell is called "the Devil's passing bell".' Alternatively, the name may come from the Old English word which gave us the modern 'dew' and may simply mean 'fortified town by a stream'.

Elland

This requires a little more effort than BRIGHOUSE, but only a little: put an *a* after the *e*, look back at the entry for NUNEATON for an explanation of the Old English word *ēa* and you arrive at 'cultivated land or estate by the river'.

Featherstone

Not so easy, unless you know that the Old English for 'four' was *feower*. Then you can take a wild guess that this means 'place of the four stones' and pat yourself on the back. The stones were probably a marker for a meeting place or possibly of an ancient sacred site.

Halifax

Possibly 'area of coarse grass in a nook of land', in which case the first part comes from *halh*, as in LUDGERSHALL, MAGHULL and elsewhere, and the thirteenth-century spelling Haliflex suggests a connection with *flax*. The idea that it means 'holy flax' is more imaginative but surely ridiculous – what could be holy about flax? The earlier belief that Halifax meant 'holy locks' or 'holy head of hair' was based on the fact that there has been a church dedicated to St John the Baptist here since the twelfth century: the name may refer to an early image of the saint, probably his severed head. There is even a rumour that John's head was brought here for burial. (Well, St Andrew's bones are said to have ended up at St Andrews in Scotland, even further from home – these holy relics were surprisingly mobile in the Middle Ages.) But the dates don't really fit and the idea appears to be too fanciful – or perhaps too grisly – for modern scholars.

Holmfirth

Firth comes from the Old English for 'sparse woodland', with no connection to the Scottish word for 'inlet'. Holmfirth therefore means 'sparse woodland near a place called Holme' (see OLDHAM). There is still a village called Holme nearby; it is mentioned, somewhat dismissively, in the Domesday Book, two hundred years before the first reference to Holmfirth. Holme is on high ground; Holmfirth lies in the valley below it and grew up near a corn mill and a bridge over the river Holme. In the eighteenth century the fast-flowing water became attractive to industrialists; woollen mills sprang up, with the result that what had once been a tiny offshoot became a substantial town, while the original Holme remained a rural hamlet.

Horsforth

This was Horseford in the Domesday Book and means exactly what that version of the name says – a ford that could be used by horses. The change from *ford* to *forth* which occurred sometime after the twelfth century is a quirk of local (Scandinavian-influenced) pronunciation. The Stainforths in North and South Yorkshire (stony ford), Yafforth in North Yorkshire (ford over the river), Rufforth near York (rough ford) and two Gosforths, one in Cumbria, one near Newcastle upon Tyne (fords frequented by geese), all developed in the same way.

Leeds

The Venerable Bede mentions Loidis, a vast forest which covered most of what is now West Yorkshire in the eighth century. The enormous number of places hereabouts ending in *–ley* ('woodland clearing') are a reminder of its former woodiness: Barnsley, Headingley, Ilkley, Keighley and Otley, all derived from personal names, and Brierley ('clearing where briars grow') are the tip of the iceberg. As it were. By the time of the Domesday Book Loidis had become Ledes, and was a substantial place: 'Twenty-seven villeins and four bordars have fourteen ploughs there. A priest is there and a church and a mill of four shillings and ten acre of meadow. It was worth six pounds, now seven pounds.' There is little information about pre-Norman settlement in the area, but the name tells us that there were people here at least a thousand years earlier: Loidis – and hence Leeds – comes from Landensis, a Celtic word meaning 'people living by the strongly flowing river'. Today the river is called the Aire, which also means 'strongly flowing' and probably derives from an even older word than Loidis. The names of two nearby villages, Ledsham and Ledston, come from the same source as Leeds, and Airton and Airmyn ('mouth of the Aire') derive from the river.

Normanton

The Normans of Normandy (the ones involved in the Norman Conquest of 1066) were descended in part from the Norsemen of Scandinavia, also known as the Vikings. Places called Normanton – and there are three in Derbyshire as well as this one near WAKEFIELD – are named not after the Normans but after the Norsemen who invaded the north of England long before the Normans invaded the south. So Normanton means 'farmstead or village of the Norsemen'.

Pontefract

Pont– is a common opening for place names in Wales, as it is the local word for bridge, taken from the Latin. It's not often found in England, with the main exception of Pontefract, which means 'broken bridge'. There is much speculation about the location of the bridge, as no great rivers run nearby, but the most likely answer seems to be that it crossed a small stream known as the Washbeck, to the east of the town. In an area prone to flooding, this might have become an important – and possibly strategic – crossing place. Certainly the tradition is that William the Conqueror was the one who broke the bridge, to prevent some enemy or other from using it. This would tally with the fact that the town's name is first recorded in 1090 three years after William's death. Pomfret – the name often given to the liquorice-flavoured cakes that originated here – is an Old English spelling and pronunciation.

Todmorden

Don't take your German friends here unless they have overstayed their welcome and it is time they went home – they'll think it means 'death murder' and may be alarmed. In Old English it is considerably less provocative: it means 'boundary valley of a man called Totta'.

Wakefield

In medieval times a *wake* was a village fair or festivity, held once or twice a year, often on the feast day of the patron saint of the local church. Centuries later, it became the norm in northern mill towns for all the mills to close down for a week so that everyone had their holidays at the same time: this tradition, known as Wakes Week, persisted well into the twentieth century. The word is also connected with wakefulness, with the idea of holding a vigil over a dead body and thence with the party held after a funeral. But as

CROSSING PLACES 2

Of course a ford was not the only way to cross a river (see the box *Crossing Places 1*, page 117).

Fordingbridge means 'bridge of the people living by the ford' and as early as 1286 the Hampshire locals had produced this belt-and-braces approach to crossing the Avon. Understandably enough: it's a substantial piece of water at this point (the current stone bridge is an imposing structure with seven arches) and relying on the water being low enough for you to cross at the ford must have been dodgy.

Wadebridge in Cornwall was originally Wade, meaning 'ford' (on the river Camel – see CAMELFORD). In the fifteenth century they built a bridge and the rest is history. This is a rare survival of an early Old English term: in other parts of the country this name would probably have metamorphosed into Bridgford.

Most other places with 'bridge' in their name are also connected with bridges. **Bridgnorth** was simply Bridge in the twelfth century and became Bridgnorth in the thirteenth, when the need arose to distinguish it from another bridge further south. **Bridgwater** was not 'place by the bridge over the water', but 'place by Walter's bridge', Walter being a twelfth-century landowner. **Trowbridge** had a bridge made from a tree trunk, **Stalybridge** was near a wood where staves were collected and **Whaley Bridge** was built near a woodland clearing near a road (the *wha–* element is related to the modern word 'way'). **Hebden Bridge** is perhaps the most alluring of all – it means 'bridge in the valley where rosehips or brambles grow'.

For other crossing places that have their own entry, see CORBRIDGE, TONBRIDGE, BRIGG, WAINFLEET ALL SAINTS and, most peculiarly, PONTEFRACT.

far as Wakefield is concerned, it is the first sense that matters: it was 'field where festivities are held'. The town still lives up to its name: it has been hosting the Wakefield and North of England Tulip Society Tulip Show for 175 years, and also holds an annual Festival of Food, Drink and Rhubarb.

Wetherby

This was a very specific sort of farm (for the *–by* ending, see the box *Farming Country* 2, page 139): the animals reared here were wether-sheep; that is male sheep, particularly castrated ones. The suggestion that in bad winters Wetherby has less snow than its neighbours because 'weather goes by' has no foundation in etymology and very little in meteorology.

SOUTH YORKSHIRE

The smallest of the four divisions, South Yorkshire is focused on former industrial centres, with a smattering of the Peak District in the west and a stretch of moorland to the east. The steel for which SHEFFIELD is famous was known in Chaucer's time, but some of the place names commemorate otherwise forgotten incidents much longer ago than that.

Askern

A number of places in the north of England have names beginning with *ask–*, from the Old Scandinavian for 'ash': examples include Askham Bryan and Askham Richard near York (Bryan and Richard having been the names of thirteenth-century lords of the manor); Askham in Cumbria, and Askrigg and Askwith in North Yorkshire (respectively 'ridge' and 'wood' where ashes grow). The *–ern* element in Askern is Old English and means 'house', so this is 'house near the ash tree'.

Conisbrough

This is 'king's fortification', the first part of the name being of Scandinavian origin. *Conis*–, 'belonging to the king', is quite a common opening in northern place names, being found in Coniscliffe near DARLINGTON ('king's cliff'), Conisholme in Lincolnshire ('dry ground in marsh belonging to the king') and, most famously, Coniston Water in the Lake District. In the case of Conisbrough, one of the early holders of the manor was Harold, the king who traditionally lost his eye (and certainly lost his life) at the Battle of Hastings, but the name is too old for it to refer to him. Conisbrough is mentioned as a fortified village in the Anglo-Saxon Chronicle for about the year 600, so it may have been established by Edwin, an early king of Northumbria. It's impossible to be sure at this distance.

Doncaster

'Roman fort on the river Don'. Don itself is an Old Celtic name meaning 'river', possibly connected with the Celtic mother goddess Danu (known as Don in Welsh). The site of Doncaster was probably chosen for two good reasons: first, it was a crossing point on the river, midway between the two larger towns of LINCOLN and YORK – if you took the more direct route, the Roman road known as Ermine Street, you had to cross the Humber in a boat, so a detour via Doncaster saved that trouble. Second, it was on the edge of the territory of the Brigantes, a powerful Celtic tribe – or loose confederation of tribes – occupying most of England north of the Humber. While many of the tribes in the south succumbed quickly and more or less peacefully to Roman occupation (with the noticeable exception of the Iceni under Queen Boudicca, see COLCHESTER), the Brigantes were made of sterner stuff and conflict with them was a regular part of Roman life for over a hundred years. So the remains of Roman fortifications are a common feature in

Brigantes country. A little to the north of Doncaster are two villages named Kirk Sandall and Kirk Bramwith. The *kirk* element means church (see KIRKBY-IN-ASHFIELD); Sandall is 'sandy nook of land'; Bramwith is 'wood where broom grows'. I mention this only because Kirk Sandall's church is dedicated to St Oswald (see OSWESTRY); legend has it that his body rested here after he was killed in battle. Which is further proof that these medieval saints, alive or dead, intact or chopped up to produce a relic here and a relic there, covered a lot of ground.

Penistone

There is some debate about what this name means, but one thing is certain – it's not what you thought when you first read it. It's probably nothing more controversial than 'farmstead on a hill', the first part coming from the Celtic *penn*, which the Anglo-Saxons translated as 'hill' (see PENRYN) and the second from the incredibly common Old English *tūn*.

Rotherham

Places beginning with *Roth–* come from a variety of sources, some connected with a clearing (places called Rothwell mean 'spring or stream by the clearing'); others to do with cattle (see ROTHERHITHE) and still others from personal names (Rothbury in Northumberland and Rotherby in Leicestershire may fall into this category). Rothers-thorpe in Northamptonshire is an outlying farm (see THORPE) connected to an advocate, because in the twelfth century the local manor belonged to the Béthune family, described in a 1937 survey of the county as 'hereditary advocates of the church of St Vedast of Arras', which at the time was a famous abbey in northern France. Rotherham, however, has nothing to do with any of these. It is simply 'homestead or village on the river Rother', with Rother being an Old Celtic name meaning 'chief river'.

Sheffield

Sheffield appears in the Domesday Book as Escafeld, 'open land on the river Sheaf'. The Sheaf, a tributary of the Don, on which the city still sits (see DONCASTER), took its name from an Old English word for a boundary – so Sheffield started life as 'open land on a river that marked a boundary', possibly between the old kingdoms of Mercia and Northumbria. Iron was mined and knives were made in the area in the Middle Ages, but Sheffield really burgeoned as a steel centre during the Industrial Revolution. The Cutlers' Hall in the centre of town commemorates the importance of 'Sheffield steel' cutlery, and the theatre that now hosts the World Snooker Championships is named after a process used to improve the quality of steel by heating it with other ingredients – in a crucible.

EAST RIDING OF YORKSHIRE

The East Riding has never been densely populated, but the Angles and Danes nevertheless managed to squabble over it. BEVERLEY – still the county town – was the only settlement of substance until the growth in trade described under GOOLE. Nowadays half the population of the riding lives in and around KINGSTON-UPON-HULL, leaving plenty of rolling hillside and a bit of Heritage Coast for tourists to enjoy.

Beverley

This is a rare instance of an *–ley* ending not meaning a woodland clearing. In this case it comes from a Celtic word meaning 'hiding place' and the whole name means 'beaver lodge'. Sadly, the only beaver remaining in the area is on the town's coat of arms. The surname Beverley originally indicated someone who came from this part of the world, and the personal name derives from that.

Driffield

Neither of the two possible meanings for this name is attractive: it is open land with either dirt (*drit*) or stubble (*drīf*). If the former, as in DROITWICH SPA, this is the Old English word that evolved into *dirt*.

Flamborough Head

Now designated a Special Area of Conservation and a mecca for birdwatchers, in the eighteenth century the site of a battle in which British forces were defeated by the American naval commander John Paul Jones, Flamborough started life as 'Fleinn's stronghold'. Tradition has it that Kormak Fleinn (whose name means 'javelin') was the brother of Thorgil Skarthi, founder of SCARBOROUGH; that he was shipwrecked down the coast from his brother's place; and that he built the first house there from the wreckage of his boat. An early belief that Flamborough referred to the 'flame' of a watchtower or beacon on the headland ignores the Domesday spelling Flaneburg: this is more likely to derive from the Old English *flaen*, 'sword' or 'arrow', which in turn is related to Kormak's Scandinavian nickname.

Goole

First recorded in 1362, this derives from a Middle English dialect word for 'stream' or 'channel', reflecting the town's position at the point where the river Ouse flows into the Humber. There must therefore have been a settlement here in the fourteenth century, but the town officially came into existence only in 1826, thanks to the Aire and Calder Navigation Company. The company had been set up in 1698 to improve the navigable waterways between the Yorkshire coalfields and the manufacturing towns of LEEDS and WAKEFIELD on the one hand, and the sea and thus a wider market for their goods on the other. In 1820 the company obtained permission – by Act of Parliament, no less – to build a canal from Knottingley, about 30 km inland, to Goole and to make two docks at the new port, with locks also giving access to the Ouse. The first ship, bound for Hamburg, left Goole in April 1828 and the Aire and Calder Navigation continued to expand and develop the port until their function was subsumed into the British Transport Commission in 1947. A far cry from a medieval channel that didn't even merit a mainstream name.

Hornsea

'Lake with a horn-shaped peninsula'. Look at it on a large-scale map and you're likely to say, 'Fair enough.'

Kingston-upon-Hull

Most of us call this place 'Hull', which is actually the name of the river on which it stands and means either 'muddy' (in which case it comes from the Old Celtic) or 'deep' (Scandinavian). The fact that the name is first recorded as late as 1193 (as 'Wyke on Hull', meaning 'farm or outlying village on the Hull'), long after both Celtic and Scandinavian influence had waned in this part of the world, makes it difficult to plump confidently for either. We know that the town was founded as a river port to allow the monks of the abbey of Meaux, a little to the north, to export the wool from their estates. Then in 1293 it was taken over by Edward I, who was interested less in wool than in supplying the armies he had sent to fight the Scots; it became known as Kingston in his honour. And lest you don't know this part of the country well and thought Hull was on the Humber, let me add that the Hull flows into the Humber and that the modern unitary authority includes bits of both.

South Cave/North Cave

Not a cave, but a fast-flowing stream, from the Old English. This was a single settlement in the Domesday Book, but over the years

Cave, as it was known, grew to the point where it justified being split in two (see APPLEBY MAGNA/APPLEBY PARVA). However, there was a practical difficulty to be overcome in giving the two new communities distinctive titles: unlike, say, CHALFONT ST PETER and CHALFONT ST GILES, both Caves had churches dedicated to 'All Saints'. Hence, presumably, the no-messing approach to the modern names.

Warter

Wearg was the Old English for 'criminal' and *–ter* is a corruption of 'tree', so this becomes 'tree for criminals' – a gallows. Nowadays Warter is a particularly pretty village owned by a single estate, and if the trees look familiar it is because some of them have appeared in paintings by David Hockney.

NORTH YORKSHIRE

The largest and most sparsely populated of the four areas, North Yorkshire nevertheless boasts some great names and lots of history. There are battles between the Romans and the incumbent Celts, important centres of early Christianity and the possibility – just the vaguest, folkloric hint – of a connection with an outlaw on the run from Nottinghamshire.

Aldbrough St John

St John comes from the name of the local parish church and is of much more recent date than the Old English Aldbrough – 'old or disused stronghold'. Two thousand years ago Aldbrough was in the heartland of Brigantes territory (see DONCASTER) and they had an important fort nearby, at the place now called Stanwick. There were all sorts of shenanigans around here in the first century AD: the Brigantian queen Cartimandua betrayed the British rebel Caratacus to the Romans; as a result she fell out with her husband,

Venutius, who took control of the stronghold at Stanwick and continued to resist the Roman occupation. It was only a matter of time, however, before the Romans prevailed, Venutius had to surrender and his fort fell into disuse – hence the name the Saxons gave it several hundred years later. Further south, near Borough-bridge ('fortified town near the bridge'), Aldborough – same derivation, slightly different spelling – had been the Brigantes' capital and after their defeat it was replaced by the Roman town of Isurium, substantial remains of which can still be visited.

Blubberhouses

The derivations of the modern words *blubber* and *bubble* are vaguely connected and have been confused in this name: it means 'houses by the bubbling stream', which raises the question, would Bubble-houses have been a more appropriate or more dignified name?

Catterick

I have no wish to be rude about Catterick, but it really isn't the sort of town you'd expect to be named after a waterfall. Yet the version recorded by Ptolemy in the second century AD is Catourac-tonion, apparently connected with the Latin *cataracta*. In fact it is more likely that Catterick was originally a fortified Celtic town whose name was based on *catu*, meaning 'war', and *ratis*, 'rampart', and that the Romans misunderstood and turned it into something they could make sense of. Camden records the existence of a waterfall on the Swale, towards Richmond, but he is trying to justify what was then the accepted explanation for the name: 'And wherefore should [Bede] call it *the towne nere unto Catarracta* if there were not there a waterfall?' Camden didn't have access to recent research: the waterfall explanation persisted into the twentieth century, with a 1915 dictionary of place names giving it as one of the very few 'real' Latin names that had survived. Certainly the city was an important one in the second century, because (again according to Camden) Ptolemy, working on the book that would be the bible of astronomy for the next thousand years, 'tooke there an observation of the heavens position', not something that many people would bother doing today. Anyway, the town was destroyed by the Danes – 'in the yeere 769 it was set on faire and burnt by Eanred or Beanred the Tyrant, who pittifully mangled the King-dome of Northumberland' – and, although there is now a sizeable garrison just outside the village, Catterick itself has never really returned to former glories.

Filey

This probably means 'promontory resembling a sea monster', an imaginative but not entirely ludicrous description of the headland of Filey Brigg, which juts a kilometre into the sea to the south of the town. The fact that the promontory has been the cause of many a shipwreck over the centuries could be said to add to its perceived monstrous qualities.

Guisborough

No one seems to know anything about Gigr, except that he was Scandinavian, but this is probably his fortified place. The priory, founded in 1119 by an ancestor of Robert the Bruce and today spelt Gisborough, seems to have taken its name from the town, which was mentioned in the Domesday Book thirty-three years earlier. Whatever the place's origins, it must have been quite some-thing in the sixteenth century: Camden describes it as a 'passing good place, and may well for pleasantnesse, delightsome variety, and rare gifts of Nature contend with Puteoli in Italy, which in regard of healthy situation it also farre excelleth'. Which may be why the mysterious Gigr decided to settle here.

Harrogate

Although *gate* normally means 'gate' or 'gap' in the south of England, in the Scandinavian-influenced north it tends to mean 'road', as it does here, and in street names such as Castlegate in YORK. The *Harro-* element is also from Old Scandinavian and means 'heap of stones', so Harrogate becomes '[place at the] road leading to the cairn'. The name is first recorded in the fourteenth century, but Harrogate's history really begins in the sixteenth, when a chalybeate (= containing iron) spring was discovered and paved the way for the town's development as a spa. There is no connection with HARROW.

Ingleby

You can tell you are in Scandinavian-dominated territory, because this name means 'Englishmen's farmstead or village'. So in the eleventh century Englishmen were rare enough hereabouts to be worth pointing out as furriners. There are, in fact, three Inglebys within about 20 km of each other in North Yorkshire: Ingleby Arncliffe, Ingleby Barwick and Ingleby Greenhow. The first is distinguished by being near a cliff frequented by eagles; the second was probably a barley farm; and the third was near a green mound. Interestingly, all three of these affixes come from Old English, so must have been added after the Anglo-Saxons had sent the Danes packing.

Knaresborough

The most likely explanation of this name is 'fortified town of a man called Cēnheard': if this were correct, it would be Old English and indicate the existence of a pre-Norman fortification. Certainly the name is recorded a hundred years before the Normans are known to have built a castle here. We know that the castle was in existence by 1170, because at that time it was held by Hugh de Moreville, one of the assassins of Thomas Becket (despite having done the deed in CANTERBURY, they subsequently turned up all over the place – see BOVEY TRACEY for another example). An alternative explanation for the name Knaresborough is 'fortification on a rocky outcrop', which is an appropriate enough description and stops us having to worry about unknown Saxons called Cēnheard.

Leyburn

The *burn* bit is the common Old English element meaning 'stream', but in this case *Ley–* doesn't mean 'wood' or 'woodland clearing'; it comes from an Old Scandinavian word meaning 'shelter' and is connected with the modern *lee*, as in the *lee side* of a ship or the Leeward Islands.

Loftus

There are two places called Lofthouse in other parts of Yorkshire; their derivation is exactly the same as Loftus and their spelling makes the meaning clear. This was a house with a loft or upper storey – unusual in the days when most people lived in cottages made of a latticework of sticks with the gaps filled in with mud plaster, in which a family would share a maximum of two rooms with its livestock. There is no mention in the Domesday Book of a grander dwelling at Loftus, but an Anglo-Saxon burial ground containing jewellery and weapons dating back to the seventh century was discovered nearby in 2005 and suggests that Edwin, King of Northumbria, and his Kentish wife, later known as Saint Æthelburh, may have spent time here. They would certainly have warranted two-storey accommodation.

Middlesbrough

This name first appears in the mid-twelfth century and it doesn't take much to work out what it means: 'fortified town in the middle'. The question then arises, 'In the middle of what?' Well, in Saxon times there was a chapel here which belonged to WHITBY Abbey; it is likely that this was a midway stopping-off point for monks travelling between Whitby and another important Christian settlement at DURHAM. Even so, Middlesbrough remained tiny until the early nineteenth century; when, in 1828, the railway pioneer Joseph Pease bought up five hundred acres (about 190 hectares) of land so that he could extend the newly opened Stockton and Darlington railway to a place that could be built up as an industrial port, there were no more than thirty people living here. So successful were Pease and the railways, however, that the population grew to 5,463 in 1841 and more than 90,000 in 1901.

Redcar

If I tell you that this name dates from the twelfth century, you'll realise (I hope) that it has nothing to do with red cars. Instead, the first part is Old English and means 'reedy' and the second comes from an Old Scandinavian word meaning 'marsh'. This isn't a common ending in place names (the Old English *marsh* seems to have prevailed in most cases where it was needed), but it does occur in Broadcarr in Norfolk ('broad marsh') and Altcar and Holker in Lincolnshire (respectively 'marsh by the muddy river' and 'hollow marsh').

Rievaulx

'Valley of the Rye' – an Old French word tacked on to an Old Celtic river name which probably means nothing more informative than 'stream'. There is no record of the place name existing before the now-ruined Cistercian abbey was built here in the twelfth century: presumably both place and abbey were named at the same time.

Robin Hood's Bay

The name is self-explanatory, but doesn't that mean he was a long way from home? Well, yes, and there are any number of implausible reasons for that. One story has it that Robin Hood kept a boat here so that he could flee the country if Sherwood Forest became too hot to hold him – though this is far from being the nearest stretch of coast and you would have thought he would be better off heading for KING'S LYNN. Another says that he was invited here by the Abbot of WHITBY to fight off Danish invaders, but, if Robin Hood lived when we all think he did, that chronology is awry by about three hundred years. Alternatively, it may be that the Robin Hood of Robin Hood's Bay isn't the 'rob from the rich, give to the poor' guy at all, but a sprite similar to Robin Goodfellow (the Puck of Shakespeare's *A Midsummer Night's Dream*). In which case, of course, he has magic powers and can do what he likes where he likes when he likes. The existence of a fishing village with this name is first recorded in the 1530s and we know that it subsequently became a favourite haunt of smugglers, but anything else to do with its origins is down to 'you pays your money and you takes your choice'.

Scarborough

This is another stronghold, probably belonging to a tenth-century Viking warrior and poet named Thorgil. Yes, it looks like a bit of a stretch to get from Thorgil to Scar, but let me help you out by telling you that he was nicknamed Skarthi, which meant 'Hare-lip'. Not a nickname many people would approve of today, but there is no suggestion that the Vikings knew or cared anything about political correctness. Just up the coast from Scarborough, Ravenscar has no connection with Thorgil, but instead means what it looks as if it means: 'rock frequented by ravens'.

Scotch Corner

The point here is that all roads lead to Scotland – provided you are heading more or less north. If you keep going straight on, the old Great North Road (now the A1 and A1M) will take you to

BERWICK-UPON-TWEED and eastern Scotland; if you veer off to the north-west you will eventually hit western Scotland. The name dates from 1860, so when it was first invented you would have been doing the journey in a horse-drawn carriage and it would have been a long way whatever your destination.

Settle

This is a rather sweet little name, because it derives from the same source as the modern word *settle*, and simply means a house or dwelling place.

Tadcaster

Like all –*casters* (see the Introduction, page 11), this was a Roman town, but who Tata or Tada was isn't known. The Romans called it Calcaria (*calx* was the Latin for 'lime'), because of the limestone that has been quarried here through the centuries and contributed to the building of York Minster. The Roman settlement wasn't a large one, but served as a staging post on the LONDON-YORK road.

Thirsk

This is thought to be the only name to derive from the unattested Old Scandinavian *thresk*, meaning a marsh, though is it recorded in the Domesday Book as normal farming land, so it must have been reasonably dry by then. An alternative suggestion, that the name is appreciably older and derives from the Celtic meaning 'house on the water', by analogy with Old Celtic river names such as Esk and Usk, is considered unlikely because very few Celtic names have survived in this part of the country.

Whitby

Whitby was a centre of Christianity from the seventh century, when an abbey was founded here (it was destroyed by the Vikings, but the ruins of its Norman successor can still be seen). The Synod of Whitby, held in 664, was the first in the country to acknowledge the authority of Rome, as opposed to the Celtic church – a decision that remained in force until Henry VIII fell out with the Pope over his divorce from Catherine of Aragon in 1533. There is no evidence, however, that the town got its name because the abbey was built of white stone (as was the case, for example, in Winterborne Whitechurch – see WINTERBORNE ABBAS). Instead it seems to be named after a Viking called Hviti. The Vikings didn't arrive until long after the abbey was founded, but they are known to have changed the name from its earlier one, Streonshalh, presumably because they didn't know what it meant (nor does anyone else for sure) or how to pronounce it (a problem with which you may have some sympathy).

Yarm

You might not see at a glance that this name means exactly the same as CREWE, but it does. Crewe's origins are Celtic while Yarm's are Old English, but both words mean 'fishing weir' or 'fish trap'.

York

If you know that the Archbishop of York signs himself 'Ebor.', you may be aware that the Roman name for York was Eboracum, a more user-friendly (to them) version of the Celtic Eburus. If you have done the tourist bit here, you will know that the Vikings called it Jorvik. Soften that *j* to help you on the way to the Domesday Book spelling Eurvic and the progression towards the modern name becomes more obvious. Add to that the fact that the letter *v* was very rare in Old English and was more or less interchangeable with a *u*, and you begin to see how the Danes' consonantal *v* disappeared over the years. So all that remains is to discover what the name meant in the first place. Probably 'estate where yew trees grew'.

Eburus or Eburos was also a personal name, so York may have started life as 'Eburos's place', but if that is the case the personal name derived from the name of the sacred tree. It wouldn't be fair, however, to finish without a passing mention of Eoforwic, the Old English name that came between Eboracum and Jorvik. Eoforwic means 'settlement with wild boar', but although there probably were boar in the area (they were all over the place at that time), the name is simply a mistake: the Anglo-Saxons confused the unfamiliar Latin with a word that they knew. As for their alternative suggestion, Eoforwiccaester, which meant 'settlement with wild boar where the Roman fort used to be', it was obviously as unwieldy in Old English as it is in the modern translation and wouldn't have lasted five minutes.

13

NORTH-WEST ENGLAND

The north-west – Cumbria in particular – is unusual in that it was settled by Norwegians rather than Danes, with subtle knock-on effects on place names. In fact the Norwegians came not directly from Norway but from their kingdom in Ireland (they captured Dublin in 838); from there it was easy for them to extend their influence over north-western England while their Danish cousins did the same in the east.

LANCASHIRE

Like CHESHIRE, this is a cut-down version of 'the shire of the obvious town': Lancastreshire is found in the fourteenth century but was too unwieldy a name to survive. Although some of Lancashire's settlements are ancient, many were tiny before the Industrial Revolution and a good handful were founded to cope with the increases in trade, industry and tourism.

Accrington

An exception to the rule that names ending in *–ington* mean 'farmstead or village of the family or followers of so-and-so'. In this case the first part comes from the Old English for 'acorn' and the whole thing means 'farmstead or village where acorns are found or stored'.

Bacup

Although this means 'valley by or below a ridge', the derivation has nothing to do with *up*: the ending is derived from Old English *hop*, meaning 'secluded valley'. In the twelfth century it was considered 'foul' or 'muddy' enough to be known as Fulebachope, but it had presumably dried up a bit a hundred years later, when the modern name is first recorded.

Blackburn/Blackpool

Both these names mean what you might think they would mean: 'dark stream' and 'dark pool' respectively. The interest lies in why one of the world's most famous seaside resorts should have been founded near a dark pool. Well, almost inevitably, it's not as simple as that. Blackpool grew up in medieval times as a collection of coastal farmsteads, by a stream (known as 'le pull') that drained the nearby peatlands into the sea. In those days the settlement was called merely Pul; although the peat would have darkened the water from earliest times, the name Blackpool doesn't emerge until 1602. The first house of any substance was built by Edward Tyldesley towards the end of the seventeenth century and it is thought that his guests were among the first people in England to make the journey – or indeed any journey – specifically to enjoy the sea air and the privilege of riding along the beach. The idea that sea air and sea bathing were good for you really took off in the eighteenth century; by the end of it visitors were flocking here and there were luxurious hotels, humbler inns and an elegant promenade. So the short answer is: it was called Blackpool long before anyone thought of building a tower or producing a stick of rock.

Burnley

If you have been paying attention to the recurring elements in names throughout this book, you might think that this meant 'woodland clearing by a stream' and you would be half right. In fact, it was originally 'woodland clearing on the river Brūn', with Brun being Old English for 'brown'. People seem always to have been very eager to tell you if a place was muddy (see BUDE, SLOUGH and YARMOUTH, to name but three), but if it meant that you couldn't drink the water this could have been a matter of life and death.

Carnforth

Famed as the setting for *Brief Encounter*, Carnforth's name doesn't live up to its romantic associations – unless you are an ornithologist. As in other places in the north of England (see, for example, HORS-FORTH), the *–forth* bit means 'ford' and in this case it was probably 'ford frequented by cranes or herons'.

Clitheroe

What remains of Clitheroe Castle, built by the Normans and rendered unusable by the Parliamentarians during the Civil War (they shot a hole through one of its sides), stands – as most castles do – on a hill, and it is this hill that gives the town its name. The origins are either Old Celtic or Old English and mean 'hill with loose stones'.

Cow Ark

Ark in this sense is found only in the north of England and means a temporary shelter, for the cowherd rather than the cows. He would have needed it in this isolated place, which was cut off from the outside world for three weeks during the harsh winter of 2009–10.

Dalton

This is a common name – there is a fistful of Daltons across northern England – for the simple reason that it is a common concept: 'farmstead or village in a valley'. The only one with an unusual addition is Dalton Piercy, near HARTLEPOOL, which is named after the Percy family, famous in these parts during the Wars of the Roses and in the Shakespearian history plays (their most famous son was the rebel Hotspur in *Henry IV Part I*).

Darwen

This has the same derivation as the various rivers called Derwent – 'place with an abundance of oak trees'. See MATLOCK.

Fleetwood

How can a wood be fleet or swift you may be wondering. Well, it can't. The Old English *flēot* meant 'pool or stream' (see FLEET), so Fleetwood should mean 'wood by a pool or stream'. In fact, Fleetwood, Lancs, was a nineteenth-century 'new town', conceived by local landowner and PRESTON MP Peter Hesketh Fleetwood. In addition to providing housing and amenities for the none-too-affluent, Peter hoped that his namesake town would be a vital seaport, transferring goods that had come from the south by rail to steamships that would take them on to Scotland. Sadly, this part of the plan was scuppered when the rail link between London and Scotland was completed in the 1850s, with the town still in its infancy.

Garstang

This weird-looking name is Scandinavian in origin and means 'spear post', probably as an indication of a meeting place. It appears as Cherestanc in the Domesday Book (another instance, perhaps, of the Normans doing their best but not quite getting it), but something nearer to the modern version – which is more faithful to the

Scandinavian original – had reasserted itself by the end of the twelfth century.

Lancaster

Lancaster sits on the river Lune, which gives it the first part of its name and probably means 'pure' or 'healthy'. We don't know a great deal about the Roman settlement that produced the *–caster* element (see the Introduction, page 11), but we know that it existed and had a public bath house. The Normans built a castle here, but Lancaster really comes into its own with John of Gaunt, a son of Edward III who in 1362 became the first Duke of Lancaster. He was one of the greatest landowners and – when he became regent for his ten-year-old nephew, Richard II – arguably the most powerful man in England. From him sprang the House of Lancaster that became the 'red rose' side in the Wars of the Roses. Lancaster's involvement rests solely in the name, however: although the wars continued for thirty years, none of the battles was fought in Lancashire.

Lytham St Anne's

The ending of Lytham does not, for once, mean 'farmstead or village'; in fact, the word has to be taken as a whole and means 'place at the sand dunes'. There was a Benedictine priory here throughout the Middle Ages (bizarrely under the jurisdiction of the not-exactly-just-down-the-road DURHAM Cathedral), but apart from that Lytham remained a small and isolated place until decent roads and a railway came along in the nineteenth century. By that time, people were aware of the health benefits of sea bathing (see SOUTHPORT and BLACKPOOL) and coastal villages were being developed as 'resorts'. This is where St Anne's comes into the story. It is not a village that has grown up round a church, but a Victorian planned town, specifically designed to attract visitors (the famous golf course was added only ten years later, when somebody realised that those sand dunes had to be good for something). Among other amenities, of course, the new town had to have a church, so St Anne's was built as recently as 1873. The two villages still regard themselves as separate entities but are officially part of the same conurbation. Their part of Lancashire is called the Fylde, which comes from the Old Scandinavian for 'field, plain' and refers to the flat alluvial plain of the Fylde Peninsula. The river that marks the southern boundary of the Fylde is the Ribble, which means, aptly enough, 'boundary'.

Morecambe

It's not every seaside town that has a comedian named after it – in fact, this may be the only one. Eric Morecambe, whose real surname was Bartholomew, was born in Morecambe and took his stage name from it. But the town itself, like so many, takes its name from its geography: Morecambe means 'curved inlet', which is a fair description of Morecambe Bay. The name is an ancient one, derived from Old Celtic, and the bay is marked on Ptolemy's map as Moricambe estuary. The town, however, is of comparatively recent origin: like many places along the Lancashire coast it blossomed when improved transport links, the popularity of sea air and sea bathing for health reasons, and the invention of holidays for the masses came together in the nineteenth century. A gazetteer of 1887 records it as 'conjoint with Poulton…a rising watering-place, with sea-bathing facilities for summer visitors, and with aquarium and gardens, and other attractions'. Then in 1889 Poulton ('farmstead by a pool or creek'), Morecambe and two other nearby villages were officially joined to create one promotable holiday destination.

Nelson

Another 'new town', formed as a mill town in the early nineteenth century by combining two existing villages, Great and Little Marsden (whose names mean 'boundary valley'). When the railway arrived in 1849 the powers that be realised that there was already a railway station called Marsden in Yorkshire – close enough to cause confusion. Nelson's station was therefore named after the local hotel which, like lots of pubs, had taken the name of Horatio Nelson in a wave of hero worship after the admiral's death at the Battle of Trafalgar in 1805.

Pendle

Penn was the Celtic for 'head' and came to be used for 'hill' (see PENRYN); *–dle* comes from the Old English *hyl*, meaning 'hill'. To call the local peak Pendle Hill is therefore doubly silly. Mind you, it sits in the Forest of Pendle, which a local walking guide describes as 'characterised by windswept moorland, rocky outcrops, deep-sided valleys (cloughs) and rolling fields'. Not much of a forest, then. For other tautologies of this nature, see the box *Say That Again?* overleaf.

Preston

Most places whose names begin with *Prest–* are associated with priests, and Preston is 'priests' farmstead'. The name appears in the Domesday Book but the connection with priests is older than that: a link with Ripon and its bishop, later canonised as St Wilfrid, goes back to about AD 700. In addition to a dozen places called Preston, other 'priestly' towns include Prescot on Merseyside and Prescott in Devon (both 'priests' cottages'), Prestbury in Cheshire ('priests' manor') and Prestwick in Northumberland ('priests' dwelling or farm'). But the most exciting is Prestbury in Gloucestershire (also 'priests' manor'), said by some to be the most haunted village in England. The hooded figure of a black abbot roams St Mary's churchyard, normally at Easter, Christmas and on All Saints' Day, but also sometimes after funerals. In addition he is seen

SAY THAT AGAIN?

One of the signs that a place name has become part of the scenery, as it were, is that its meaning is duplicated, indicating that the person who added the second part didn't realise what the first part meant. Avon, for example, comes from the Celtic word for 'river', so it has always been unnecessary to refer to 'the river Avon'. Throughout England we find names where this happens, and sometimes not only once but twice. BEACHY HEAD, GRASMERE and PENDLE are tautological names that have their own entries; others include:

Bredon, Worcestershire, combines an Old Celtic word for 'hill' with the more familiar *–don*, from the Old English for 'hill'. To refer to Bredon Hill compounds the tautology. The same applies to the Mendips, in Somerset, whose name already means 'upland hill'. Within the Mendips there is a peak called Pen Hill, which again says the same thing twice.

Canvey Island, Essex. Canvey on its own means 'island associated with the family or followers of a man named Cana', but that had been forgotten by the time a directory of Essex described 'Canvey Island' in 1848. Until the seventeenth century it was in fact five islands, but these were linked as a result of land reclamation by the Dutch 'water engineer' Cornelius Vermuyden, who was also largely responsible for the draining of the Fens. **Mersea Island**, also in Essex, is a similar tautology: despite the difference in spelling, the *–ey* of Canvey and the *–ea* of Mersea come from the same root and Mersea means 'island in the pool'.

Cheadle, Cheshire, combines the Celtic for 'wood' with the Old English for 'wood'. Using a more recognisable word for *wood*, Cheetwood in Lancashire and Chetwoode in Berkshire do the same.

> **Cheddar**, Somerset, means 'gorge' or 'ravine', so Cheddar Gorge is a duplication of effort.
>
> **Ferryhill**, Durham, is what pretentious French teachers used to call a *faux ami*. *Ferry* in this instance has nothing to do with a ferry boat (if it did you might wonder what it was doing on a hill); it comes from the Old English *fergen*, 'wooded hill'. Having been Feregenne in the tenth century it had become Ferye on the Hill by the fourteenth.

at an old cottage whose front garden was once a monks' burial ground. Scoff if you dare.

Rawtenstall

An 1870s gazetteer describes Rawtenstall as 'not long ago, a secluded village; consists now of regular and well-built streets; is a seat of petty sessions, and a polling-place; carries on cotton and woollen manufactures; and has a r. station with telegraph, a post-office under Manchester, a hotel, a mechanics' institution, a church, four dissenting chapels, a Roman Catholic chapel, and four large public schools'. Not bad for a place that started life as 'rough cow-pasture'. The Old English *rūh* from which the first syllable comes is the source of the modern word *rough*.

CUMBRIA

This came into existence in 1974, when it absorbed the former counties of Westmorland, Cumberland and part of Lancashire. Westmorland was 'the home of the people west of the moor' (that is, the Yorkshire moors), while Cumberland and the older form

Cumbria trace their ancestry back to the ancient conflict between the Celts and the various invaders from Roman times onwards. Cumberland was 'the land of the Cumbrians' and Cumbria is a Latinised form of it. The Cumbrians, of course, were the Celts or Britons; the word is related to the modern Welsh word for Wales, Cymru.

Ambleside

This name is more complicated than it looks, because it is made up of three Old Scandinavian words: *á*, meaning 'river', *melr*, 'sandbank' and *saetr*, 'summer pasture'. So the sum of it is 'summer pasture by the river sandbank'. An eleventh-century spelling, Amelseta, is close to the original elements; by the 1390s this had evolved into Amylsyde and by 1671 to Amblesyde. The practice of moving animals on to higher ground in summer to make use of pasture that wasn't available at other times of the year is thought to have been brought to this part of the country by the Norsemen; they are also credited with the introduction of the hardy Herdwick sheep that are now considered indigenous to the Lake District and make use of the highest grazing on the fells.

Aspatria

This is 'Patrick's ash tree' and refers to St Patrick, best known as the patron saint of Ireland but in fact a native of Cumbria. He was sold into slavery and sent to Ireland as a youth, but escaped and travelled widely in Cumbria, converting pagans and baptising them at, among other places, the holy well at Aspatria. The well still exists, in the churchyard of St Kentigern's. There is no record of an ash tree going back to Patrick's time (the fifth century), but as 250 years would be a decent lifespan for an ash, this is disappointing without being surprising.

Barrow-in-Furness

Barrow is a mixture of Old Celtic and Old Scandinavian, meaning 'island promontory'; Furness, the name of the surrounding district, is also Old Scandinavian and means 'headland by the rump-shaped island'. The island of Walney, just off the Furness peninsula, is today longer and thinner than most rumps, but perhaps the sea has eroded its shape over the last nine hundred years. Walney itself may mean 'island of the killer whales' or 'island of shivering sands' – either of them surely a more enticing description than 'rump-shaped'. Another place that has '-in-Furness' affixed to its name is Broughton, which means 'farmstead by a brook'.

Bassenthwaite

Thwaite, which crops up in a number of names in areas of Scandinavian influence, means 'clearing or meadow' and Bassenthwaite once belonged to a family called Bastun. Other *–thwaite* names tend to be of a practical nature, reflecting the sort of thing a medieval settlement might do with a clearing or meadow: grow flax in it (Linthwaite), grow oats (Haverthwaite), keep calves (Calthwaite), build a church (Curthwaite). More evocative is Armathwaite – 'clearing of the hermit'. There was a Benedictine nunnery here from the eleventh century and the name Ermithwait is found in the thirteenth, so this probably applies to the nuns living in seclusion.

Carlisle

You have to use your imagination a bit here, because Carlisle evolved from the fourth-century Luguvalium – not obvious at first sight. This was the Roman name for their settlement, and it came from an Old Celtic personal name which in turn derived from Lug, the god of skills (see LUTON). The earliest Roman fortress in the area was made of timber and has long since vanished; the first stone one was built in the second century at the western end of Hadrian's Wall, the massive fortification designed to mark and defend the northernmost boundary of the Roman Empire. But as we know (if we have read the introduction to this book), the Romans abandoned Britain by the fifth century and left the way clear for successive waves of invaders. The north-west of England became part of the kingdom of Rheged, whose inhabitants spoke Cumbric, a now-vanished Celtic language closely related to Welsh. When they described a city as fortified, therefore, they didn't tack *–caster* on the end as the Saxons did, but – using their own approach to word order – put the Celtic word *caer* at the front (this is the same *caer* as is found in modern Welsh names such as Caerphilly and is mentioned under CHESTER). Thus by the twelfth century Luguvalium had dropped its Latin ending, taken on a Celtic beginning and become Carleol. From that to the modern spelling is but a step, but it still means 'place associated with someone named after the god Lug'.

Cleator Moor

Another name that reflects the importance of medicinal plants (see, for example, ARUNDEL and DULWICH), this was 'hill pasture where burdock grows'. Burdock was used in the treatment of coughs and catarrh, skin complaints, digestive problems and arthritis, so knowing where to find a ready supply was the medieval equivalent of having the address of the all-night pharmacy.

Cockermouth

Cocker was Old Celtic for 'crooked river' and you would think that Cockermouth would be at the mouth of it. Certainly that is what the name means, but in fact the Cocker doesn't have a mouth: what happens at Cockermouth is that the Cocker flows into the larger and longer Derwent (for the meaning of which, see MATLOCK). It was this handy position at the confluence of the rivers that led the Romans to establish a camp here and use it as back-up for their efforts to keep the Scots safely on the other side of Hadrian's Wall (see CARLISLE). In fact, the Roman camp was just up the road at Papcastle, whose name means 'Roman camp occupied by a hermit'. The only known hermit in the area was the man later canonised as St Herbert; according to Bede, he was a friend and disciple of St Cuthbert, Bishop of LINDISFARNE. Herbert lived on the island now named after him, in Derwentwater, and after his death his cell there became a place of pilgrimage. But Papcastle is about 25 km across the fells from Derwentwater, so it is a matter of speculation whether Herbert went to the Roman camp in winter when an island in the middle of a lake was just too cold and damp to bear, or whether another hermit was squatting at Papcastle and has vanished without trace from the history books.

Egremont

In the midst of all the Scandinavian and Celtic influence, here is a name that comes from the French, *aigre mont*, meaning 'sharply pointed hill'. Although the Danes had a settlement here, the Scots took over after the Danes left; the Norman (and therefore French) influence starts in about 1092 when William II decided to claim it back. The castle whose ruins still dominate the town dates from shortly after this period.

Grange-over-Sands

'Grange' is a outlying farm, generally a place used to store grain, and often belonging to a religious order. In this case, it belonged to Cartmel Priory, which dates back more than eight hundred years and, as the rest of its name suggests, overlooks the sands of Morecambe Bay.

Grasmere

This is probably a tautological name, as the *gras* bit means 'lake with grassy shores' and *mere*, 'lake' was a later addition for the benefit of those who had forgotten. Nearby Windermere is less poetic: it is simply 'lake belonging to a man named Vinandr', while Rydal Water, which lies between the two more famous lakes, was 'valley where rye is grown'. Presumably to feed Mr Vinandr, or possibly his livestock.

Helvellyn

This probably derives from the ancient Cumbric language (see CARLISLE) and means 'yellow moor'. The moorland here is actually no more or less yellow than it is anywhere else in the area, but maybe the sun fell on it in a certain way on the day in 1577 when the name was first recorded.

Kendal

This name has undergone quite a journey to reach its current form. It was originally an early version of Kirkby – 'village with a church'. By the eleventh century this had become Kircabikendala, the addition indicating that it was 'in the valley [dale] of the river Kent'. (Kent in this instance is not related to the county name but is probably from the same unknown Old Celtic source as the Kennet – see HUNGERFORD.) However, a name as long as Kircabikendala was doomed from the start and by the fifteenth century mention of the church had been dropped to leave Kendale.

Keswick

'Farm where cheese is made or sold'. There was a market in Keswick from 1276, about the time when the name is first recorded, and cheese markets continued until the early twentieth century. The other Keswicks in England – there are two in Norfolk and an East Keswick near Leeds – were also originally 'cheese towns'. See the box *Farming Country 2*, page 139.

Millom

This odd-looking name means nothing more than 'place at the mills'. It's a dative plural. You may not know or care what that means, but it is the reason the name isn't Mill or Miln.

Penrith

Opinions vary on this one, but let's start with the aspects where the experts are in agreement. One, the name comes from Cumbric, the Celtic language spoken in Cumbria up to about the eleventh century (see CARLISLE). Two, the *pen–* element is the common Celtic one meaning 'hill' or 'chief' (see PENRYN). But which comes first, the adjective or the noun? If the adjective goes before the noun, as it regularly does in Modern English, then the name would mean 'chief ford', with the second part coming from another Cumbric word. But, say some, that's not the way Cumbric worked. Cumbric put the adjective *after* the noun, making it much more likely that *pen–* means 'hill' and that *–rith* means 'red', as in REDRUTH. Additional arguments in favour of this latter explanation include the fact that there is a red sandstone hill on the site of the earliest settlement, while the nearest ford is 2 km away. Also, there is a village called Penruddock nearby, and this could easily mean 'little red hill'. But, as so often, it's easy to be dogmatic but impossible to be sure.

Scafell Pike

Fell comes from the Old Scandinavian for 'hill' or 'upland moor', so is really just a Lake District alternative to 'hill'. *Pike* is related to *peak*, and *Sca–* comes from a word meaning 'summer pasture'. Which all adds up to 'peak of the hill with the summer pasture'. But you may have noticed that Scafell looks nothing like AMBLE-SIDE, which also has 'summer pasture' hidden in its name. If so, let me reassure you that the sources are two different words: the one relevant to Scafell may have indicated that the pastures were level once you got up to them.

Sedbergh

This ending is nothing to do with a fortified place; it means a hill and is related to the modern German word *berg*. Sedbergh means 'flat-topped hill' and if you choose to pay it a visit you will see that the hill is still there, and still has a flat top.

Skiddaw

Too big and imposing to be left out, Skiddaw unfortunately has nothing very satisfactory to say about its name. One suggestion is that it comes from the Old Scandinavian meaning 'overhanging hill', another that it is Cumbric for 'shoulders'. Skiddaw's overall shape makes either explanation a possibility, but there seems to be no consensus.

Unthank

Now this is pleasing: it really does mean 'thankless' or 'unthankful'. So it is either land occupied by squatters, who forgot to say thank you (never mind pay rent), or land that was unrewarding to cultivate. There are several other places with this name: of the one in Northumberland, an 1870s gazetteer wrote (and this is the entry in its entirety), 'UNTHANK, a township in Alnham parish, Northumberland; 6½ miles NNW of Rothbury. Acres, 172. Pop, 37. Houses, 7.' Its author had doubtless found his visit there a thankless task.

14

❦

NORTH-EAST ENGLAND

Early English scholars, start here. This is the home of the monasteries, the great centres of Christian learning without which we would know almost nothing about anything between the Roman period and Alfred the Great. It's also a place where the Vikings wreaked a goodly portion of their havoc and where, in the following centuries, border clashes between England and Scotland were everyday occurrences. And there it all is, quietly recorded in the place names…

DURHAM AND TEESSIDE

The southern part of this region is made up of an ancient county and a short-lived county whose name is now used in a looser sense for the areas on either side of the river Tees. The boundaries of Yorkshire to the south and Northumberland to the north are clearly defined: this section covers the area in between.

Barnard Castle

This doesn't mean anything more complicated than 'Bernard's castle', but Bernard de Balliol and his successors are worth a line or two. Bernard's father Guy had 'come over with the Conqueror' (posh people continued to claim that their ancestors had done that for about seven hundred years) and had remained in favour with his son, William II, who gave him the land on which the castle stands. It was Bernard who built it, starting in about 1112, and it became a powerful stronghold while Bernard fought both for and against successive Scottish kings. John de Balliol, in whose name Balliol College Oxford was founded, was probably a grandson. From the thirteenth century the castle and lands changed hands on a number of occasions, according to the whim of the monarch. Its last great contribution to the history books came in 1569, when it was besieged by an army rebelling against Elizabeth I, with the intention of putting Mary Queen of Scots on the throne. Although those holding the castle were eventually starved out, the eleven days' delay was crucial in allowing Elizabeth's forces to get their act together: the 'Great Rebellion' was suppressed. Thereafter the castle was allowed to fall into ruin. By that time, however, it had come into the possession of the Dukes of Cleveland, who took their title from the surrounding district: it means 'area where there are hills or cliffs', with the same derivation as the modern *cliff*.

Bishop Auckland

The eleventh-century name for this place was Alclit, which probably originated in the Old Celtic for 'rock or hill above the Clyde'. For this to make sense, Clyde ('cleansing river') has to be an earlier name for the river now called Gaunless, a tributary of the Wear. Most experts think this is the case, though there is also a suggestion that Alclit was a misspelling of Aclit and therefore connected with oaks (see ACTON). Whatever the 'mists of time' origins, some centuries later the name became confused with the Old Scandinavian *auka*, 'to increase' (related to modern *eke*). In that language Auckland meant 'extra land' and that is the spelling that has stuck.

Moving on to more solid ground, there is no doubt that the bishop in question is the Bishop of DURHAM, to whom the land was given by King Cnut in 1020 and who had a hunting lodge built here. This bolthole has grown over the years into Auckland Castle and has been the bishop's official residence since 1832. The name Gaunless comes from the Old Scandinavian for 'useless, profitless' – perhaps because the river was too sluggish to power a mill, or too dirty to support fish life. I like to think of this spoken in a dismissive, contemptuous tone, meaning 'that waste of space of a river'. And, to tie up the last loose end, Wear probably means 'winding, bendy', which is an apt description of the river's meandering course.

Chester-le-Street

This combines two common souvenirs of Roman times, the fortress and the road. The name Ceastre doesn't appear until the twelfth century (much later than, say, LEICESTER), but we know that the Romans had a fort called Concangis here from about AD 160. It was situated above the unnamed road that runs north to NEWCASTLE UPON TYNE, on a piece of high ground that made it easy to monitor passing traffic. The designation 'le Street', to distinguish this place from CHESTER in Cheshire, is first recorded in the fifteenth century. Despite the recentness of the name, the history of the settlement goes back a lot further: it was the first place the monks of LINDISFARNE settled on the mainland when Viking raids caused them to abandon their 'holy island' in the eighth century. They built a minster to house the bones of St Cuthbert (which they had, inevitably, brought with them) and it was here that the Lindisfarne Gospels were translated from Latin – a landmark in ecclesiastical history, as it was the first ever rendering of the gospels into English. (When I say English, it was actually Northumbrian – tenth-century Geordie – so more or less impenetrable to the modern non-scholarly eye, but a big step forward at the time.)

Durham

In the eleventh century this was Dunholme, which gives a clearer idea of its meaning: *dūn* is the Old English for 'hill', found in many many names featuring the modern spellings *don* or *down*; *holme* is Scandinavian for 'island or promontory' (see OLDHAM). Put them together and you have a fitting description of the rock on which Durham's castle and cathedral sit. Like almost every other place name, this evolved over the centuries, becoming at one time Dunhelm, the name still used by the Bishop of Durham. The *r* had appeared by the end of the twelfth century to give something very close to the modern spelling. This is the result of what one authority called 'the liquidity of the liquids'. 'Liquid' in this context means a flowing sort of consonant, particularly *l* or *r* but also *m* and *n*. The way these sounds are produced makes them readily interchangeable or liable to be dropped; two examples of this phenomenon (*n* becomes *r*, *l* disappears altogether) can be seen in the change from Dunholme to Durham. Or so the phoneticists say.

Hartlepool

Bede calls this place Heruteu, 'deer's island', though the headland on which the old town sits is a peninsula nowadays. The *-eu* is a variant on the *-ey* ending, meaning 'island', common throughout the country (see RAMSEY, SELSEY and many more) and *herut* soon evolved into *hart*, with the same meaning as the modern word. The *pool* was added in the twelfth century, referring to the substantial bay that is partly enclosed by the peninsula. Anyway, it means 'peninsula by the bay where deer are seen'.

Peterlee

Named after a man called Peter Lee. What could be simpler? He was a local miners' leader and this was a 'new town', created after the Second World War to improve the housing conditions of miners.

Pity Me

There is a (surely apocryphal) story about the monks escaping from LINDISFARNE after the Viking raid, carrying St Cuthbert's coffin with them. Weary towards the end of their journey to DURHAM, they accidentally dropped the coffin and the saint's corpse cried out, 'Pity me!' Much more likely is that the name was deliberately chosen to be spoken with a heavy sigh by the person who had to work this unproductive land.

Spennymoor

This obviously refers to a sort of moor, probably an enclosed one, either fenced or surrounded by hedges. One early spelling, however, has it as Spendingmore and it seems a shame that this didn't catch on.

Stockton-on-Tees

The *stock* in this name takes us back to outlying farmsteads or hamlets (see the box *Farming Country 2*, page 139), so this is probably 'farmstead belonging to an outlying hamlet'. Like many rivers, the Tees has an ancient name, probably meaning 'surging'.

Tow Law

The ending –*law* or –*low* (as in HARLOW) means 'rounded hill' and in this case Tow comes from a supposed Old English word *tot*, meaning 'lookout'. Most places beginning *Tot–* come from personal names (Tottenham and Totnes are two examples), but the lookout theme recurs in Totland on the Isle of Wight, Tostock in Suffolk and Great and Little Totham in Essex. The name of Tow Law gives a clue as to its location: on an exposed site some three hundred metres above sea level, with a good view of anyone who happened to be passing. Although the name derives from Old English, suggesting the existence of a settlement in the first millennium AD, there was only one house here at the time of the 1841 census. Then coal and iron works moved in, so that by 1851 the population was almost two thousand. It peaked at just over five thousand in 1881, but with the demise of its core industries it is now back to 1851 levels.

NORTHUMBERLAND AND TYNE & WEAR

The county of Tyne & Wear was created in 1974, but the name is used in a not very specific way to designate the area around these two rivers. Northumberland is of ancient provenance, although it is only a small part of the ancient kingdom of Northumbria, 'the land north of the Humber', which once stretched as far as the Forth, north of Edinburgh.

Alnwick

This is 'farm or trading place on the river Aln', and Aln is yet another of those Old Celtic river names whose meaning has been lost. But never mind that. You can forgive a place for having a run-of-the-mill name when it has a castle as cool as this one. It was built in the eleventh century by a family called de Vescis, acquired by the Bishop of DURHAM (who seems to have been more of an estate agent than a cleric for much of medieval history) and sold in 1309 to a member of the Percy family. The Percys, as you will know if you have seen Shakespeare's *Henry IV Part I* or read the entry for DALTON, became Earls and later Dukes of Northumberland and had a lot of clout in this part of the world for a long time. The Hotspur Tower, named after the most famous of the Percy family and once part of the walls that enclosed the town, still forms an arch across the main street and makes any motorist wish they had left the car in the park and ride.

Bamburgh

Another fortified town, recalling this area's – shall we say military? – past. This was initially 'Bebba's town', named after the wife of Æthelfrith, first king of a united Northumbria. The area had previously been divided into two kingdoms, Bernicia and Deira. Æthelfrith's grandfather, Ida the Flame-bearer (didn't they have great names?), ruled Bernicia, a kingdom centred around the Tyne and the Wear but with expansionist ideas. Ida established his capital at Bamburgh in 547 and was the first to fortify it; it was his grandson's conquest of neighbouring Deira in 603 that united most of northern England. St Oswald (see OSWESTRY) was one of Æthelfrith's sons – he brought peace (and Christianity) to the area, and it is in Bamburgh that the legend of his hand not decaying arises. Sitting down to dinner with St Aidan, Oswald felt the need to give his food to the starving beggars in the street outside; Aidan, deeply moved, took Oswald's right hand and said, 'May this hand never perish.' When Oswald was killed and his body parts scattered to the four winds, his head and hands were brought back to a shrine in Bamburgh – which rather puts paid to the story that they are in Bardney, but so be it.

Berwick-upon-Tweed

Berwick means 'barley or corn farm' – it would have been an outlying part of an estate, where grain was grown and stored. Tweed means 'powerful river'. But what Berwick is famous for is not grain, but being transferred from England to Scotland and back again through centuries of border skirmishes. At the end of the twelfth century Richard I even sold the town to the Scots in order to raise money for his next crusade. His brother and successor John fought successfully to get it back; two generations later Edward I fortified it to keep the Scots out, but it kept changing hands until 1482, when it finally officially became part of England. Even so, it retained the status of a 'free burgh' until 1855, which meant that it had to be mentioned separately – as part of neither England nor Scotland – in Acts of Parliament. A more interesting claim to fame than that people used to grow grain here, I feel.

Blyth

This is a rather sweet name: it means 'blithe', in the positive sense of 'cheerful, gentle', rather than 'heedless, regardless of the consequences'. The town is named after its river, and the name evokes an image of a river flowing gently along, getting on with the pleasant business of being a river and making everyone's life a little more cheery as it passes by.

Corbridge

This was originally 'the bridge at Corstopitum', Corstopitum being a Roman fort in the vicinity; it was used as a supply depot for the armies building and guarding Hadrian's Wall and was called Corchester for a while after the Romans departed. There was a ford across the Tyne here long before a bridge existed, which is why the site was chosen. The first known bridge was built in 1235, but as the name is recorded nearly two hundred years before that, another – presumably timber, certainly perishable – bridge or bridges must have preceded it: this was for many centuries the only place between CARLISLE and NEWCASTLE where you could cross the Tyne. What the original name meant is unclear, although Ptolemy mentions a town called Coria belonging to the Otalini or Otadini tribe and Corstopitum may be a Latinised corruption of those elements. Tyne is easier: it means 'flowing' or just 'river'.

Gateshead

Not a gate but a goat: this means 'headland frequented by wild goats'. Bede suggests that the goats might have been involved in some pagan ritual; Camden thinks it's more likely that there was a pub called the Goat's Head in the area. Or, hey, there may just have been a few goats wandering about.

Haltwhistle

This sounds as if it should have come into being with the arrival of the railways, but in fact it dates back to at least the thirteenth century. *Twistle* derives from the Old English for 'junction of two streams' (or 'fork in two streams', depending on whether you think of them as coming or going), and *halt* comes either from the French *haut* meaning 'high', or from the Old English for 'head', here used in the sense of 'hill'. In either case, this is a settlement on high ground, above the point where a smaller stream meets the South Tyne.

Hetton-le-Hole

The twelfth-century spelling Heppedun brings us nearer the meaning of this name: first, it is not a farmstead (*tūn*) but a hill (*dūn*); second, it is a place where hips or berries (probably brambles) grow. The addition le-Hole seems to indicate that the hill sat in a hollow, which is, on the face of it, daft, but in fact differentiates this village from the now much smaller Hetton-le-Hill. The two were subdivisions of a medieval parish, one of them further up the hill than the other, and the larger settlement grew up in the lower and more sheltered parts. And just to reinforce the fact that two very similar names can mean completely different things, Hetton in Yorkshire is recorded in the Domesday Book as Hetune, and means 'farmstead on a heath'.

Hexham

'Homestead or village of the warrior'. This is a much reduced form of the seventh-century Hagustaldes ham, which shows the origins more clearly. *Hagustald* meant specifically a younger son who was granted land outside the central settlement, which would of course have been inherited by his elder brother.

Jarrow

Distinguished by being the birthplace of the Venerable Bede, this has the far from distinguished meaning 'home of the marsh people'. However, its history is undeniably venerable: a monastery, dedicated to St Paul, was built here in the 680s, less than ten years after a brother monastery, dedicated to St Peter, had been built at the mouth of the Wear, giving rise to a town that added all these factors together and came up with the name Monkswearmouth. Bede entered St Peter's at the age of seven and died at St Paul's in 735, at the age of sixty-two, having spent his entire life at one or other of these establishments. He tells us that they were built 'on the understanding that the two houses should be bound together by the one spirit of peace and harmony' and, remarkably, in an area known for its little local difficulties (see, for example, BERWICK-UPON-TWEED), this seems to have happened. Certainly Bede was able to write his great works here and give us much more insight than we would otherwise have had into the history of Britain from the beginning of time to the eighth century. Well done, Jarrow, for all your marshiness.

Lindisfarne

Lindsey is an old name for the northern part of Lincolnshire, probably deriving from a local tribe. Lindisfarne is thought to owe its name to people who travelled here from Lindsey, –farne coming from either the Old English for 'traveller' or the Old Irish for 'domain'. Since the twelfth century it has also been known as Holy Island, because of the monastery that was founded here in the seventh and its associations with, among others, St Oswald and St Cuthbert, whose names and legends crop up elsewhere in this book (see BAMBURGH, CHESTER-LE-STREET and OSWESTRY).

Morpeth

Who would have thought that this gentle border town would have one of the most exciting and yet one of the most frustrating names in the book? It almost certainly means 'path where a murder or murders took place', but no one seems to know why. It may well have been the scene of many bloody encounters during Anglo-Scottish skirmishes over the centuries, but there is no record of a specific murder. Even Camden doesn't speculate on it: he confesses, 'Nothing I have of any antiquity to say of this towne but that in the yeere of Christ 1215 it was set on fire by the inhabitants themselves in spitefull malice to King John.' A fascinating snippet on its own, but no help to us, as the name Morpeth is recorded well before that, in 1138.

Newbiggin-by-the-Sea

Bigging is Middle English for 'building' or 'house' and there are several places in northern England with this name. We know that the Danes renamed an existing settlement when they landed here in 875, but what the new building was is not on record. Nor is there any more useful information to be found about the Newbiggins in Cumbria and Durham. The name of the famous airfield Biggin Hill in Kent may be from the same source, but if it were it would be the only example of this word in the south; it is more likely to come from a personal name.

Newcastle upon Tyne

Not hard to interpret, but worth a mention nonetheless. This was historically an important crossing point on the Tyne. The Romans constructed a bridge and called the fort built to guard it Pons Aelius, 'Hadrian's bridge', Hadrian's full name having been Publius Aelius Hadrianus. A bit further west was the most substantial of several Roman sites in the area; the Anglo-Saxons called it Beonnam-Wall

NOT ROCKET SCIENCE

In the place-names minefield, it is a huge relief to come across some that are completely self-explanatory. NEWCASTLE is one; others include: **Hedge End**, Hampshire, was once even more explicit: Cutt Hedge End indicated that the hedge was clipped.

Ivybridge, Devon, and **Ivychurch**, Kent, were covered in ivy.

Longparish, Hampshire, and several places called **Longtown** or **Longton** are all long.

Loudwater, Buckinghamshire, is named after the stream which flows – noisily – nearby.

The newness of places such as **Newbury**, Berkshire, **Newmarket**, Suffolk, **Newhaven**, Sussex, and **Newquay**, Cornwall, is relative – the first two are both recorded before 1200, whereas the new harbour at Newhaven was built in the sixteenth century and the new quay at Newquay in the fifteenth. The various **Newports** scattered around the country are less self-explanatory, in that the *–port* generally means 'market town' (see LANGPORT) rather than 'port'.

Northchurch, Hertfordshire, **Northfield**, West Midlands, **Northwood**, Greater London, and loads of other places beginning north, east, west and south were originally to the north, east, west or south of…something.

Redhill, Surrey, is not a hill so much as a slope, but one with red soil.

Sevenoaks, Kent, is 'the place where seven oaks once grew', though sadly there is now no record of them.

Street, Somerset: as in STRATFORD-UPON-AVON and other places mentioned under that entry, this means a Roman road. Or street.

Whitchurch, Hampshire and Shropshire, and other 'white' place names often indicate that the building was made of stone, so was more substantial, more important and altogether posher than the rest of the village. Places called **Whitehaven** or **Whitfield** had white, chalky rocks or soil.

It's perhaps a little unfair to include **Woodbridge**, Suffolk, in this box because its meaning isn't entirely obvious. Although the *wood* means 'wood' and the *bridge* means 'bridge', it is unclear whether the name refers to a wooden bridge or to a bridge near a wood. However, lots of other places beginning with *wood–* are more straightforward: **Woodend**, **Woodford**, **Woodland**, **Woodleigh** ('clearing in a wood'), etc. Even with more complicated names such as **Woodmansterne** in Surrey ('thorn tree by the boundary of the wood') and **Woodplumpton** in Lancashire ('farmstead in the wood where plum trees grow'), *wood* almost always means, comfortingly, 'wood'.

('within [Hadrian's] wall'). The name stuck: Benwell is now a western suburb of Newcastle. As for the castle, like most castles it appeared in the Norman period. William the Conqueror met with a lot of resistance in the north-east in the years immediately following the Conquest and he built castles all over the area to assert his authority. By the early 1070s he had started work in YORK, Richmond and DURHAM, so Newcastle, begun in 1080, was probably regarded as 'newer' than any of those three. That castle, made of wood, was replaced in the twelfth century by Henry II. However, the name Newcastle pre-dates this, so the 'new castle' was not Henry's stone one.

Ponteland

Unlike PONTEFRACT, this isn't a Latin or Celtic reference to a bridge: it's named after the river Pont, which means 'valley'. So Ponteland is 'cultivated land by the river in the valley', the 'river' element coming from the Old English *ēa*, 'stream' (see NUNEATON), which is tucked away in the middle of the name.

South Shields

This is *shield* in the sense of a shelter or temporary building, in this case a fisherman's hut. The name does not appear until the thirteenth century, but before then there had been a Roman settlement here, followed by a seventh-century nunnery dedicated to St Hilda (whose name survives in the present church built on the same site). After the nunnery was raided by the Vikings in the ninth century, the town's next claim to fame was as a fishing port – hence the accommodation that gave it its name. Fishermen's huts spread north along the coast, so that by 1313 Shields had to call itself South Shields to distinguish it from North Shields on the opposite bank of the Tyne.

Sunderland

The core meaning of this name is not disputed: it is an estate that is detached – sundered – from something else. An element of doubt arises when you ask, 'Why?' 'Set aside for some special purpose' is one interpretation, though it has also been suggested that the city grew up from two early settlements 'sundered' by the river Wear. If this is true, the two settlements were Bishopswearmouth, the property of the Bishop of DURHAM, and Monkswearmouth (see JARROW).

Wallsend

The reference is to Hadrian's Wall, whose easternmost point this marks. The name dates from the eleventh century, but there was a

Roman fort here long before that. Hadrian's Wall didn't in fact end at Wallsend; having run in a more or less straight west-east line across from the Solway Firth, it now turned south and extended a further kilometre or two, as far as the Tyne. There was no ford at that point, so the river and the wall between them would have been enough to keep out all but the most determined Scots.

Washington

With the greatest possible respect to any American readers, this isn't a very exciting name: it means 'village or farmstead associated with the followers of a man named Hwaessa'. But for five hundred years the local manor, Washington Old Hall, was the residence of the ancestors of George Washington. One William de Hertburne moved here in the early part of the twelfth century and called himself Wessyngton after his new home. Although his descendants later moved to Sulgrave in Northamptonshire ('grove in a narrow valley'), they stuck to this surname, changing its spelling as time went by, and took it with them when they moved to the future United States. The first US president and the state, federal capital and umpteen other places named after him can therefore trace their ancestry back to what is now the county of Tyne and Wear, where, in 1113, the family acquired land from the Bishop of DURHAM and put down roots in a place where Hwaessa was already long forgotten.

Wooler

Another example of regional pronunciation causing confusion: further south places associated with springs or streams managed to hang on to the name 'Wells'; this one has been mangled into 'wool'. The ending probably comes from the same root as BOLSOVER and other places mentioned in that entry, so that Wooler means 'ridge or promontory by the stream'. Nearby is the Wooler Water, the substantial stream that first gave the village its name and then was named after it.

GLOSSARY

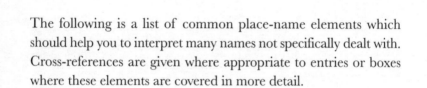

The following is a list of common place-name elements which should help you to interpret many names not specifically dealt with. Cross-references are given where appropriate to entries or boxes where these elements are covered in more detail.

Bech	ridge, raised ground, *see* **Wisbech**
Beck	brook, stream; hence a valley with a stream flowing through it
Bold, bottle	house, dwelling, *see* **Nobottle**
Borough	hill, burial mound, *see* **Marlborough**
Borough, burgh, bury	stronghold, fortified place
Bourne, burn	spring, stream
Bridge, brig	bridge, *see* **Crossing Places 2**
Brom, broom	broom
By	farmstead, village (in areas of Scandinavian influence), *see* **Appleby**
Caster, cester, chester	old (usually Roman) fort
Combe	narrow valley
Cot	shelter, hut

Dal, dale	valley (mostly in areas of Scandinavian influence)
Dean, den(e)	valley (mostly in areas of Anglo-Saxon influence)
Din, don, dun	fort, often a hill fort
Don, down, dun	hill
Ea, ey	river, *see* **Portsmouth**
Ea, ey, ye	island, dry land in a marsh, *see* **Portsmouth**, **Chertsey**
Fel, field	field, open land
Firth, frith	sparse woodland, *see* **Chapel-en-le-Frith**
Font, hunt	fountain, spring, *see* **Cheshunt**
Ford, forth	ford *see* **Crossing Places 1**, **Horsforth**
Gate, yat, yate	gap, pass, *see* **Margate**
Hall, hull	nook, *see* **Ludgershall**
Ham	homestead, village, *see* **Farming Country 1**
Hamm	land in the bend of a river, partially enclosed land
Ham(p)ste(a)d	a combination of *ham* and *stead*, meaning approximately village, *see* **Moretonhampstead**
Hampton	usually, a combination of *ham* and *ton*, meaning 'homestead'; sometimes a combination of *hamm* and *ton*, meaning a settlement partially enclosed by water; sometimes *high* and *ton*, giving 'high farmstead', *see* **Southampton**, **Northampton**

Hanger	slope, particularly a wooded one, *see* **Tring**
Hat, heath	heath, heather
High, hea(n)	high, important
Hoe, hol, hough	a 'heel' of land; hence a hill spur or ridge, *see* **Houghton Conquest**
Holm(e), hulme	island, piece of dry land in a stream or marsh; promontory, *see* **Oldham**
Hop(e)	island in a fen; small enclosed valley
Hurst, hirst	wooded hill, woodland
Hythe	landing place, *see* **Hythe**, **Rotherhithe**
Ing(s)	belonging to, associated with or characterised by a person, his followers or dependants. *See* **Whose Place Is It Anyway?**
Kir(k)	church (in areas of Scandinavian influence), *see* **Kirkby-in-Ashfield**
Law, low	mound, small hill, *see* **Harlow**
Lea, leigh, ley	clearing in woodland, glade, *see* **Bromley**
Mar, mere, more	boundary, 'march', *see* **March**
Mar, mere, mor	pool, lake
Mars, mers	marsh
Mead, mede	meadow
Med, mid	middle, *see* **Milton Keynes**
Mond, mont	mound, hill, *see* **Richmond**
Moor, mor, mur	moor
Naze, nes(s)	headland, cape

Oare, Or(e)	river bank; border, edge of a hill, slope
Or(e), Over	hillside, ridge, slope, *see* **Bolsover**
Pen	hill, headland, *see* **Penryn**
Pol, pool	pool, lake, *see* **Blackpool**
Port(h)	port, market town, *see* **Langport**
Rick, rigg	strip of land, *see* **Chatteris**
Ridge, rig(g)	ridge
Set(t)	dwellers (around a certain place), *see* **Somerset**
Shep, ship, skep, skip	sheep
Shot(t)	projecting piece of land, end of a wood, *see* **Bagshot**
Slade, slate	small valley
Stan, sten, stone	stone, *see* **Stansted Mountfitchet**
Ste(a)d	place, site of a building, farm
Stock, stoke	outlying farm, *see* **Farming Country 2**
Stow	meeting point, often a holy place, *see* **Padstow**, **Bristol**, **Felixstowe**
Strat, street	Roman road, *see* **Stratford-upon-Avon**
Thorp(e)	outlying farm, *see* **Thorpe**
Thwaite	clearing, meadow, *see* **Bassenthwaite**
Toft	homestead (in areas of Scandinavian influence), *see* **Farming Country 2**
Ton(e), town	enclosure, farmstead, manor, *see* **Farming Country 1**
Tor	rocky outcrop
Tre, trow, try	tree, particularly as a marker or meeting place, *see* **Coventry**

Wade	ford, wading place, *see* **Crossing Places 1**
Wal(s), walla	foreign, Celtic – used by the invading
War(e), were	weir, *see* **Wareham**
Wark	work, fortification, *see* **Newark**
Was(h)	marsh
Wath, with	wood, forest
Wath, with, worth	ford (in areas of Scandinavian influence) Anglo-Saxons to describe a place inhabited by the natives, *see* **Walton-on-Thames**, **Wallasey**
Weald, wold	wooded upland, *see* **Cotswolds**
Well	spring, well, *see* **Wells**
Wich, wick	dwelling, specialist farm (especially a dairy farm), trading place, *see* **Farming Country 2**
Wood	woodland
Worth(y)	enclosure, farm, *see* **Farming Country 2**

BIBLIOGRAPHY

This book would have been impossible to write without the help of the books listed here and much less enjoyable without the many, many websites dedicated to local history and tourism.

Books about place names

John Ayto & Ian Crofton, *Brewer's Britain and Ireland* (Weidenfeld & Nicolson, 2005) – particularly the place-names information by Dr Paul Cavill

Flavell Edmunds, *Traces of History in the Names of Places* (Longman's Green, 1872)

Eilert Ekwall, *The Concise Oxford Dictionary of English Place-names* (Oxford University Press, 4th edition 1960)

Margaret Gelling, *Place-Names in the Landscape* (Dent, 1984)

Margaret Gelling, *Signposts to the Past* (Phillimore, 3rd edition 1997)

Dominic Greyer, *Far from Dull* (Sort Of Books, 2004)

James A Johnston, *The Place Names of England and Wales* (John Murray, 1915)

Fred McDonald & Julia Cresswell, *The Guinness Book of British Place Names* (Guinness, 1993)

A D Mills, *The Oxford Dictionary of British Place Names* (Oxford University Press, 2003)

Charles Whynne-Hammond, *English Place-Names Explained* (Countryside Books, 2005)

Other reference books
William Camden, *Britannia* (David & Charles, 1971 facsimile of the 1695 edition)

Juliet Gardiner & Neil Wenborn, eds, *The History Today Companion to British History* (Collins & Brown, 1995)

Christopher Hibbert, *The English: A Social History 1066–1945* (Grafton, 1987)

Simon Jenkins, *England's Thousand Best Churches* (Allen Lane, 1999)

Knud Mariboe, *The Encyclopaedia of the Celts* (Celtic Chronicles, 1997)

Kenneth O Morgan, *The Oxford Illustrated History of Britain* (Oxford University Press, 1984)

Dr Ann Williams & Professor G H Martin, *Domesday Book: A Complete Translation* (Penguin, 1992)

Websites
The ones I found most useful for information about specific places, people and incidents include:

www.amblesideonline.co.uk

www.englandsnortheast.co.uk

www.birminghamuk.com/historicbirmingham.htm

www.bishopscastle.co.uk

www.visitblackpool.com

www.blackrodtowncouncil.org

www.st-botolphs.com/botolph

www.celtnet.org.uk/gods

www.chesham.gov.uk

www.aboutderbyshire.co.uk

www.claycross.org.uk

www.bellinnbrass.co.uk/CleoburyMortimer.htm

www.dover-kent.co.uk

www.earlshiltonandbarwell.co.uk

www.thepotteries.org

www.beautifulbritain.co.uk

www.faversham.org

www.localancestors.com

www.oxford-shakespeare.com

www.herefordwebpages.co.uk

www.kirby-le-soken.co.uk

www.britainexpress.com/counties

www.exmoor-nationalpark.gov.uk

www.maldon.co.uk

www.nantwichmuseum.org.uk

www.newforest.hampshire.org.uk

www.homepages.nildram.co.uk

www.newtonnoss.co.uk

www.peasepottage.info

www.polegate-tc.co.uk

www.plymouthdata.info

www.romseyabbey.org.uk

www.deerings.co.uk/reigate_history

www.north-herts.gov.uk

www.megalithic.co.uk

www.shanklinchine.co.uk

www.shipstononline.org

www.worcestercitymuseums.org.uk

www.yorkshire-england.co.uk/YorkCity

In addition, www.genuki.org.uk and www.british-history.ac.uk provided a wealth of information on almost any place name I cared to search and www.visionofbritain.org.uk gave me invaluable access to nineteenth-century gazetteers and other early travel writing, including that of Daniel Defoe.

INDEX OF PLACE NAMES